Praise for *Practicing Our Faith: A Way of Life for a Searching People*

"I firmly believe that the way we bathe a child or discuss family matters at the dinner table reveals who our God is. This book is a valuable contribution to our understanding of such everyday spirituality within the contact of traditional Christian practices such as hospitality, asceticism, and hymn-singing. Deceptively simple and down-to-earth, these authors provide potent surprises. Dorothy Bass's observation that 'slaves cannot take a day off but free people can' startled me into a new comprehension of the workaholism that permeates American culture. *Practicing Our Faith* strikes me as a book as wise as grandparents, a good guide to living within our families and communities with integrity and generosity."
—Kathleen Norris, author of *Dakota: A Spiritual Geography* and *The Cloister Walk*

"*Practicing Our Faith* is a book written by a remarkable community of people—remarkable not only because it includes some of the most insightful Christian voices of our time, but because its members prayed and talked and worked together to create this volume, modeling the way the church is meant to do its work. As their title suggests, this book emphasizes not just the theory but the practice of the Christian life, and it does so in fresh and lovely ways: it is a book that can help us understand what it might mean to become 'the Word made flesh' in the course of everyday life. Equally important, the practices explored here go far beyond the individual—and sometimes isolating—techniques often advocated by spiritual texts into ways of reaching out to others, of strengthening our communities and institutions, of helping to heal the world. *Practicing Our Faith* is a book that should be widely read, and more: it should be put into action."
—Parker Palmer, author of *A Hidden Wholeness, Let Your Life Speak,* and *The Courage to Teach*

"Millions of Americans claim to be interested in deepening their spirituality, but many are swimming contentedly in shallow waters. The essays in this highly readable volume challenge us to practice our faith with greater dedication and imagination. Drawing inspiration from biblical tradition and from contemporary literature as well as their own experience, the authors show how such practices as hospitality, keeping Sabbath, forgiving, and singing, among others, can forge more deliberate and rewarding connections with the sacred."
—Robert Wuthnow, Princeton University

"Here is a resource that can enrich the religious live of the entire church. Its strong sensitivity to the holiness of the body, the interplay of the communal and the personal, the Jewish traditions informing Christianity, and the inseparable domains of the biblical and the mystical are precisely what we need as we prepare to enter the twenty-first century. Profound thanks to all who made it possible."
—Maria Harris, author of *Fashion Me a People* and *Proclaim Jubilee!*

"This book vigorously, knowingly, and at times eloquently addresses the hugely important matter of how we ought to live this life—those of us who continue to believe that Christ's teachings matter in that regard. Here are wonderfully suggestive and edifying essays that will help 'people of faith' put their beliefs and convictions to that ultimate test of *conduct*—how we call upon our ideals in the everyday lived life that is our great opportunity, but also our demanding test, and at times, trial."
—Robert Coles, author of *The Spiritual Life of Children*

"For years the religious book market has been flooded with volumes about 'spirituality' but people are still uncertain what it would mean to 'live like a Christian.' This is a unique response to that uncertainty, a down-to-earth description of twelve practical ways of being Christian. Its authors draw from historical tradition as well as from present-day paradigms of Christian behavior to distill a wisdom that is expressed, not in theoretical explanation, but in daily living. It would be a much different world if people were to follow the guidelines of this book.
—Bernard Cooke, Loyola Professor of Theology Emeritus, Holy Cross College.

The Practices of Faith Series
Dorothy C. Bass, Series Editor

Practicing Our Faith:
A Way of Life for a Searching People
Dorothy C. Bass, Editor

Receiving the Day:
Christian Practices for Opening the Gift of Time
Dorothy C. Bass

Honoring the Body:
Meditations on a Christian Practice
Stephanie Paulsell

Testimony:
Talking Ourselves into Being Christian
Thomas G. Long

A Song to Sing, A Life to Live:
Reflections on Music as Spiritual Practice
Don Saliers, Emily Saliers

PRACTICING OUR FAITH

A Way of Life for a Searching People

Dorothy C. Bass, Editor

M. Shawn Copeland   Craig Dykstra

Thomas Hoyt Jr.   L. Gregory Jones

John Koenig   Sharon Daloz Parks

Stephanie Paulsell   Amy Plantinga Pauw

Ana María Pineda, RSM   Larry Rasmussen

Frank Rogers Jr.   Don E. Saliers

JOSSEY-BASS
A Wiley Imprint
www.josseybass.com

Published by Jossey-Bass
A Wiley Imprint
989 Market Street, San Francisco, CA 94103-1741   www.josseybass.com

Jossey-Bass books and products are available through most bookstores. To contact
Jossey-Bass directly call our Customer Care Department within the U.S. at 800-956-
7739, outside the U.S. at 317-572-3986 or fax 317-572-4002.

Jossey-Bass also publishes its books in a variety of electronic formats. Some content
that appears in print may not be available in electronic books.

Credits are on p. 229.

Library of Congress Cataloging-in-Publication Data

Practicing our faith : a way of life for a searching people / Dorothy
  C. Bass, editor. — 1st ed.
      p.   cm.
    Includes bibliographical references and index.
    ISBN 0-7879-0336-1 (alk. paper)
    ISBN 0-7879-3883-1 (paperback)
    1. Christian life.   I. Bass, Dorothy C.
  BV4501.P64   1997
  248.4—dc21   96-45782

FIRST EDITION
HB Printing   10 9 8 7 6 5 4 3
PB Printing   10

Contents

Preface

Every summer, my family visits a retreat center high in the mountains. My husband delights in the hiking and fishing; I thrive on the absence of phones, televisions, and grocery stores; and the children revel in the freedom they have to roam about unsupervised in a small, safe, mostly outdoor community of friends. All of us enjoy the natural splendor of this place. But there is also something stronger and deeper that keeps us going back, something harder to describe. When we are there, we slip into a way of life that comes pretty close to our vision of how things are supposed to be. As staff members, we work; we consume appropriately, eating lower on the food chain and doing without the goods and gadgets that usually clutter our lives; we worship daily. In other words, we enter a community shaped by shared practices that make sense, and as we adjust to them, we feel ourselves becoming a little different, a little better.

Back home, we find patterns of shared life that are less coherent, less morally clear. But we jump right in; the kids are back to school and their playmates, while we adults return to jobs, to housework, to worship, to friendship. But now we are doing these good things in a divided, fast-paced society. Here, eating and consuming are not patterned for the good of creation. Work and play and prosperity are out of balance. Expectations coming from different parts of our lives conflict with one another. It is hard to keep our moral and spiritual bearings. We yearn once again for a way of life that is whole, and touched by the presence of God.

Many people today share this yearning, or are on a search like the one that led my family to the mountains. And many share in the sense of fragmentation that settles in once we are home. How can we live faithfully and with integrity here, where the pace of existence is so fast and life's patterns are changing all around us? Can we conduct our daily lives in ways that help us not just to get by but to flourish—as individuals, as communities, and as a society, in concert with all creation and in communion with God?

These questions are in the hearts and minds of many seekers who are exploring spirituality today. Whether they grew up beyond religious communities or left the religious households of their childhood, they are now searching for some context of larger belonging and some pattern of believing and valuing that is richer and deeper than that offered by the wider culture.

And many thoughtful Christians are also pondering these questions. We yearn for a richer and deeper understanding of what it means to live as Christians in a time when basic patterns of human relationship are changing all around us. We want to know what Christian faith has to do with our work, with friendship and marriage, with the way we raise our children, with public and political life, with how we spend our money. Some Christians cut the search short, perhaps after finding that when they ask, they get stock answers that are no real help at all. But most of us continue to look for greater insight into how our faith can help us discern what we might do and who we might become.

This book offers people who are asking such questions help that is rooted in Christian faith and tradition. For some readers, what it contains will be a new discovery; for others, a fresh way of thinking about cherished beliefs. The authors invite both sorts of readers, as well as the many who find themselves somewhere in between, to explore a Christian way of life that can be lived with integrity at the dawn of the twenty-first century.

We invite you, in particular, to think with us about *practices*. Practices are those shared activities that address fundamental human needs and that, woven together, form a way of life. Reflecting on practices as they have been shaped in the context of Christian faith leads us to encounter the possibility of a faithful way of life, one that is both attuned to present-day needs and taught by ancient wisdom. And here is the really important point: this encounter can change how we live each day.

AUDIENCE

The book is addressed not only to seekers on journeys of the spirit, and not only to committed Christians searching for ways to practice their faith more fully. It is also addressed to people of every faith who are concerned about human flourishing, including people in the helping professions and those who guide public policy. Educators concerned about bridging the gap between theory and practice will also find useful insights here.

OVERVIEW OF THE CONTENTS

The first chapter, "Times of Yearning, Practices of Faith," considers the spiritual hunger of our day and suggests that thinking about Christian practices can help contemporary people envision a vital and authentic way of life. It also explains the terms and sets forth the purposes of the book.

Our exploration of specific practices begins in Chapter Two with a story of birth and the practice of honoring the body, acknowledging in this way that we come to all the practices not just spiritually—as some books about faith would have it—but as embodied beings. This exploration ends in Chapter Thirteen not with death (the practice of dying well comes *next to last* here) but with singing, the practice in which our very breath sounds the truths of our lives and responds with beautiful music to the active presence of God. In between are other practices that add essential strands to the tapestry of life.

The practice of hospitality comes early to welcome readers to this book, just as we all need to welcome one another in life; in Chapter Three, we consider how our lives can be patterned to provide *posada,* a place of rest, for one another. This practice leads us to think in Chapter Four about our households, and about the importance of our economic practices to the well-being of all who share this planet that is our home. The practice of saying yes and saying no follows in Chapter Five, where we retrieve ancient wisdom that insisted that if we want to say yes to God and to life abundant, we must also say a related no to other things. This practice, which will be important if we are to persevere in living out any of the others, is strengthened by the disciplines of prayer, examination of conscience, and small faith-sharing groups. Keeping Sabbath, the subject of Chapter Six, forms us to say yes to regular rest and worship and no to a society and economy that force—or lure—many of us to work too hard.

The three practices that follow focus on our urgent need for speech that is truthful, decisions that are well-considered, and communities that are structured to permit the just and full participation of all. We are guided by a variety of Christian models—the Black Church, the Society of Jesus (Jesuits), the Society of Friends (Quakers), and the young churches led by the apostle Paul—as we reflect on the importance of giving truthful testimony (Chapter Seven), making discerning choices (Chapter Eight), and shaping worthy communities (Chapter Nine). The practice that follows these in Chapter Ten—forgiveness—is one without which none of them, or indeed any other practice, could continue for long. In the practice of forgiveness, Christians participate in the divine activity of reconciliation, making God's forgiveness palpable by forgiving one another. The strength of God's reconciling love also provides the foundation of the practice discussed in Chapter Eleven: healing. Dying well, the subject of Chapter Twelve, rests on this same foundation; the practice shapes us in lament, hope, judgment, and mercy, not only in our last hours but as we respond to the reality of human mortality through all the years of our lives. As already noted, we conclude our exploration of specific practices with singing.

Chapter Fourteen, "Growing in the Practices of Faith," provides guidance for strengthening our participation in the way of life set forth in the book.

GUIDING PURPOSES

We have chosen the twelve featured practices because they are practices that human beings simply cannot do without, particularly at this time in history. Many forces make it difficult to discern and persevere in life-giving forms of practice today. Hospitality and Sabbath get squeezed out of our lives, and testimony and discernment are lost amid the din of sound bites and opinion polls. But the Christian community bears wisdom about these practices, and learning that wisdom will help us, and the world, to flourish.

Practicing Our Faith offers reflection on practices as a way of connecting our faith with our daily lives. It also opens a path of spiritual formation; taking part in practices that have been shaped by the Christian community over the centuries in response to God, we develop virtues and experience growth in our spiritual lives. The book's approach represents a refusal to leave our beliefs in the realm of theory, insisting that they can make a difference in our lives.

THE AUTHORS AND OUR HOPES FOR THIS BOOK

This book originated in Craig Dykstra's insight that the idea of "practices" provides a helpful way of addressing the yearning of contemporary people for deeper understanding of and involvement in the redemptive practice of God in the world. He developed this idea in his work as a Christian educator, drawing especially on the philosopher Alasdair MacIntyre's work on social practices. When he became vice president for religion at Lilly Endowment Inc., he invited me to join him in leading a seminar of theologians and educators to think further about practices and to develop a book that would share this idea with others.

The eleven theologians who joined us soon became our friends. We had not known them all before, nor had they known one another, but from the beginning our conversations had a special quality. We talked about the practices in our lives, in our institutions, in our families, as well as about the philosophy, history, sociology, and theology of practices. We grew excited about sharing this idea with others. We prayed together.

This book is now finished. At the same time, what is here is only a beginning. It is an invitation to think about practices in your own life, including practices we have not included. It will stimulate your imagination by offering stories from faith and tradition that run counter to some of our society's patterns. It will encourage you to reflect on how you spend your weekends, how you pray, how you offer care to others, and much else. Unlike some books on spirituality, this one does not offer rules or set forth numbered steps to wholeness. Rather, it initiates a conversation that we hope will spread to many contexts, each of which presents unique opportunities for thinking out and living the practices of faith.

ACKNOWLEDGMENTS

As the book's editor, I want to extend personal thanks to all of the authors for their wisdom, perseverance, and friendship. Craig Dykstra deserves most of the credit for this book, not only because he got it started but also because of the clarity of his vision and the steadiness of his leadership throughout. Stephanie Paulsell was an important conversation partner and editorial collaborator. Our editor at Jossey-Bass, Sarah Polster, has provided excellent guidance. Mary C. Boys and E. Brooks Holifield, friends and sages, have contributed as advisers to the Valparaiso Project on the Education and Formation of People in Faith, of which this book is one product. Susan Briehl, Thomas Droege, Katherine Dyckman, and Thomas G. Long were generous and helpful consultants. Beth Schoppa managed group meetings and manuscript preparations with care and grace. Jeanne Knoerle, James P. Wind, Kevin Armstrong, Larry Parks Daloz, Paul Teresa Hennessee, Janet Lynn Kerr, Robert Wood Lynn, Bobbie Miner, Rodger Nishioka, Kay Bessler Northcutt, Evelyn L. Parker, Barbara Patterson, Edith Prendergast, and Rosendo Urrabazo offered valuable commentary. Margaret Franson and Bruce Berner gave important advice. I also thank Judy Shoffner for secretarial support, as well as Jansie McMahan and Kathy Yerga. I am deeply grateful to Lilly Endowment Inc. for its generous support of this book, and to Valparaiso University for providing a congenial and stimulating home for this work. And to my dearest partners in the practices of Christian faith, Mark, Martha, John, and Kaethe Schwehn, gratitude and love.

Valparaiso, Indiana   Dorothy C. Bass
October 1996

PRACTICING OUR FAITH

Chapter 1

TIMES OF YEARNING, PRACTICES OF FAITH

Craig Dykstra and Dorothy C. Bass

I never thought I'd be living this way," she says. "Somehow I imagined that life would be simpler." She has reached forty, and she thinks she should have her life together by now, but things are just not right. Too few evenings include nourishing suppers shared with loved ones; too many are given over to the demands of paid work or housework, or lost to worry and exhaustion. Her closest friends are spread across several time zones. The old neighbors she entrusted with the house key are gone, and she barely knows the new ones. She finds community here and there, and she volunteers to help out as she can, but she is wary about getting too involved. Showing up at a PTA meeting, she has learned, probably means getting stuck with a fundraising assignment, so increasingly she stays away, in spite of her intense concern about her children and all the others. She does not feel right about this. "This is not how I intended to live my life," she sighs, turning from one task to the next.

The sighs of this woman and so many of us today come only in part from having too much to do. Even more, these sighs are born

1

of our yearning to understand what the too-much-to-do adds up to. We long to see our lives whole and to know that they matter. We wonder whether our many activities might ever come together in a way of life that is good for ourselves and others. Does all this activity make a difference beyond ourselves? Are we really living in right relation to other people, to the created world, and to God?

These concerns engulf the unemployed as well as the busy professional, the retiree as well as the young parent, the recent immigrant as well as the lifelong citizen. Lacking a vision of a life-giving way of life, we turn from one task to another, doing as well as we can but increasingly uncertain about what doing things well would look like. All the while, an uneasiness lies just beneath the surface—an uneasiness made of personal restlessness, worry about our loved ones, and apprehension about the well-being of the world.

With this book, we and eleven other authors who have known this uneasiness invite you to join us in envisioning a way of life that is whole, a way of life that can be lived with integrity in our time. We write because we believe that Christian faith offers hope and help to people who long for such a way. Each author is different; we come from a variety of Christian traditions, regions, races, and backgrounds. But we all perceive that the search for how to live aright at this time in history is an extremely urgent one. In all the communities we know, people yearn for deeper understanding of how to order human life in accord with what is true and good. And beyond this desire, we recognize another reason for urgency: the good of all people, indeed of all creation, may depend on our ability to order our lives well.

LIFE-GIVING WAYS OF LIFE

A Catholic priest recently told a gathering of friends about a time when he arrived in Israel late on a Friday afternoon, just as everything was about to shut down for the Sabbath. Public transportation was no longer available, and the house where people were expecting him was fifteen miles away. So he picked up his suitcase and started to walk. He did not get far before a family saw him and invited him to spend the Sabbath with them. He accepted their invitation, and they all had a wonderful time. When Saturday evening came, he found his bus and went on his way.

After the priest finished his story, a Jewish friend said that he had a similar story to tell. As a long-haired college student in the late 1960s, he was traveling through Spain. One night, he got off a train in a village that was already asleep. A little frightened, he approached the only lighted place. It turned out to be a monastery, and the monks received him gladly. After his departure, he discovered that they had quietly slipped some coins into his pocket as he slept.

In both of these stories, we get glimpses of ancient traditions sustaining ways of life that shelter and nourish people, ways of life ready to receive strangers who are passing through. The hospitality these two young men received came from communities structured with hospitality in mind. In each of these places, hospitality was more than an individual act of kindness—it was sustained by a way of life.

What would happen in our society today if young men like these were wandering through? Perhaps they would be fortunate and find a safe place to rest. But they, or others not so different from them, might not. For is there not a crisis of hospitality in our society? It is tragically evident in homelessness and widespread hostility to immigrants. But it affects almost everyone in less noticeable ways as well. A stranger smiles, and we cautiously turn away. In our retreat from hospitality, we find that even friends and relatives sit at our tables less often than they used to.

ON NOT GOING IT ALONE IN A TIME OF CHANGE

Today, the shared ways of life that sustain hospitality are changing all around us. And change is also affecting the other basic activities we depend on for our well-being. Change touches us in our homes, workplaces, hospitals, and schools; it tests our relationships and shapes our desires, altering our sense of what we can expect from others and what we should expect of ourselves. On the grand scale, change shows up in major technological advances or global shifts in population. But in the end it reaches into the kitchens and bedrooms even of people who rarely travel and never use a computer. The basic activities of life are shifting all around us, and we are being pushed in directions we never intended to go.

These shifts have set many people on spiritual journeys, in search of solid ground. But here too, change complicates matters, for now a dazzling array of religious and therapeutic options is available. It is hard to know what is of value, and harder still to settle into a steady way. So great is the need for insight that people look for it in many places—sometimes, indeed, in many places all at once. What will it be? Eastern meditation or Western psychotherapy, twelve-step groups or self-help books, spiritual retreats or private prayer? Some of us invest our hopes in spiritual journeys that are private and inward-looking, only to find that the very same forces that prompted the journey also work against finding a nourishment that is rich and enduring. Dislocated and disconnected, we suppose that *self*-help offers our best hope. Lacking shared beliefs, we conclude that our *private* preferences are the closest we can come to the truth of matters. When this happens, the solo quest only mimics the disconnectedness that gave it birth.

The fact is that inward journeys are not enough to meet our need. Our lives are tangled up with everyone else's in ways beyond our knowing, "caught," as Martin Luther King Jr. put it, "in an inescapable network of mutuality, tied to a single garment of destiny." The simplest economics teaches this truth about life in the global village. So does the science of clean air and wholesome food. And so do the desires of our hearts: who would wish to eat a feast alone, while others starve? And who will not someday find themselves starving—if not for food, then for health or dearest companion? We need to cooperate if we hope to find not just contented states of mind but ways of living that are good for ourselves and others, nearby and around the world.

FINDING COMPANIONS

How important it is to have companions as we seek life-giving ways of life! This, after all, is a basic tenet of Christian faith and life: through Christ, we belong to God and become brothers and sisters to one another, sharing Christ's love for all people. Christians know that we are not made to be alone. Yet today we too are uncertain about the shape of our way of life. With the ordinary things we do each day changing all around us, even we who have belonged to the church all our lives wonder how to do these things well—how to do them, in Christian terms, *faithfully*.

Many Christian people seem to be unaware of the rich insights and strong help the Christian tradition can bring to today's concerns. Hungry, they look elsewhere without ever exploring and appreciating what their own tradition can offer. We write this book in part to answer this hunger with nourishment drawn from the deep wells of Christian history, belief, and experience.

The community of people gathered around Jesus Christ has explored the contours of a faithful way of life over the centuries, and it continues to do so all around the world today. This community, like everyone in it, is flawed, and there has been much stumbling and sinning along the way. But the church has also gathered wisdom and skill as this people has tried to understand and live in response to the mysterious grace of God in creation, the redemptive presence of Christ, and the ongoing work of the Holy Spirit. There is tremendous diversity within this far-flung community's explorations—and that diversity exists also among the authors and the intended readers of this book. But the search to walk aright in each new time and place is one that unites us all.

In *Practicing Our Faith,* we invite you to learn from the wisdom of this community by reflecting on Christian practices. *Christian practices are things Christian people do together over time in response to and in the light of God's active presence for the life of the world.* Look at the table of contents, and you will see what sorts of things we mean. Honoring the body. Hospitality. Household economics. Saying yes and saying no. Keeping Sabbath. Testimony. Discernment. Shaping communities. Forgiveness. Healing. Dying well. Singing our lives. These are ordinary activities, the stuff of everyday life. Yet all of them, no matter how mundane, can be shaped in response to God's active presence. And all of them, woven together, suggest the patterns of a faithful Christian way of life for our time.

PRACTICES: A WAY OF THINKING
ABOUT A WAY OF LIFE

A way of life is a big and often baffling thing. Imagine being set down among a group of people whose way of life is completely unfamiliar to you. It would be nearly impossible to comprehend its meaning all at once, or to see how it all holds together. And so you might try to make sense of it piece by piece: this is how they eat, this is how they trade, this is how they raise their children. Gradually, you would begin to see the patterns of this way of life in the details of how people do a variety of things with and for one another.

This book follows a similar method. Rather than examining a Christian way of life as a whole, we intend to survey some of the most important activities that compose it. One of our reasons for doing this is the same as yours would be on your arrival in the unfamiliar land: things are confusing, and we want to be clear about what is going on. But we have other reasons as well. First, we want to avoid abstractions as much as possible. The changes that are sweeping the world unsettle life at its most basic levels, and we want to offer help directly at this point of need. Second, we are writing this book not for the idly curious but for people who hope to strengthen their own ways of living. Christian practices provide concrete opportunities to do so.

Why call these activities "practices" rather than using a more familiar term or no special term at all? In choosing this word, we are drawing on a concept more familiar to philosophers and social scientists than to most other readers. Even those familiar with it will find that it has a special meaning in this book. We know some explaining will be needed to show its usefulness, but we think the effort is worthwhile. Learning a new term often helps us to think in new ways, even when the things we are thinking about are as old as can be.

Practices address fundamental human needs and conditions through concrete human acts. Young men traveling alone do not need to be greeted with a sermon on hospitality; they need to be beckoned inside, given some supper, and shown where to sleep. The hosts may or may not be able to articulate why they do these things, though in fact they are carrying on long traditions rooted in the Bible. They are simply practicing hospitality. And the other practices are like this; they provide concrete help for human flourishing. Each is the human place where people cooperate with God in doing what needs to be done.

Practices, therefore, have practical purposes: to heal, to shape communities, to discern. Oddly, however, they are not treasured only for their outcomes. Just taking a full and earnest part in them is somehow good in itself, even when purposes that are visible to the human eye are not achieved. If a patient dies unrelieved in spirit as well as body, do healers abandon the practice the next time? No, they do not, for they understand what they do as part of the practice of God. They are doing it not just because it works (though they hope it does), but because it is good. The observable outcome is, in a sense, beyond them; a different satisfaction comes just from taking part.

Practices are done together and over time. Enter a Christian practice, and you will find that you are part of a community that has been doing this thing for centuries—not doing it as well as it should, to be sure, but doing it steadily, in conscious continuity with stories of the Bible and in frequent conversation about how to do it better. You join by jumping in where you are: learn the hymns, volunteer to welcome the homeless, seek companions who will support you in prayer as you say yes to God and no to the destructive forces in your life. Once in, you find that a practice has a certain internal feel and momentum. It is ancient, and larger than you are; it weaves you together with other people in doing things none of us could do alone. But each practice is also ever new, taking fresh form each day as it subtly adapts to find expression in every neighborhood and land.

Moreover, *practices possess standards of excellence.* The Christian practice of household economics is not just a matter of adding a warm spiritual glow to the work of homemaking. Instead, it is a matter of permitting the light of God to shine on the work we do and the money we spend, so that we can shape them in response to God's activities in creating and providing for the care and redemption of the earth and all its inhabitants. The challenge lies in figuring out what this means with enough specificity to make a difference. Part of the figuring out requires soul-stretching theological conversations with others: say, an eighteenth-century Quaker accountant, a Catholic worker of the 1930s, and an environmental scientist of the 1990s. With these acquaintances and with people closer at hand, we also turn to the Bible for guidance.

This process is important. Because practices are so spacious and flexible, we need to be prepared to think about what it means to do them well rather than badly. Does our way of life include the Christian practice of honoring the human body? Do we recognize God's image in all of the human bodies we see, or do we pay exaggerated but shallow obeisance to certain bodies while permitting others to be battered and discarded? Thinking about this practice, we discover evidence that what we have been doing violates life and rejects God's magnificent acts on behalf of human bodies in creation, incarnation, and resurrection. Both our own failings and the failings embedded in economic or political structures set obstacles in the way of practices that are good for all people. Thinking about practices can help us to see how destructively the basic activities of human life can be organized—globally, in American society, in our churches, in our homes. Moreover, if we are willing to risk further change, this kind of thinking can guide us into renewed ways of life, which humanity so sorely needs at the present difficult turn in the history of this world we inhabit together.

Finally, when we see some of our ordinary activities as Christian practices, we come to perceive how *our daily lives are all tangled up with the things God is doing in the world.* Now we want to figure out how to pattern our practices after God's, and it becomes our deepest hope to become partners in God's reconciling love for the world. We are never able to do this perfectly, at least not for any length of time. Even so, when we set ordinary daily activities in this context, they are transformed, and so are we. A meal becomes a time of forgiveness. A day of leisure becomes a day of contemplation. An illness turns into an experience of solidarity with the poor. An occupation becomes a vocation. Giving becomes an expression of gratitude. A burial becomes a time of thanksgiving.

PRACTICES: REHEARSING A WAY OF LIFE

One thing about practices is that they are very down-to-earth. When people engage in a practice, they don't just talk about it, though words often play an important part. People-at-practice do things. They make gestures and touch one another. They raise their voices in song and open their arms in welcome. They recruit the ordinary physical stuff of nature into the practice. Practicing forgiveness, for example, the members of some churches wash one another's feet, remembering how Jesus washed the feet of Peter on the night before his death. They do it tenderly, but with bodies as well as spirits: water ends up on the floor, backs get sore, trousers get soggy, bunions are there for anyone to see, and someone has to launder the towels afterward. Similarly, those who enter the Christian practice of dying well hold the hands of those who face death or bring casseroles to the bereaved. From one practice to another, oil is rubbed in, food is set out, water is splashed, embraces are shared. Every practice is made up of many small gestures like these.

In public worship, the Christian community takes all these gestures and does them on a grand scale. We use the familiar elements of everyday life—food, water, oil, embrace, word—to proclaim and celebrate what God is doing in the world and in our lives. Worship distills the Christian meaning of the practices and holds them up for the whole community to see. We confess our failure to do them well, receive assurance of God's grace, hear stories and speak words that relate our practices to God's own creative and redemptive work, and go out strengthened to live more faithfully.

Worship is to daily life, a wise pastor has said, as consommé is to broth. In liturgy at its best—in the common work of the people assembled to hear the Word of God and celebrate the sacraments—the meaning of all the practices appears in a form that is thick and tasty, darker and richer than what we get in most everyday situations. In Holy Communion (or, as it is also called, the Lord's Supper or the Eucharist), every one of the Christian practices finds guidance. The worshipers experience the extravagant hospitality of God at the table and commit themselves to extend God's welcome to others; they collectively say no to what is harmful and yes to what is good; they keep the Sabbath holy in a joyful celebration of Christ's resurrection.

A Christian community at worship is a community gathered for rehearsal. It is "practicing" the practices in the same way a child practices catching a ball or playing scales. You may not think you need this skill, we tell the child, but stay in the game and the time will probably come when you do. The rhythms of worship—through the hour and through the year—set a common pace, one that worshipers follow even when it doesn't feel like it fits. Lent comes, but you are not feeling somber; or Easter, and you cannot rejoice. But the rhythms of worship must be endured in spite of your moods, and you go along. Later, when a Lenten time comes, whatever the season, you remember the songs of lament you learned and are grateful.

One of this book's authors told of attending the funeral of his father, a United Methodist minister. This son was too sorrowful to join in the hymns by which this congregation thankfully returned his father to God's care; he could only sit and mourn. Though he was barely sensible of this at the time, in later years he understood that the community had sung not only on its own behalf but also for him, and he was grateful. He had been included in their shared practices of dying well and singing our lives, even when he was too weak to do what he thought was his share of the work.

WEAVING THE PRACTICES TOGETHER

One more thing about practices: they are all interrelated. This is something that needs emphasizing in the present climate, when many people try to cobble together a religious and moral life out of lots of disparate pieces. It also needs emphasizing in a book that has many separate chapters on many apparently separate practices. All are related. Some readers will be attracted to a certain practice while others are drawn to different ones, depending on their experiences of life so far. That is fine. Start where you can.

In real life, however, it is very difficult to separate the practices. They flow into one another, each one making a space for God's active presence that then ripples out into other parts of life. When simplicity orders the economics of our households, our hospitality can focus on persons rather than display, we can say no more heartily to the appeals of advertising, and we can more readily welcome the quiet joy of the Sabbath. When we more fully honor the physical bodies of our fellow human beings, we can care for them more tenderly in sickness and at the time of death. Decisions made in communities that practice truthful testimony can be more discerning, and participatory communities that are shaped by justice can become places where all of the practices flourish. As we take part in God's activity by joining in all of these practices, we will sing together, grateful that we know forgiveness and are free to live reconciled to God and one another.

Thus focusing on even a single practice can lead you into a new way of life. Get started on one and you find yourself in the middle of another. This book discusses only twelve; many other practices, tied to other dimensions of human experience, would be part of a finished tapestry. We urge you to name and think about other important practices that are not in this book.

LOOKING AHEAD

The heart of this book lies ahead, in the twelve practices we invite you to consider. The authors have chosen practices that are essential for life on this planet as the twenty-first century begins. These are practices people need, sorely and surely, if fullness of life is to increase. They are also practices that are in trouble, like the practice of hospitality. Change has shaken our ability to help one another in these life-giving practices, and we need to think anew about how faith can shape them.

The chapters are united by the authors' shared belief that practices find their deepest expression in the activities of God. The Sabbath keeping to which this book invites you began on God's own glad day of rest. Honoring the body expresses humanity's creation in the image of God. Our hope when life ends rests on Christ's victory over death. Christian faith holds the authors, and the book, together in a common venture.

At the same time, the authors do not speak with just one voice. There exists within Christianity a wonderful variety of voices, and thirteen of them speak individually here. You will hear in our voices the distinctive tones of Catholics and Protestants, women and men, teachers and ministers. Our voices come from many places—one from El Salvador and San Francisco's Mission District, another from small-town Minnesota and New York City, and others from different regions of the United States. Readers attuned to the accents of theology will notice in various chapters inflections common to the heirs of Martin Luther, John Calvin, John Wesley, and Thérèse of Lisieux. The thirteen of us found the variety of our voices to be a source of great delight. We hope that readers will too. And then, we hope, you will set about to speak whatever help this book contains in the voice of your own community.

With this book, we invite our readers to think and act together in the midst of this time of change. Some are still searching for a community with whom to practice a life-giving way of life. Others are already woven into the community gathered by Christ and now share this community's search to fathom the depth and extent of God's grace as we practice our faith in our own unique moment in history. We hope that this book will help us all as we grow in a way of life that is informed by the wisdom of the Christian tradition, alert to the needs of our time, and responsive to the gracious presence and startling promises of God.

Chapter 2

HONORING THE BODY

୶

Stephanie Paulsell

I once served as a Lamaze partner for a friend in my church. Together we attended weekly birthing classes, practiced panting and deep breathing, and learned massage techniques. When my friend's water broke one morning, we met at the hospital with great excitement.

We soon learned, however, that things would not go according to the plan we had prepared in our classes. Although the bag of waters cushioning the baby had broken, my friend's body did not respond with the contractions necessary for the baby to be delivered. She walked up and down the halls of the hospital, trying to encourage labor

---
୶

For it was you who formed my inward parts;
you knit me together in my mother's womb.
I praise you, for I am fearfully and wonderfully made.

PSALM 139:13–14

13

through exercise, but her body did not respond. Finally, she agreed to an induced labor.

The breathing exercises we had learned to help my friend through a natural childbirth seemed superfluous now. The regular ebb and flow of labor pains was replaced by relentless drug-induced contractions that barely left her time enough to catch her breath. The baby's father and I stayed with her through the night, massaging her sore body, giving her our hands to grip as she suffered contraction after contraction, holding her in our arms during the rare moments free of struggle. I had difficulty remembering, at times, that a baby was coming, that my friend was laboring to bring new life into the world.

After a long and difficult night, my friend began pushing the baby out. The nurse, the midwife, the baby's father, and I all gathered around her, holding her legs, rubbing her arms, urging her on with our voices. As exhausted as she was, seeing the baby's head appear allowed my friend to reach for the strength she needed. And when, with one final, powerful act of loving will, she pushed her daughter out into the midwife's waiting hands, we all burst into tears of joy and relief and wonder. I remember thinking, over and over, as we stood there half-weeping, half-laughing: this must be the way God made the world, this must be the way God made the world . . .

For those who have been present at the moment when a new human being emerges entire from the body of another, such a reaction will not seem surprising. The wondrous act of one person giving birth to another can easily lead us to think of divine creativity. My friend's courageous and difficult laboring for her daughter recalled for me the words of Paul in which he speaks of the labor of each person, and indeed of all creation, to be re-formed in God's image: "We know that the whole creation has been groaning in labor pains until now; and not only the creation, but we ourselves, who have the first fruits of the Spirit, groan inwardly while we wait for adoption, the redemption of our bodies" (Romans 8:22–23).

The Christian practice of honoring the body is born of the confidence that our bodies are made in the image of God's own goodness. "Your body is a temple of the Holy Spirit within you," Paul wrote to the church at Corinth (1 Corinthians 6:19). As the place where the divine presence dwells, our bodies are worthy of care and blessing and ought never to be degraded or exploited. It is through our bodies that we participate in God's activity in the world, just as my friend united her creativity to God's own during the birth of her child. And it is through daily bodily acts—bathing, dressing, touching—that we might live more fully into the sacredness of our bodies and the bodies of others.

SHARED VULNERABILITY

To hold a newborn child in one's arms is to know both the sacredness and the vulnerability of the body; indeed, it is to know that there is an intimate connection between sacredness and vulnerability. But although it is easy to sense that connection at the moment of birth, and even at the moment of death, between those liminal moments can come days and years of great confusion.

The poet Jane Kenyon speaks of our "long struggle to be at home in the body, this difficult friendship." Part of the difficulty is that any practice that honors the body's sacredness can also be used to demean it. Adorning our bodies with beautiful clothing can shape our identities as individuals, help us delight a beloved, and mark important passages in our lives, but it can also be practiced in ways that perpetuate oppressively limited ideas of beauty. Our sexuality can nourish relationships and lead us into an intimacy that itself speaks of God's presence, but it can also be deployed in selfish or violent ways. Ascetic religious practices can awaken a desire for God in our bodies and bring us into solidarity with our suffering neighbor, but they can also be used to deny the goodness of the body.

The practice of honoring the body challenges us to remember the sacredness of the body in every moment of our lives. We cannot do this alone. Because our bodies are so vulnerable, we need each other to protect and care for them. A woman giving birth needs others to help her; adolescents struggling with sexual pressure need a community that insists on the autonomy of bodies made in God's image; those living with bodily illness need others to care for them and touch them in ways that heal and soothe. Our fragile bodies require communal attention, and so honoring the body is a shared practice, one that requires the participation of all.

The practice of honoring the body comes to life not only in relationships with those we know and love. It also makes inescapably visible the world's wounded bodies. It makes us notice and care about the bodies of children murdered in our cities, the bodies of women and girls raped in Bosnia, the bodies of people living with AIDS. The practice of honoring the body keeps these wounded bodies visible not as objects but as persons made in God's image. The practice of honoring the body leads us to prophetic action by forming us as persons who love every human body and the ravaged body of the earth itself. Shaped by the things we do with and for one another every day—eating and drinking, bathing and touching, dressing and undressing—the practice of honoring the body allows us to rediscover the sacredness of our own bodies and to shape communities committed to protecting the bodies of others.

When we honor the bodies of others, we are also drawn into God's work, as Matthew's Gospel affirms when Jesus tells his followers that whenever they feed the hungry and clothe the naked, they minister also to him. Embodiment is central to the Christian faith. The Christian emphasis on the incarnation of God's presence in Jesus and the Christian understanding of community, which describes the church as the body of Christ, both put embodiment at the center of Christian meaning. Jesus' command that we love our neighbor as we love ourselves makes it clear that our faith has everything to do with how we live as embodied people. And when we gather to worship, we do things together that bring this command to life: in the meal of communion, we eat and drink, gathered together by Christ's own wounded body; in baptism, it is our bodies that are bathed in cleansing water; in the passing of the peace, we touch one another in love and hope.

RETRIEVING AN AMBIGUOUS LEGACY

This is not to say that Christianity's history in regard to the body has been untroubled. Unfortunately, that history can pose serious problems for people who turn to Christian faith for guidance in this practice. From its origins, there have always been Christians who have found the human body scandalous and repugnant. Some early

Christians believed that Jesus' own body must have been an illusion, since a mortal human body surely could not bear within it something as precious as divinity.

Such perplexity about the body continued as Christianity developed. Early Christians looked for clues about humanity's relationship to God in the body's most vulnerable moments: the moment of sexual desire and the moment of death. Some believed that death revealed our separation from God most fully, and that sexuality represented God's sympathy for our mortality because it offered a remedy, through procreation, for death. Others thought that sexuality itself was the clearest sign of our distance from God, because sexual desire can assert itself insistently even when the individual wills otherwise. The Christian practice of honoring the body thus took shape within the very human concern over how the basic physical realities of death and sexual desire can rob us of our freedom. At its best, the early Christians' difficult friendship with human embodiment aimed to restore human freedom in the face of these powerful forces.

With their commitment to freedom came a profound sense of responsibility for the protection and nourishment of other bodies. Bodily vulnerability is something we all share—rich and poor, male and female, slave and free. Many early Christians preached that knowledge of such shared vulnerability must lead us to solidarity with every other human body, especially the bodies of the poor. These Christians knew that what is suffered by one can be suffered by all, and that every body is a fragile temple of God's Spirit and worthy of care.

Early Christians teach us to pay attention to the ways in which our bodies are central to our freedom and to our life in God's presence. They also call us to solidarity with others—especially those

──── ⁀Ĺ ────

He whom we look down upon, whom we cannot bear to see, the
very sight of whom causes us to vomit, is the same as we are, formed
with us from the self-same clay, compacted of the same elements.
Whatever he suffers, we also can suffer.

Saint Jerome

who suffer. Unfortunately, a destructive fear of women and suspicion of the goodness of sexuality are often bound up with that legacy. Like any powerful practice, the practice of honoring the body can be deformed.

It is our task to retrieve and reinterpret the practice of honoring the body for our own age. We must do this in a way that corrects the deformations of the practice in the past and helps us honor the body in the future. There are so many forces in society that dishonor the body. If we are unable to shape a way of life that honors the body in every moment, we will lose something vital to human flourishing. We can receive help for this task both from the long history of Christian tradition and from the lives of those who are giving this tradition new life in our time. From our ancestors and our neighbors, we learn to glimpse the sacredness of the body in the most ordinary rituals of our daily lives—bathing, dressing, touching.

BATHING

Bathing is one of the most fundamental ways we honor our bodies. Whether we shower or soak in the tub, bathing requires an intimacy with our own bodies. Bath time is also a time of vulnerability, as we cannot offer our bodies this care without stripping them of the clothing that usually affords them a kind of protection. Times of bathing are opportunities to bless and honor the body and to perceive the sacredness at the heart of its vulnerability, as Gospel stories about bathing show.

Luke's Gospel tells a story about an unnamed woman, identified only as "a sinner," who entered a house where Jesus was having supper and began bathing his feet with her tears and wiping them dry with her hair. She goes on to kiss his feet and anoint them with ointment. The host is embarrassed and wonders what kind of prophet Jesus could be if he doesn't resist the touch of a sinful woman.

It is the woman herself, however, who seems to be the prophet in this story. Through the bold extravagance of her actions, the woman turns the simple act of bathing another's feet into a prophetic act. Her loose hair, which the host interpreted as a sign of her sinfulness, becomes a sign of loving intimacy. The bath she gives to

Then turning toward the woman, [Jesus] said to Simon,
"Do you see this woman? I entered your house; you gave me
no water for my feet, but she has bathed my feet with her tears
and dried them with her hair. You gave me no kiss, but from
the time I came in she has not stopped kissing my feet. You
did not anoint my head with oil, but she has anointed my feet
with ointment. Therefore, I tell you, her sins, which were
many, have been forgiven; hence she has shown great love."

Luke 7:44–47

Jesus becomes a sign of God's Spirit who wrenches from us our most passionate offerings. As the woman bathes him, a sense of recognition seems to pass between Jesus and the woman. He recognizes her as one whose sins have been forgiven. She recognizes him as dangerously vulnerable, leading her to give tender attention to a body that will soon be brutalized.

In John's Gospel, we see Jesus on his knees, bathing the feet of his friends. Again, this is seen as a shocking act, one normally required only of non-Jewish slaves, and Peter at first wishes to resist. Jesus responds by explaining that their community must be shaped by such acts of generosity: "If I, your Lord and Teacher, have washed your feet, you also ought to wash one another's feet" (John 13:14). Here, bathing becomes a sign of community in which each member takes responsibility for the well-being of every other.

Attention to our bodies during bathing can help to nurture a sense of the body as worthy of love and care by reminding us of our creation in God's image. A mother of two daughters remembers that, as a teenager, she was plagued by outbreaks of acne. One day, when she felt unable to leave the house because of anguish over her face, her father led her to the bathroom and asked if he could teach her a new way to wash. He leaned over the sink and splashed water over his face, telling her, "On the first splash, say, 'In the name of the Father'; on the second, 'in the name of the Son'; and on the third, 'in the name of the Holy Spirit.' Then look up into the mirror and remember that you are a child of God, full of grace and beauty." This woman has integrated her father's reverence for the body into her own daughters' bath time, making each bath a baptismal act. While they wash, they sing blessings over each part of their bodies, remembering that they are children of God, made in God's image.

Not long after the birth of my friend's daughter, our church community gathered on the feast of Epiphany for her baptism. As we remembered the magi whose gifts had no other purpose than to delight the senses, we welcomed this child into the household of God through the ancient ritual of baptism. Having been present at her birth, I felt I understood for the first time the magi's desire to offer extravagant gifts to a baby who was full of possibility and to a woman who had blessed us all by struggling to bring a new life into being.

The ritual of baptism welcomes the body along with the spirit into the community of faith. By giving the community an opportunity to bless the body, baptism undergirds the practice of honoring the body, a practice that can shape a way of life that protects the body, that delights in the body, that cherishes the body as part of God's good creation. It was a privilege to be present as this child was bathed in the waters of new life.

ADORNMENT

Clothing our bodies not only offers a way of protecting ourselves from the gaze of others, but has long been a source of delight for human beings. Graduates adorn themselves in academic robes that distinguish them as students who have completed a program of study. Brides and grooms adorn themselves gloriously for one another to prepare for and heighten the moment when they exchange their vows. The more special the occasion, the more careful we are about how we dress ourselves and what our dress says about us.

Adornment is not just a secular practice. In the Book of Exodus (28:2), God commands Moses to "make sacred vestments for the glorious adornment of your brother Aaron." The newly baptized are often dressed in white robes symbolizing their new life in Christ. Members of some religious orders wear simple garments that bear witness to their vocation. Members of Amish communities dress simply out of a commitment to direct their attention toward

*As God's chosen ones, holy and beloved, clothe yourselves with
compassion, kindness, humility, meekness, and patience. Bear with
one another and, if anyone has a complaint against another, forgive
each other; just as the Lord has forgiven you, so you also must
forgive. Above all, clothe yourselves with love, which binds
everything together in perfect harmony.*

COLOSSIANS 3:12–14

God and one another rather than fashion. The practice of wearing "Sunday-go-to-meeting" clothes to church is born of the ancient impulse to take special care with one's appearance when entering God's presence. How and with what we adorn ourselves can help shape our identity and heighten our experience of worshiping God.

Adornment can also be overemphasized in ways that obscure that experience. Sometimes it becomes a symptom of what is wrong with Christian communities. Wearing nice clothes to church may appear to be more important to some Christians than practicing the Gospel values of hospitality to the stranger, solidarity with the poor, and inclusion of those cast out by society. It is all too easy to satisfy the impulse to adorn ourselves, even to adorn ourselves for God, in wholly commercial ways.

Some families who want to resist such consumerism have begun to include creative ways of "dressing for church" as part of their preparation for worship. Rather than allowing the fashion industry to dictate what it means to "dress up," these families encourage their children to ready themselves for worship by adorning themselves with some garment or object that is special to them—perhaps a piece of jewelry made by a friend or an outfit that reflects and heightens the child's own sense of self. This approach to adornment helps children learn to resist the pressures of an industry that tries to dictate the dress of even the very young. Intentional, shared attention to adornment also allows children to develop their own sense of what is beautiful and pleasing. By helping children use their own developing aesthetic sense and sense of self to worship God, we encourage children to see their own uniqueness, and not some imposed notion of beauty, as intrinsic to what it means to be made in God's image.

Our relationship to bodily adornment not only allows us and our children the freedom to decide what is beautiful, but it also has implications for the literal freedom of others. News reports in 1995 of Thai garment workers enslaved in the United States in a barbed-wire-encased apartment where they were forced to sew around the clock made that very clear. Enslavement to the commodification of adornment makes this other, more terrible slavery possible. God intends all of us to be free. The practice of honoring the body requires habits of adornment that make us vigilant about the effects our choices have on others.

TOUCHING

The boundary of skin that our bodies place between us can be bridged through the touch of another. Our culture cries out for ways of understanding and teaching what is and is not an appropriate way of touching, what are and are not loving, generous ways of moving back and forth across the boundaries that our bodies establish between us.

The stories about bathing give us some insight into how we might teach ourselves and our children about appropriate touch. Indeed, in touching ourselves as we bathe, we can learn to touch others with love and care. The mother who sings joyfully with her children about the blessedness of the body as they bathe teaches them that appropriate touch seeks to honor, not diminish, another. The woman who weeps over Jesus' feet shows that, although touch can be extravagant and surprising, its power lies in its gentleness. Jesus' own washing of the feet of his disciples teaches us that it is appropriate to cross the boundaries between us only from motives of generosity and not from a desire to please ourselves alone.

Ritual acts of touching, such as foot washing and exchanging signs of peace in worship, offer us opportunities to learn to touch one another in peace and love. A student living alone in Italy for a year reports that she attended mass every evening in the small town where she lived, to worship God not only through word and sacrament but through touch. Living alone, she often went all day without feeling a human touch. The ritual moment of passing the peace

The capacity to give one's attention to a sufferer is a very rare
and difficult thing; it is almost a miracle; it is a miracle.

SIMONE WEIL, *Waiting for God*

was the high point of the service for her, because it provided a safe space for her to touch and be touched by other people—even people whom she did not know.

The longing to be touched reminds us again of our shared vulnerability and how we need one another in order to honor the body. We are perhaps never more aware of our shared bodily vulnerability than when we are ill or when we are in the presence of those who are ill. Because of this, it is all too easy to render the ill invisible, because to be truly present to those who suffer, we have to remember our own capacity for suffering.

It is understandable that those who are ill often feel that their bodies have betrayed them. A group of friends in a Chicago church responded to this reality when one of them became terminally ill. As he grew sicker, his body first became a stranger and then an enemy to him, a source of nothing but anguish. In the last months of his life, he told his friends of his feeling of having been abandoned by his body. They began reading about and training themselves in therapeutic touch. They began to gather regularly in his home, to stroke his hands and feet, to touch his skin, to gently offer him a sense of his body as a source of comfort, not of pain alone. Through these sessions of therapeutic touching, he found himself more able to speak freely about his illness and his inevitable death. Through the practice of touching, his friends found themselves able to respond with compassion rather than fear, with openness rather than denial. And when their friend died, they found comfort in their grief through the healing touch of one another.

The group has since gone on to offer the gift of therapeutic touch to others in need of compassionate attention. Through this practice, they find themselves able to be present to those who are suffering, to experience the vulnerability of their own bodies, and to offer comfort that is rooted in a fragility that is shared by us all.

SEXUALITY

The practice of honoring the body is perhaps nowhere more urgently needed than in the realm of sexuality. As early Christians knew, our sexuality is a source of both great pleasure and great vulnerability. Because of this, honoring the body means that we will be always moving between affirmation and renunciation, between, as another chapter in this volume puts it, saying yes and saying no.

A few years ago, a "posse" of high school boys was discovered to have been competing for "points" by having sex with girls in their classes. When interviewed, many of the girls said they had felt obliged to participate. Our young people desperately need ways of resisting the coercive power of others over their sexuality. They need communities that honor the body by nurturing the powerful sense of self required for such resistance. They, and we, need to find ways of nourishing among us a sense of reverence for our own and others' bodies.

Such reverence can flourish only in homes and religious communities where sexuality is discussed and celebrated. When families and communities honor the body, people are formed in freedom, solidarity, and love rather than anger and frustration. Our efforts to help young people refuse others' demands on their bodies and to postpone their own gratification must be taken out of the context of "dos and don'ts" and put into the context of our hope that they will have the ability to love well and to find deep satisfaction in their sexuality as adults. This is most possible in communities where loving, committed partners model reverence toward and delight in one another's bodies. Rituals that mark the growth and development of young people can undergird the practice of honoring the body by providing community affirmations of the goodness of the body and the changes that occur in the course of its sexual development.

Jewish biblical scholar Tikva Frymer-Kensky has begun to end the silence around such changes in her collection of prayers for pregnant women and women seeking to become pregnant. She begins her book with prayers about menstruation, linking women's monthly cycle to the spiritual cycles of faith communities and the cycles of history and of lifetimes. She rejects the interpretation of menstrual blood as unclean and instead embraces it as an agent of cleansing, just as blood was used by Aaron and his sons to purify the altar in biblical Israel. Her prayers about menstruation celebrate God's covenant with women as bearers of life and the ways in which women are united by their monthly cycle to women of every time and place.

Churches and families can use such prayers to affirm the changes in sexually developing bodies. Even just a few words of acknowledgment can contribute to a sense of reverence about these changes. One woman remembers that on the evening of the onset of her first menstrual period, her father came into her room, sat on the edge of the bed, and told her how proud he was of her. She remembers feeling embarrassed and now realizes that her father was probably equally embarrassed. His willingness to speak in spite of their mutual discomfort, however, left her with a sense of the blessedness of her body that has persisted throughout her life. She hopes to have children herself and to pass on to them the reverence for the body that her father showed for her own.

As we move between affirmation of the goodness of the body and refusal of anything that diminishes or degrades the body, we must learn to repudiate the ways in which our culture values and protects some bodies more than others because of race or gender or sexual identity. When we renounce the privilege that attaches to some bodies and makes possible the denigration and violation of others, we proclaim that all bodies are reflections of God's good creation, deserving of reverence and care.

WORSHIP

Increasing our awareness of the sacredness of the body promises to deepen our relationship to others and help us respond to one another's suffering with genuine compassion. Such awareness can also open paths for us to explore our relationship to God as embodied creatures. The flesh that was formed and shaped and loved by God is the same flesh that longs for God. "O God, you are my God, I seek you," the psalmist writes. "My soul thirsts for you, my flesh faints for you, as in a dry and weary land where there is no water" (Psalm 63:1). Our desire for God is not only a desire of the spirit, but also of the body.

For Christians, communal worship provides opportunities to honor the body through rituals that deepen our experience of the body's sacredness in everyday life. The Lord's Supper reminds us that every time we gather with others to nourish our bodies, we have an opportunity to draw closer to one another and to God. Exchanging signs of peace with our bodies reminds us that we must touch others only in peace and love. Adorning ourselves for worship, kneeling in prayer, drawing our breath in song all remind us that we come to God as embodied people.

The movement of the liturgical year also honors the body as central to our search for God. The liturgical calendar is a record of embodiment, as it takes shape around the life of Jesus and the community he called into being. Fasting during Lent, foot washing on Maundy Thursday, celebrating the Easter Vigil at midnight unite us with Christians of every age who have sought to enter bodily into the narrative of Jesus' life and death.

During Easter, it is Jesus' resurrected body that teaches us, perhaps more than any other image in Christianity, that bodies matter. In the resurrection narratives of the New Testament, Jesus insists on his body: "Look at my hands and my feet," he says in Luke's Gospel. "See that it is I myself. Touch me and see." Offering his hands and feet for inspection, Jesus gives his followers the foundation of the new vision that will be required of them as they strive to follow him when he is no longer walking and talking by their side. "Touch me," he says, "and *see.*" Jesus offers his body as the lens

---

∿

She seemed to see Jesus Christ, so glorious that no human heart could conceive of it. . . . This glorious body was so noble and so transparent that one could clearly see the soul inside of it. This body was so noble that one could see oneself reflected in it more clearly than in a mirror. This body was so beautiful that one could see the angels and the saints, as if they were painted on it.

Margaret of Oingt, *Mirror*

Practicing Our Faith

through which the disciples must look if they—and we—are to respond to the world's needs with love.

The Christian practice of honoring the body requires that we view the world through the lens of Jesus' wounded but resurrected body. His broken body brings into focus the bodies of the sick and the wounded and the exploited. His resurrection shows us the beauty God intends for all bodies. As we love and suffer, as we seek God and each other, with our bodies, we remember that every body is blessed by God, deserving of protection and care.

Chapter 3

HOSPITALITY

❧

Ana María Pineda

For many decades, the Mission District of San Francisco has been a home and a welcome *posada* (shelter) for a diverse population of Hispanics and Latinos. Over the years, it has taken on the aged familiarity of the neighborhoods its inhabitants left behind in their Latin American countries of origin. Its streets bustle with activity as people attend to the daily needs of family and work and as children come and go to school. Throughout the day, the bells of St. Peter's announce the presence of the church. The Mission District teems with life, as the culture and customs of the Latino world fill its days with vitality.

On this December evening, children of every age process down Twenty-Fourth Street, some with lighted candles in hand and others carrying on their shoulders statues of Mary and Joseph. Each Advent, the young and the old reenact the story of Joseph seeking lodging for his young wife, Mary, who is weary from travel and heavy with child. For nine nights in a row, children and adults assume the identity of the weary couple or of the innkeepers, processing around the inside of the church or throughout the neighborhood, moving

29

En nombre del cielo,
buenos moradores,
dad a unos viajeros
posada esta noche.
(In the name of God,
we ask those who dwell here,
give to some travelers
lodging this evening.)

Traditional Song for *Las Posadas*

---

from one designated site to the next. This is the beloved ritual of *Las Posadas.*

At each station, an ancient exchange is repeated. Those playing the role of Joseph approach the inn, knock on the door, and say in a loud voice, *En nombre del cielo, buenos moradores, dad a unos viajeros posada esta noche.* From inside, a chorus of voices responds, *Aquí no es meson sigan adelante; yo no puedo abrir no sea algun tunante* (This is not an inn; move on—I cannot open lest you be a scoundrel). As Joseph moves from one inn to the next, the innkeepers grow angry and even threaten violence, while the night grows colder and the young couple's weariness turns to exhaustion. *Venimos rendidos desde Nazareth, yo soy carpintero de nombre José* (We are tired traveling from Nazareth; I am a carpenter named Joseph), the anxious husband implores. Finally, he even reveals his wife's true identity, begging for *posada* for just one night for *la Reina del Cielo,* the Queen of Heaven—to no avail.

For eight days, the scene is reenacted. Finally, on the ninth day, the eve of Christmas, Joseph's request moves the heart of an innkeeper, who offers the young couple all that he has left—a stable. Yet the stable is enhanced by the love with which the innkeeper offers it, and this humble place becomes the birthplace of Jesus. In an outpouring of joy and festivity, those gathered on the final night celebrate the generosity of the innkeeper and the *posada* given to Mary and Joseph in song and dance, food and drink. Candy and treats from the piñata shower the children, and the community recalls anew how the stranger at one's door can be God in disguise.

Every December, Hispanic communities relive in their flesh the Gospel truth that "the Word became flesh and lived among us" (John 1:14). "He was in the world, and the world came into being through him; yet the world did not know him. He came to what was his own, and his own people did not accept him" (John 1:10–11). In *Las Posadas,* they ritually participate in being rejected and being welcomed, in slamming the door on the needy and opening it wide. They are in this way renewed in the Christian practice of hospitality, the practice of providing a space where the stranger is taken in and known as one who bears gifts.

STRANGERS IN OUR MIDST

Although *Las Posadas* is a beautiful, engaging ritual, the reality it addresses is a painful one: the reality of human need and exclusion. When the ritual takes place in the Mission District of San Francisco, many of the participants—once refugees themselves—remember their own experience as strangers. Through the ritual, the community affirms the goodness of taking people in, and those who once needed *posada* are reminded to offer it to others.

This is a lesson that is needed in other communities as well. The need for shelter, for *posada,* is a fundamental human need. None of us ever knows for sure when we might be uprooted and cast on the mercy of others. Throughout human history, there have been times when people were dislocated, becoming vulnerable as they journeyed far from home. Sometimes there have been people to take them in, and sometimes not.

Just as the human need for hospitality is a constant, so, it seems, is the human fear of the stranger. Unfortunately, the fear of "the strange one" has a long history in human societies. The stranger seems to portend danger—sometimes of physical harm, but also because the stranger represents the unknown, a challenge to the familiar constructs of our personal world. And so we human beings try to keep strangers at a distance; we avoid risky encounters or we try to neutralize the stranger's power in order to protect our own. Some societies try to appease strangers with gifts; others exclude or even destroy them.

These fundamental human needs and fears confront contemporary men and women intensely. As the world shrinks and mobility increases, we encounter strangers frequently. But this has only heightened our fears. Those who enjoy comfort and shelter edge their way around homeless strangers. Those whose health is presently strong turn away from the gaunt, blemished faces of those living with AIDS. The prosperous never enter the poverty-stricken neighborhoods that abound with gang violence, drug abuse, unemployment, and welfare dependency. "Strangers" do not belong in the world in which the "comfortable" move with relative ease. And so there is no room for those who do not conform to mainstream standards or speak the mainstream language. Access to borders and to basic resources—shelter, employment, education, and health care—is cut off, as the powerful respond to genuine human need with an inhospitality fueled by fear.

Ironically, it is not just hospitality to the "stranger" that is in peril in our society. We are short not only of tables that welcome strangers but even of tables that welcome friends. In a society that prizes youthfulness, the elderly are often isolated from the affection and care of their own families. In many busy families, children find no after-school welcome home, and spouses find little time to host one another over supper. And when we become estranged—separated by grievances large or small, or simply crowded out of one another's lives—we all too often become "strangers" even to those we once loved. Can we move beyond strangeness and estrangement to learn the skills of welcoming one another and to claim the joy of homecoming?

STRANGERS, GUESTS, AND HOSTS IN THE BIBLE

In the traditions shaped by the Bible, offering hospitality is a moral imperative. The expectation that God's people are people who will welcome strangers and treat them justly runs throughout the Bible. This expectation is not based on any special immunity to the dangers unknown people might present—far from it. Rather, it emerges from knowing the hospitality God has shown to us.

When an alien resides with you in your land, you shall not oppress the alien. The alien who resides with you shall be to you as the citizen among you; you shall love the alien as yourself, for you were aliens in the land of Egypt: I am the LORD your God.

LEVITICUS 19:33–34

The Hebrew Scriptures (called by many Christians the Old Testament) tell the story of the descendants of Abraham and Sarah, who answered God's call to journey far from home in search of a promised land. Later, after years of exile and slavery in Egypt, these descendants were a refugee people, wandering in a wilderness, and later still they were forced into captivity again and sent off to a distant land. As a result, their laws always required them to deal justly and compassionately with the strangers among them. "You shall also love the stranger," God instructs the people through Moses, "for you were strangers in the land of Egypt" (Deuteronomy 10:19). Resident aliens must be judged and protected by the same laws that govern insiders, and strangers must be treated with the same respect one would wish for oneself. Just as God protected the people of Israel when they were refugees, so God insists on proper care for other aliens now, judging harshly those who treat them ill. God's people will be a people whose just hospitality flows from gratitude for God's past care and from their own painful memories of refugee life.

Hospitality was also a crucial practice among the early Christians. One New Testament word incorporates a profound truth: *xenos,* the word that means "stranger" in Greek, also means "guest" and "host." This one word signals the essential mutuality that is at the heart of hospitality. No one is strange except in relation to someone else; we make one another guests and hosts by how we treat one another. There is a common English word that uses this same root: *xenophobia,* fear of the stranger, which is often associated with extreme nationalism or intense "my group is better than your group" attitudes. Turn this word around and make a little change, however, and you get the New Testament word for hospitality: *philoxenia,* a love of the guest or stranger. *Philoxenia* can also mean love of the whole atmosphere of hospitality and the whole activity of guesting and hosting. Indeed, within a philoxenic circle of mutuality, unexpected transformations can occur. This happens again and again when Jesus eats with others. He arrives at a wedding as a guest, but when the wine runs out, he provides more and becomes the host (John 2:1–11). Martha invites him to her house to be her guest and wears herself out with serving, but he teaches her that on this day it is better to sit and receive (Luke 10:38–42).

This circle of mutual hospitality can embrace and transform the people who enter it. The early church, which met in houses, grew up turning hosts into guests and guests into hosts. The apostle Paul, whose ministry involved traveling from one house church to another, looked forward to the nourishing hospitality that awaited him in each place, just as the young churches looked forward to the gifts he would bring to them.

We need to think about how similar transformations can happen in our own lives, as those we thought were our guests end up hosting us instead, giving us the gifts of their presence. Work for the homeless, for example, frequently begins with the thought that a privileged person can help someone in need. Often, however, the ostensible hosts discover that they have received from the homeless at least as much as they have given.

This notion that the guest—even a strange one—may bear surprising gifts and may indeed be a Holy One leads to a third biblical perspective on hospitality. "Do not neglect to show hospitality to strangers, for by doing that some have entertained angels without knowing it," says the Letter to the Hebrews (13:2). Abraham's warm welcome to three men who visited his tent (Genesis 18) was an ancient example; these guests brought with them the astounding news that Abraham's aged wife, Sarah, would bear a child. Later, the idea that the face of the stranger is indeed the face of Christ appears in Matthew's Gospel (25:38). When it is most fully realized, hospitality not only welcomes strangers; it also recognizes their holiness. It sees in the stranger a person dear to and made in the image of God, someone bearing distinctive gifts that only he or she can bring.

Becoming a Hospitable People

Many of us know that we should offer hospitality, but we wonder whether we can. Hospitality is made up of hard work undertaken under risky conditions, and without structures and commitments for welcoming strangers, fear crowds out what needs to be done. Hospitable places where guests can disclose the gifts they bear come into being only when people take up this practice and grow wise, by experience, in doing it well. In the face of overwhelming human need for shelter and care, and in the face of our own fear of strangers, we need to develop ways of supporting one another in the practice of hospitality.

Today, communities of many cultures are doing this hard work in response to concrete needs. In 1986, for example, a group of concerned Central Americans in San Francisco came together to create the organization CARECEN (Central American Resource Center) to provide legal defense for Central Americans who were negatively affected by a new immigration law. Relying heavily on volunteers, CARECEN expanded over time to provide a wide range of services, particularly to Latinos who had little or no access to basic health care. The Spanish-speaking staff and volunteers took an approach to health and medicine informed by Hispanic culture, and Latinos felt welcome. In many instances, staff and volunteers had themselves benefited from CARECEN's services, so the stresses and pressures experienced by clients were familiar to those who now

꒦꒦

To offer hospitality to a stranger is to welcome something new,
unfamiliar, and unknown into our life-world. . . . Strangers have
stories to tell which we have never heard before, stories which
can redirect our seeing and stimulate our imaginations. The stories
invite us to view the world from a novel perspective.

Thomas Ogletree, *Hospitality to the Stranger*

found themselves at the giving end. Those who had first come as guests now found themselves in the privileged position of being the hosts.

As the organization grew, CARECEN found itself in need of a new *posada,* a site where the expanding services could be housed. Not surprisingly, they turned to St. Peter's parish, whose welcoming spirit was well known even though it was obvious that the physical plant had little space to spare. On less than a city block in a densely populated neighborhood, the parish grounds included the church, a small parish hall, the parish convent, the rectory, and a two-storied elementary school, all in constant use for meetings, a homeless shelter, and a small community-run co-op. The only extra space was in the convent, which had once housed twenty members of a religious community of women who had taught in the elementary school and worked in the parish; it now housed only five. After considerable discussion, all concerned agreed to see if the building could be architecturally modified to make room for both the services of CARECEN and the religious who continued to work in the parish. It could. The convent, while remaining a home for the religious women whose order had given service to the parish community for over a hundred years, widened its doors to respond to the medical needs of Latinos.

In spite of its limited resources, this parish continually looks for ways to extend hospitality, helping both guests and hosts to grow stronger in the many aspects and the richness of this practice. Here, hospitality extends beyond feeding the hungry and sheltering the homeless; here, it also involves creating space where people can learn how to receive and give. In neighborhoods across the nation, the church is often in a good position not only to gather families around the Eucharist each Sunday but also to prepare them to expand the circle of those who are made welcome in their communities. Unfortunately, the church's walls sometimes seem to shut people out instead of welcoming them, and even what happens inside those walls can have the effect of excluding others. Often churchgoers are uncomfortable with people whose spiritual devotions are unfamiliar or with people whose ethnicity, class, or age group is different from their own. Each Christian community must struggle to find ways of creating a *posada* where all can become free to receive and give.

Preaching and liturgy must speak a welcoming message to those both inside and outside church walls.

In San Jose, California, the Portuguese community celebrates the practice of hospitality annually on the Feast of the Holy Spirit. Once again, the walls of the church broaden to embrace the larger community as the parish members process through the city streets. The procession leads into a shared liturgy and ends with a parish-sponsored meal to which everyone in the neighborhood is invited. The meal in itself is a significant part of the celebration; traditionally, it has been seen as an expression of a community's responsibility to make provision for those who have less. This celebration is no small challenge, for the parish church is located in a working sector of the city that is growing less familiar to those who have lived there for decades. At a time when this church is struggling to serve people discharged from a nearby mental institution and to adapt to the increasing ethnic diversity of its neighborhood, this procession, liturgy, and meal strengthen its members in the practice of hospitality.

In San Francisco and San Jose, as in all large cities, economic problems have given rise to delinquency, gangs, and violence. All these factors make hospitality to the stranger challenging and often formidable. Nevertheless, these West Coast communities have brought together their creativity and talent to find ways of participating in the Christian practice of welcoming the stranger, the alienated, the homeless, the other. While alert to the importance of prudent and thoughtful consideration, they have found ways to bolster the effectiveness of individual practices of hospitality through the strength of community. What would be a daunting undertaking for any single individual is addressed by committed groups of people who together discern how to extend hospitality and provide *posada* to the stranger. Similar examples of congregational hospitality exist all over the world.

WEAVING HOSPITABLE PATTERNS OF LIFE

Over five decades ago, Antonio and María left their homeland to seek greater security for their young children. Life in the United

States was different from anything they had ever experienced before, and making ends meet required hard work. María abandoned her profession as an elementary school teacher to work in a laundry, while Antonio dreamed of being able to support the family on his salary and of sparing his young wife the hardship of working in a foreign country. They longed to return to their native land, and every year Antonio and María reminded their children that they would one day return home. As the years progressed, their own home became a *posada,* a haven for other relatives and friends who arrived in the U.S. pursuing the same dreams that had once brought them here. The door to María and Antonio's home was always open to those in need of a friend or a place to stay; it is difficult even to estimate how many enjoyed the warmth of their welcome over the years. Their *posada* now boasts a houseful of young Latino professionals who fill it with grandchildren and continued commitment to the Latino community.

Every holiday, and especially Christmas, has been a special occasion to gather as an extended family to celebrate and give thanks for many blessings. And every holiday brings Charles to the warmth of this home and family. Somewhere along the way, Charles appeared as a friend to one of the boys. Who exactly he was, or how he lived, or where his own family was—these questions were never asked. A solitary man, not well-off, somewhat of a hanger-on, Charles appears empty-handed and alone each holiday season. So different from the robust members of the family, he comes seeking human warmth and care; he arrives, the continual stranger in background and culture, at the front door of María and Antonio's home, where he is received unquestioningly and given loving, generous *posada.*

To welcome the stranger is to acknowledge him as a human being made in God's image; it is to treat her as one of equal worth with ourselves—indeed, as one who may teach us something out of the richness of experiences different from our own. The stranger's gifts may come to a family circle or to a society. Yet the undocumented foreigner—the alien who crosses over the borders of narrow and provincial worlds—is too often not greeted with hospitality or even acknowledged as a human being in God's image.

It is perhaps less difficult for marginalized communities to reach out than for those long-settled to do so. Those who have been strangers themselves have developed an empathy for others who confront a similar reality. Within the biblical story, however, it is clear that all God's people are spiritually descended from migrants and wanderers, and that all are called to hospitality. In spite of the difficulties and threats encountered on the streets of U.S. neighborhoods today, Hispanic families want their children to know how to respond to the needs of the poor, the alien, the marginalized, and the physically challenged—and indeed, this undergirds the relatively low rate of homelessness in the Hispanic community. People do take one another in, taught to do so both by example and by the annual return of *Las Posadas.* The members of other communities need to learn from this, so that they can participate more fully in the Gospel practice of hospitality.

HOSPITALITY, PERSONAL AND PUBLIC

In contemporary society, opportunities to practice hospitality abound. They appear at many levels, from public policy deliberations to barely noticeable acts of personal kindness. In 1987, for example, ministers of Catholic communities in the Archdiocese of Chicago responded to the Immigration Reform and Control Act of 1986 with a statement setting forth the Christian responsibility to immigrants. The statement challenged all believers to resist unjust treatment of the men and women who seek refuge in this land and invited communities to give the finest of their resources for the compassionate care of the immigrant. The authors of the statement committed themselves not only to denounce the abuse of basic human rights, including raids on workplaces, but also to educate communities to respond to the needs of the alien, the widow, and the orphan in their midst. This statement challenged Christians to join together in attending to the needs of the stranger in ways that would go beyond anything a single person could do.

Perhaps one of the most powerful insights into the dynamic of hospitality comes from seeing the liberation, joy, and support experienced by those who have sought and found *posada,* those who have been the outsiders and who have been taken in by Christians who recognized in their faces the face of Jesus. Such a one is Refugio. In following her in her story, we may walk in the steps of a stranger

*Then the king will say to those on his right hand, "Come, blessed
of my Father, take possession of the kingdom prepared for you
from the foundation of the world; for I was hungry and you gave
me to eat; I was thirsty and you gave me to drink; I was a
stranger and you took me in."*

MATTHEW 25:34–35

seeking shelter and safety. We may understand both fear and hope, finally seeing the shadowed face of the Christ behind the visage of those who seek refuge and count on Christian hospitality.

Refugio fled one night from her home in Central America, bringing her three small children with her. She was uncertain of her future but convinced that she could no longer stay in the abusive marriage she had endured for more than a decade. The profile of her battered nose gave silent testimony to the beatings that had been regularly inflicted on her by her husband. She had withstood the beatings for the sake of the children—or so she had believed until one day the children became the objects of her husband's uncontrollable rage. It was then that she gathered up courage to leave her husband. It was a risky proposition, but the welfare of her children required it of her.

For weeks, Refugio had plotted how and when she would escape. Her husband's family was prominent in the community, and all signs of impropriety were suppressed. Refugio could not confide in relatives or friends. It had taken her this long to summon up courage to leave the situation, and she could not chance losing the opportunity to seek out a new life. In her mind's eye, Refugio reviewed the list of friends and acquaintances whom she knew had left for the United States. To whom could she turn, and who would offer her the help that she needed? Finally, one morning as she awakened from her uneasy slumber, the face of a distant relative crystallized before her. She had forgotten that he had left their town some time ago and now lived somewhere in the United States. Refugio would have to search out his relatives and discreetly discover his whereabouts.

Eventually, she managed to locate and contact him. She hoped that he would understand the urgency of her request and the need to hold it in confidence. Anxiously, she awaited his reply; at last, a cryptic message was delivered to her. It conveyed news that arrangements had been made for her to settle in a city on the West Coast. Her relative indicated that for her safety, it was best that she not travel to the city where he lived but rather settle in the Latino sector of a larger city. Refugio had heard the name of the neighborhood mentioned before. She had hoped that her relative would offer her the protection of his proximity, but she understood all too well the wisdom of his decision to locate her elsewhere.

Time passed slowly as she painfully attended to the detailed preparations her departure required. Finally, the day arrived. She was filled with the dread of exposure. What if her husband discovered her plans? What if some relative had become suspicious or had noticed her increasing anxiety? At the designated hour, she and her children boarded a small van. They crouched down in the van as they were driven across the U.S. border. From there, they traveled for what seemed an eternity. Refugio was filled with self-doubt. Perhaps it had not been such a good idea to leave her husband. What would she do in this strange land? She could not speak the language. She did not have much money, and what would she do once it was spent? As the children began to fret and cry, her fear increased, and she felt helpless to assure them that all would be well. Finally, overcome by weariness, Refugio fell asleep.

It was dawn when Refugio awoke. The first rays of sunlight warmed the neighborhood of small houses and apartment buildings. Over them loomed a church steeple that seemed to cast a protective shadow on the neighborhood. As the van drove down the narrow streets, Refugio caught glimpses of street signs with Spanish names and store after store bearing the names of cherished homelands that had been left behind—Little Habana, Acapulco, Jalisco, El Tazumal, Borinque. . . . The sleepy neighborhood seemed to be awakening: people waited on the corner for buses to take them to work, storekeepers bustled around putting out their merchandise, cars wove their way through the narrow streets. Refugio was caught up in the sounds and rhythm of a Latino neighborhood. It seemed to soothe her anxious heart, bringing a growing sense of tranquility to her spirits and offering her weary body a place to rest.

This traveler had at long last found a resting place, lodging for herself and her children. Refugio found herself humming a song from her childhood:

> Me llamo José,
> vengo con María mi esposa que espera niño.
> Vengo a pedir posadas.
> (My name is Joseph,
> I come with Mary, my wife, who is expecting child.
> I come asking for welcome.)

It was a melody Refugio would recall later that year as she celebrated the season of Jesus' awaited birth. In her new neighborhood, she and her children would join her new community in *Las Posadas*. The stranger taken in had become the host opening her doors in Christian welcome.

Las Posadas is more than ritual. It crystallizes the community's experience of being nourished and challenged daily by the central Christian mystery—namely, that the stranger at our door can be both gift and challenge, human and divine. All Christians are called to the practice of hospitality. What is important is that each community discover how to practice that hospitality in ways that are relevant to its own situation.

Chapter 4

HOUSEHOLD ECONOMICS

❧

Sharon Daloz Parks

Whatever the form of our household—an urban apartment, an upscale residence in the "burbs," a farmhouse, a nursing home, a trailer, a brownstone, or the office where we find ourselves "living"—our homeplaces define basic ways of life. We count on the predictable motion of moving into, through, and from "our space." The way we routinely approach our home and fumble for key or doorbell is coupled with a sometimes surprisingly fierce sense that it matters to us whether or not we have a Christmas tree in our window in December or candles on the table on Friday evening and food—indeed, the food we particularly like—in the fridge and cupboard. Home is where we let down and rest well—or fitfully. Home is where we figure out primary patterns of nurture and productivity, habits of need and desire, forms of rage and forgiveness, ways of "taking time" and discovering the people who "count" for us. Our households are anchoring places where, over time, we craft the practices by which we prosper or fail to prosper.

For most, "economics" suggests something quite different: money, markets, investment, trade, taxes, profit, loss, and the cultivation of

Always be sure that when your kids are helping in the kitchen
they are having a good time. We either cook for each other
or we starve, there are no other rules.

The Frugal Gourmet

wealth understood in those terms. As such, "economics" in the complexity of the contemporary world is presumed to be something understood only by the experts—economists, bankers, brokers, budget directors, accountants, attorneys, and other financial advisers. In fact, the word *economics* is grounded in a much broader set of meanings.

Like the words *ecumenical* and *ecology, economics* is rooted in the Greek word *oikos,* meaning household, and signifies the management of the household—arranging what is necessary for well-being. Good economic practice—positive ways of exchanging goods and services—is about the well-being, the livelihood, of the whole household.

RECONSIDERING THE
WELL-BEING OF THE HOUSEHOLD

We are undergoing a profound reordering of our shared planet-household, our economic-ecological-ecumenical life. While the notion of "home" in American culture has shrunk from meaning one's town or region to meaning only one's own house or apartment, at the same time, paradoxically, it has become less possible to isolate our individual households from the world around them. As we try to defend the security of our *private home,* we are simultaneously rediscovering the economic-ecological truth of our profound interdependence within the small *planet home* we share.

The technologies of travel and communications have spawned a global marketplace; ecological awareness is teaching us about our interdependence; and the global commons is becoming our shared homeplace. In this new global commons, prosperity becomes problematic when we seek only the prosperity of our individual households, neighborhoods, businesses, and corporations. When we turn

on the faucet in the sanctity of our safe haven, we are not as confident as we used to be that the water we drink is safe. Whether we eat
"in" or "out," we wonder how our current agricultural practice may
affect the safety and quality of our food supply. We become stuck in
our wondering because the relationships among the city waterworks,
the Environmental Protection Agency, plumbers, farmers, fertilizer
companies, truckers, supermarkets, municipal bonds, and the com-
modities exchange have become dauntingly complex.

Meanwhile, two economies are emerging: the Global North
and the Global South, representing a growing gap between the
wealthy and the poor. Like an hourglass, these economies divide us
into hemispheres; they bifurcate our cities and rural communities and
sever the bonds of extended families. As these two polarized economies emerge, the human conscience forms a fragile bridge between
them. Indeed, people of good conscience are increasingly troubled by
the steady advance of a debilitating culture of economic anxiety,
poverty, violence, environmental degradation, refugee-migratory
labor on an unprecedented scale, and the growth of a third, criminal
economy. Whether we are professional, working class, or underclass,
the recognition of these two (or three) economies is fueling our anxieties and our compassion. We are aware of manifold forms of economic injustice that we both create and fear.

BUSYNESS AND CUMBER

Many feel that the most we can do is simply keep up, managing as
best we can. Our calendars are bursting, and we are busy; even children are busy. We are working more and faster, in part because the
incentive structures in our present economy have a bias toward either
long work hours or multiple part-time jobs. We work at these jobs
to secure our sense of belonging and well-being, increasingly defined
by access to the goods and services we need and want.

One consequence is what early Quakers called "cumber." Billions of marketing dollars are spent worldwide to make a dazzling
array of products and services attractive, even "necessary." Moreover,
the market has become ubiquitous. Once, we only *went* to market.
Now the market comes to us—to our homes, workplaces, and public

The [United States] is among the wealthiest countries in the world,
and yet it is filled with people, rich and poor, who are anxious
about their future and who feel that they don't have enough.

SARAH VAN GELDER, "Real Wealth:
Redefining Abundance in an Era of Limits"

spaces through television, telemarketing, magazines, catalogues, and
online services. We wear advertising on our clothing and plaster it
on every facade of our common life. And it works. Americans now
spend more time shopping than citizens of any other nation, and we
spend a higher fraction of the money we earn.

The consequent cumber affects our ways of life. The stuff we
accumulate requires our energy and attention to secure, maintain,
and finally to discard, and the pervasive advertising-entertainment
images of a consumer culture lodge in our souls, shaping our desires
and agendas. These conditions give rise to a toxic economic anxiety
described by Douglas Meeks, a biblical theologian, as a double jolt-
ing sense of "scarcity and satiety." It appears that we must compete
in a world of scarce resources, continually fearing that we do not
have enough, even though we feel bloated with cumber and guilty
about a standard of living well above that of most of the *oikumene,*
the whole inhabited world. There is a growing awareness that Spirit
is inviting us as a household of faith to reconsider the management
of our planet home.

A provocative Old Testament scholar challenged a group of laity
and clergy, saying: "I'm really not interested in your 'story of faith.' I
want to know about your 'story with money.'" And another has said,
"Show me your checkbook, and I will tell you what you believe." Behind each of these comments lies the ancient wisdom that where our
treasure is, there our heart is also. Further, our practice of household
economics needs to be a part of the conversation-communion we
share in the household of faith. But this is not easy to do. We may discuss the church budget, perhaps our individual contribution, and in
some cases the tithe. In casual conversation, it may be mentioned that
"we got a good deal" or "found it on sale" or even "decided we couldn't
afford it at this point." Yet a visitor from another country observed

that in the United States, he might in the course of casual conversation during a car ride be told the details of the car owner's forthcoming surgical operation, but he would be less likely to be told (and it would be rude to ask) how much the car cost or how much the owner makes. In the domain of economic life, we typically remain strangers to one another—each of us essentially alone with our sense of busyness and cumber, fear and guilt.

SPIRIT IN MATTER

One of the reasons it is difficult to talk about either the satisfactions or the stresses of our economic life is that any linkage between faith and economics inevitably awakens a degree of apprehension. If we were really faithful, we suppose, we would have to sell all that we have and give it to the poor (Mark 10:21). We presume that something difficult and unattractive would be required—we would be asked to move from material comfort to a supposedly spiritual but surely less comfortable way of life. But the choice that is faithful is not necessarily between the comfortable and the uncomfortable. For Christians, the move that is faithful is not from the material to the spiritual but rather from materialism to incarnation.

Incarnation is a theologian's way of speaking about Spirit dwelling in matter. Along with many other traditions, Judaism and Christianity understand the inner secret of Creation to be the indwelling of God within it. The whole of Creation is the place of God's presence. God is "home" here. Spirit is incarnate—within us, among us, beyond us, beneath us—in the motion and matter of Life Itself, giving dignity and value to every element of Creation. Every being participates in the household of God and is included in the economic imagination of God. The great gulfs we have created between

ॱ৶

The breath of God is only one of the divine gifts that make us living souls; the other is the dust. Most of our modern troubles come from our misunderstanding and misevaluation of this dust.

WENDELL BERRY, *Sex, Economy, Freedom and Community*

the spiritual and the material, between religion and commerce, between businesspeople and environmentalists, are products of a false consciousness, an unexamined and inadequate economic faith.

Thus as we cross the complex economic frontiers of the twenty-first century, we can draw on the legacy of a great host who have gone before us and who, like us, have sought to practice the economic implications of "God with us."

TREACHERY AND TREASURE

To be sure, the economic history of religious tradition is ambiguous—filled with economic treachery, from Jacob's stealing Esau's inheritance to the participation of missionaries in the economic colonization of continents. But religious tradition also holds treasures of insight and practice that can prompt, inform, and guide contemporary communities of faith as we face both perennial and unprecedented economic realities.

For people of biblical faith, ancient covenants have grounded and guided economic practice. In the Book of Exodus, for example, we learn that when the Children of Israel were in the wilderness, God provided manna sufficient for each day, but if it was hoarded, it rotted. Later, if a neighbor borrowed your oxcart and left a coat in pledge, you had to be sure to give the coat back before sunset, even if the neighbor was not finished with the oxcart; this was especially binding if the neighbor was poor. A millstone could not be taken as a pledge because it was essential to a person's livelihood. The practice of economic compassion was extended to livestock and land, which should have "rest." Baby birds might be taken, but the mother bird must be left to care for the remaining eggs and to produce further young.

In the Christian Gospels, Jesus fed the hungry, countered the assumption that the wealthy had found special favor with God, and grieved the oppression of all who sought to secure treasures on Earth that were vulnerable to corruption. From its inception, the Christian church has practiced in imperfect though often powerful forms a practical, material care for each other and for "widows and orphans"—society's vulnerable ones.

Throughout much of Christian history, economic care for others appears to take the form of charity, arising from the belief that unjust socioeconomic structures are the inevitable consequences of a fallen humanity. Yet when we examine the tradition more closely, faithful people (particularly in transitional periods of history) have again and again been called to ways of life that had economic consequences in structural terms. For example, the call to the desert, the development of religious orders, their subsequent renewals, the Protestant Reformation—all were re-formations of life that gave rise to new economic patterns and structures. Likewise, in the twentieth century, from the establishment of settlement houses in Chicago to the bus boycott in Montgomery, Alabama, religious insight has prompted changes in economic arrangements. The young Dorothy Day glimpsed the mystical relationship between the household of God and the struggle of those living in poverty; she founded a soup kitchen in New York City's Bowery district, feeding each guest as if he or she were the Christ. With Peter Maurin, she established the Catholic Worker Movement, which has borne a prophetic economic witness across several decades. A conviction of incarnation has continually informed the faithful economic imagination in both personal and institutional-political terms.

Today, most of us do not deal with oxcarts; it is unlikely that we would be offered a millstone as collateral; we don't usually collect birds from their nests, debating whether to take the eggs also. We do, however, face unprecedented economic-environmental challenges. How can we, members of a planetary commons on the cusp of the twenty-first century, learn to practice household economics that are aligned with the economy of God?

SIMPLICITY AND MUTUAL AID

Over the centuries, the practices of simplicity and mutual aid have been expressions of the desire for faithful living. The strength of these practices is clearly evident in celibate orders within most religious traditions, whose members share common households and vows of poverty. For many today, this model remains evocative but does not compellingly translate into the realities of contemporary life.

Do not be conformed to this world, but be transformed by the renewing of your minds, so that you may discern what is the will of God—what is good and acceptable and perfect.

ROMANS 12:2

There are, however, two examples of Christian communities that, while embracing both single and married life, have also offered gifts to the economic imagination: the Religious Society of Friends (Quakers), a people formed in the turbulence of seventeenth-century England, and the Mennonites (along with their cousins, the Amish), Anabaptists formed in the struggles of the sixteenth-century Reformation in Europe. Both groups have developed keen insights into the spiritual, moral, aesthetic, and prophetic potential of the practice of simplicity, as Quakers would speak of it, and the practice of nonconformity and mutual aid, as the Mennonites would speak of it.

The practice of simplicity is an orientation to life that can, over time, foster a sense of right proportion and right relation within the dynamic and interdependent household of the whole earth community. Practicing simplicity is not, however, simple. One Friend remarked, "The testimony of simplicity is fraught with dilemmas." Mere streamlining, budget cutting, reengineering, throwing out, living without, sacrificing, and returning to earlier, more "simple" patterns—all in the name of "simplicity"—can be useless, counterproductive, even cruel behavior. It is difficult to simplify life by leaving a too demanding job if the move means losing access to group health insurance. It may be complicated to change the purchasing practice of your company when low cost and low environmental impact must both be taken into account. To choose simplicity as a practice is to live into complicated questions without easy answers, taking one step at a time, one step that may make another step possible.

For example, a young Quaker woman at college wrote home via E-mail: "I've been meaning to write about Christmas (and there is nothing like a smidgen of E-mail procrastination before biting into Beowulf). I still don't know exactly what I want for Christmas, but the main thing is I DON'T WANT JUNK. This is really important. I've been feeling lately like I have way too much STUFF. An idea

Poverty has a very human face—one that is very different from "simplicity." Poverty is involuntary and debilitating, whereas simplicity is voluntary and enabling. Poverty is mean and degrading to the human spirit, whereas a life of conscious simplicity can have both a beauty and a functional integrity that elevates the human spirit.

DUANE ELGIN, *Voluntary Simplicity*

might be blank tapes or good pens or nice colored paper or something really useful. I'm working to break the chains of consumerism—starting with myself." Then, struggling for clarity, she added: "P.S. I think that to say 'don't give me any gifts this year, donate it all to charity' is not good because it keeps the other person from having the pleasure of giving, which is the most important part. It's just that people feel compelled to give even if they don't have a certain gift in mind that they want to give and know the other person would love.

"Do you see?" she asked. "I've been trying to get rid of my stuff by giving it to other people on their birthdays, etc. It's not unloading my old junk on others, it's just that if someone has given me a cute little green plastic frog, I'm trying to keep the cycle going of things that are fun at first and then just sit there. Anyway, I can't decide if this sounds like a rude thing to ask. It's just that I simply can't keep tons of junk and I'm trying to avoid it. Does this make sense?"

During the same holiday season, a Jewish businessman suffered a major factory fire and attracted national attention because he chose, nevertheless, to give his employees their end-of-the-year bonus, two months' salary, and six months of health insurance. Further, he announced that the factory would be rebuilt in the same community.

In differing ways, the college student and the businessman were both recognizing, with the Quaker teacher Thomas Kelly: "Prune and trim we must, but not with ruthless haste and ready pruning knife, until we have reflected upon the tree we trim, the environment it lives in, and the sap of life which feeds it."

This kind of discernment is never ending. Accordingly, Friends do not have creeds, but they do have "queries." Among those that relate to economic life are these: "What are you doing as individuals or

Confronted by this economic complexity, and seeking clarity for the future, we can rightly ask ourselves one single question: How does our economic system affect the lives of people—all people?

NATIONAL CONFERENCE OF CATHOLIC BISHOPS,
A Pastoral Letter on Catholic Social Teaching and the U.S. Economy: Economic Justice for All

as a Meeting: To aid those in need of material help? To create a social and economic system which will so function as to sustain and enrich life for all? Do you keep to simplicity and moderation in your speech, your manner of living, and your pursuit of business?"

The practice of simplicity does not mean that all must conform to a single style, but Friends have historically avoided "adornments" and have attempted to acquire only things that are "needed," resisting "bondage to fashion." Moreover, Friends struggle to recognize that the practice of simplicity touches every aspect of life, affecting not only money but also time. Again quoting Thomas Kelly: "A life becomes simplified when dominated by faithfulness to [only] a few concerns. Too many of us have too many irons in the fire. We get distracted by . . . our interest in a thousand and one good things. . . . Quaker simplicity needs to be expressed not merely in dress and architecture and the height of tombstones but also in . . . opposition to the hurried, superficial tendencies of our age."

As we sort out the issues of time and money in a complex world, it is instructive to observe that neither Quakers nor Mennonites have chosen a "hair shirt" asceticism. Quakers, particularly in England, not only embraced the Industrial Revolution, they led it and prospered. Their prosperity was a manifestation of the wider economic reordering of their time. But their distinctive achievements may be attributed, in part, to their practice of simplicity, which enabled them to reinvest more of their profits in their businesses. Further, the Quaker belief that "there is that of God in everyone" led to enlightened labor practices and thus higher productivity; and their practice of truth telling and simplicity of speech created a reputation for trustworthiness in business dealings.

Although the Mennonites in Holland and Germany similarly prospered from the Industrial Revolution, Mennonites elsewhere (particularly the Old Order or Amish) are often admired for their faithful resistance to it—maintaining an agrarian way of life. In differing forms, Quakers and Mennonites together leave us a legacy of two vital questions as we enter the twenty-first century and reconsider our practice of household economics: the question of "right labor" and the question of "right technology."

RIGHT LABOR

An exemplar of the "simplicity that there is in Christ" and its implications for "right labor" is the American Quaker John Woolman (1720–1772). He was a talented businessman and sought to "sell things really useful." But he was troubled by the common practice of selling on credit, particularly its implications for poor people. Regarding his own household, he wrote: "A query at times hath arisen: Do I, in all my proceedings, keep to that use of things which is agreeable to universal righteousness? And then there hath some degree of sadness at times come over me, because I accustomed myself to some things which have occasioned more labor than I believe Divine wisdom intended for us."

Step by step and not without struggle, the question of right labor led him to change his work and to travel among Friends to awaken the conscience of the wider community. He called attention to the complicity of Friends in the low wages of laboring men and "the women who spin in factories." It was the growing custom to travel and send letters by stagecoach, but he refused to use them after he learned that the night travel sometimes meant that the postboys froze to death, people were run over in the dark, and the horses were so overworked that they, too, met untimely deaths. "So great is the hurry in the spirit of this world that in aiming to do business quick and to gain wealth the creation at this day doth loudly groan!"

His concern for right labor inevitably led him to resist slavery. After some turmoil of mind, he declined to write the section of a will that treated a slave as property to be inherited, and later he refused to wear clothing dyed with indigo, a slave product. Woolman's choices about right labor were a part of the catalyzing work of Spirit that led American Quakers a century before the Civil War to slowly relinquish the practice of slavery. Friends laid down familiar ways of life, moved to new regions, learned alternative forms of agriculture, and thus reordered their practice of household economics.

Today we encounter stagecoaches only in theme parks, and we like to think of slavery as a thing of the past. Yet the issues of wages, layoffs, employee benefits, third and fourth world labor, immigrant exploitation, animal rights, industrial toxins, and the correlation of the rates of unemployment and incarceration are all issues of right labor that are surely as lively and conscience-disturbing as in the days of Woolman.

RIGHT TECHNOLOGY

Preserving a communal and agrarian way of life, Old Order Mennonites have believed that they should not be conformed to this world but live "as in the Kingdom of God." Their practice of economics is guided, in part, by the question, What will this new tool (technology) mean for our community? Old Orders have said a definite no to automobiles and television, and they have given a halting, muted yes to telephones, computers, and rollerblades. Telephones may be used at a pay station but not in their homes. Many busy, cumbered Americans are fascinated by these distinctive communities who have preserved ways of making and keeping life human that have elsewhere disappeared.

We live in a world where economic life is dramatically driven by technological development. Whereas some assume that salvation

───────

We don't have to slavishly emulate, say, the Old Order Amish,
who use no cars, electricity or alcohol; but we can profitably
ask why it is that they suffer depression at less than
one-fifth the rate of people in nearby Baltimore.

Time, AUGUST 28, 1995

───────

is to be found in technology and others see technology as inevitably destructive and beyond our control, Mennonites can help us perceive our power to create tools/technology as requiring the same development of ethical wisdom as other forms of power. This means discerning in what ways a given technology affects both the natural and social ecology, and then making choices.

A single mother of four living on a limited income was given a dishwasher. After a family conference, they sold it and took an otherwise impossible family vacation. Individuals and families are beginning to ask not only *what* should and should not be watched on TV and *when,* but *where* the TV should be located. For example, some families will not place the TV in an eating area or in other parts of the home where they would otherwise be in conversation with each other. At the same time, they resist giving every family member a separate TV. Many families are asking the same kinds of questions about computers.

As social environments become increasingly dominated by technology, consumers are resisting the omnipresent video screen, some restaurants are creating "cellular-phone-free" sections, and some organizations are designating periods of pause and quiet during which time interoffice phone activity is curtailed.

Like the rest of us, Mennonites now make their way into the twenty-first century where the economic waters are sometimes full of rapids, sometimes murky; it is easy either to become trapped in backwaters and stagnant places or to merely "go with the flow." Yet though most Mennonites today have departed from agrarian ways of life, they continue to ask themselves what it means to live as signs of the Kingdom or Commonwealth of God. Having learned the value of mutual aid in the tradition of barnraisings and the like, they actively seek to practice forms of household economics that in an industrial and postindustrial age honor the reality of the interdependence of all life. Guidelines are emerging:

- "Communal property" (including the natural environment) is for the benefit of all.
- Ostentation in material things is to be avoided.
- Occupations and professions that deflect from the commitment to the community's life and witness are to be avoided.

- The profit motive in economic transactions is to be held in relationship to other motivations and outcomes.
- Mutual aid should be distinguished from charity, and resources shared in ways that recognize interdependence with others rather than fostering the perpetual dependence of many on a few.

FIGURING IT OUT WITH OTHERS

Traditional religious orders, Quakers, and Mennonites all know something crucial: as lone individuals, it is very difficult to change our economic patterns. We are social beings. Moreover, the exchange of goods and services is a profoundly relational activity. Recognizing that the practice of household economics is formed and transformed in community, Quakers and Mennonites encourage us to undertake the challenges of economic faithfulness together.

Traditionally, in Meeting for Worship, Friends sit in silence together, listen to the movement of Spirit, speak out of the silence, and thus minister to one another, seeking unity. The practice of simplicity walks hand in hand with shared practices of worship and discernment and is a manifestation of the desire to live in what Friends speak of as Truth revealed in fidelity to the guidance of the Inner Light of the Christ. Paradoxically, Friends have found that centering their life in Truth enables them to shed cumber, and that shedding cumber enables them to perceive divine order more adequately.

Reflecting a different pattern of corporate discernment, a Mennonite church in the Midwest requires as a condition of membership that everyone belong to a small group of a dozen or so people that meets regularly. (Mennonites also practice tithing, the giving of "first fruits," and this congregation has chosen to give an additional 2 percent—1 percent each for domestic and international aid—as an acknowledgment of their disproportionate wealth as middle-class North Americans.) At least once a year, within their small group, they discuss their individual and collective practice of household economics. This typically involves reflecting together on how much income they have and how they earn, invest, and spend it. One group began this discussion by sharing their 1040 tax forms with each other.

In materials prepared by the National Religious Partnership
for the Environment, pointers for congregation-based environmental
action include a new concept: environmental tithing—*encouraging*
congregants to reduce by one-tenth the amount of power and
water used in homes and houses of worship.

Occasionally, one man reports, "dollars do change hands," but usually the discussion serves as a discernment process. Years ago, his family sought wisdom regarding which of two homes they should buy, either of which would have met their needs. One cost twice as much as the other, but the more expensive home was closer to the college where they were teaching. He believes that purchasing the less expensive home has without question been the better choice. But he does not think that they would have made that choice alone, apart from their community of faith.

"GOD, MAKE US TRULY ALIVE"

Such practices can be found elsewhere as well. For example, a group of young professionals in a Presbyterian church in the Pacific Northwest discovered that the potential of each of their lives was hampered because of low-grade but real economic anxiety. They all decided to contribute to a common fund that could be used to help support any one of them who took an economic risk in order to enhance the quality and contribution of his or her life. After two years, no one had yet drawn on the fund, but several reported that they had taken risks they would not otherwise have taken if the fund had not been there.

The Church of the Savior is an ecumenical church in Washington, D.C., rooted in the Protestant tradition. Though most members appear to be living comfortable enough professional lives, they believe that Christian commitment requires a "cultural conversion," and that a practice of church that does not include commitment to the poor is "heretical." Thus they have placed certain practices at the core of their common life, adopting them as disciplines required for membership: they covenant with God and each other to spend one hour a day in prayer, meditation, and devotional reading; to worship with their gathered community once a week; to participate in a mission group that is responsive to the claims of the poor; and to tithe their gross income as a basis for "proportional" sharing of their livelihood.

These communities of faith suggest that whenever an economic witness has been distinctive, attractive, and informing, it has been practiced in a manner that corresponds to the ancient prayer of Christian asceticism, "God, make us truly alive." They have found a "hearth place" in the household of God, a point of orientation that reorders their relationships with time and money—the vectors at the core of embodied, incarnate life. They practice household economics in a manner that we might describe as cultivating a spirituality of "abundance and enoughness."

As we enter a new century fraught with unprecedented economic-ecological challenges and find ourselves grappling with busyness and cumber, fear and guilt, these communities of faith invite us to ask ourselves a set of strategic queries: How do we learn to talk together about the practice of household economics? What is "abundance," and what is "enoughness"? What are "right labor" and "right technology"? How are we to order our common life on this small planet that is our home?

Chapter 5

SAYING YES
AND
SAYING NO

❧

M. Shawn Copeland

The Christian life is like an athletic competition, the apostle Paul once wrote. A great prize awaits those who run their race well, but the running requires great exertion. "Athletes exercise self-control in all things" in order to win their contests, even though their prize is only a laurel wreath that will soon wither. Christians ought to run their race with just as much exertion and self-control, Paul urged, for they pursue a prize that is "imperishable" (1 Corinthians 9:24–25).

Many of us long to grow stronger in the Christian life. But are we really ready to exert ourselves? Being spectators comes much more easily. We prize the football player's skill and strength; we admire the dancer's trim, toned body; we applaud the pianist's dexterity. But when it comes time to actualize our own plans for physical exercise or for rehearsals, too often we prove halfhearted and fickle. The slogan "No pain, no gain" cuts close to the bone. We are conditioned by our modern culture to count on immediate results; we want the gain, but we shrink from the pain. If we find it difficult to respond to the demands of athletic and artistic training, then it is not surprising that we find it difficult to engage in the Christian practices so sorely needed for the development and growth of the interior or spiritual life.

Throughout Christian history, it has been clear that spirituality is not a spectator activity. Tough decisions and persistent effort are required of those who seek lives that are whole and holy. If we are to grow in faithful living, we need to renounce the things that choke off the fullness of life that God intended for us, and we must follow through on our commitments to pray, to be conscientious, and to be in mutually supportive relations with other faithful persons. These acts take self-discipline. We must learn the practice of saying no to that which crowds God out and yes to a way of life that makes space for God.

TRAINING FOR FAITHFUL LIVING

"I do not run aimlessly, nor do I box as though beating the air," Paul wrote, continuing the athletic image (1 Corinthians 9:26). It was the apostle's passionate concern to nurture women and men in living worthy and holy lives in expectation of the Lord's return. That, he knew, would require them to be deliberate and purposeful, for saying yes to life in Christ would mean saying no to that which harms. Christians who wish to inherit the kingdom of God must curb their appetites and passions, he told the young church in Galatia; they must renounce "fornication, impurity, licentiousness, idolatry, sorcery, enmities, strife, jealousy, anger, quarrels, dissensions, factions, envy, drunkenness, carousing, and things like these" (Galatians 5:19–21).

In these instructions, we see a practice that has been a constant part of Christian life through the centuries: Christian asceticism. The word *asceticism* comes from the Greek root *askesis,* signifying exercise or training. For Paul and other early Christians, the practice of asceticism came to mean strenuous effort for moral perfection. Vigilant hope and expectation were at the center of the rigorously disciplined life they chose. Drawing heavily on their rich heritage of Jewish religious practices, these earliest followers of Jesus imposed arduous physical observances on themselves for the sake of gaining the abundant life he offered them. Irrespective of social status or wealth or cultural attainment, they shared a communal life centered on uncompromising faith in Jesus as Lord. They gathered to remember Jesus, and they zealously met the needs of strangers, the infirm, the imprisoned, and the poor. The way these women and men lived gave rise to a distinctive Christian way of being in the world, or Christian spirituality.

SPIRITUALITY: CHOOSING LIFE

Our spirituality is our capacity to relate to God, to other human beings, and to the natural world. Through these relationships, we give meaning to our experience and attune our hearts and minds to the deepest dimensions of reality. Thus spirituality is integral to the ways in which we live our lives. It is about the kinds of persons we are and the kinds of persons we hope to become.

Far too often, however, our attention to these deeper questions wanders, and our spirituality stagnates. We find ourselves merely drifting along. But then some painful event or demand for decision jolts us. We look up and find ourselves on a path that mocks our deepest longing, a road to joy that suddenly takes a treacherous curve. And it is no longer possible merely to drift along. At such times, we find out that only we ourselves can decide what we, by our choices and commitments, are to make of ourselves. We are compelled to acknowledge the persistent yearning, the subtle pull toward a new and different way of living. We are drawn on by questions: What is most necessary in our lives? For what are we living? What does it mean to be a human person?

~~

a man must choose
he is not a spray of
flowers nor of birdsong
nor the fall of dry twigs
in a rising wind

FRANCIS SULLIVAN, "Vision with Its Outcome"

Saying Yes and Saying No

Struggle, growth, and transformation are then our reality, and we become alert to our spirituality. And the practice of saying yes and saying no is part of its fabric, for without this practice there can be no struggle, growth, and transformation. The practice challenges us to make ever more conscious our decisions about our world views, our lives, our very selves. Slowly, perhaps painfully, we discover for ourselves that our struggle against unhealthy egoism and self-centeredness, against the materialism and acquisitive individualism of our society, against the apathy and indifference of our culture, is really a struggle about just who we are and who it is we hope to become. Learning how and when to say yes and no is a practice that is crucial in our attempt to choose life. It is an essential part of our growth before, with, and toward the divine.

THE AMBIGUOUS LEGACY OF CHRISTIAN ASCETICISM

The annals of Christianity are filled with stories of women and men who committed themselves to unusual and intense acts of renunciation out of the desire for God. The monastic path was laid out in the third century, when an Egyptian named Anthony went into the desert seeking space for solitude and prayer. "Do not trust in your own righteousness [and] control your tongue and your stomach," he advised a spiritual seeker who joined him there. Confidence in God, humility, prayer, solitude, and fasting: such were Anthony's life and counsel. A little later, a monk named Simeon Stylites climbed onto a narrow stone pillar in the Syrian desert to fast and pray, hoping to lift himself literally above the enticements of the world and closer to God. Much later, in another well-known act of radical spiritual discipline, the fourteenth-century English mystic Julian of Norwich retreated into a small stone cell in fasting and prayerful contemplation. Her reputation for personal holiness attracted a steady stream of pilgrims who sought her guidance and prayers. These three are among the many thousands of Christians over the centuries who have explored monastic spirituality, forging a tradition that continues to develop today.

These women and men disturb us. By contemporary standards, they seem odd, perhaps even mentally unbalanced. We tend to be repelled by the monastics' rejection of ordinary contact with the world, by their diet of bread and water, by their disdain for the joys of friendship, marriage, and parenting. It is easy to forget that they withdrew from the world not because they were afraid, but because they were stirred by a deep love of God.

Other forms of Christian asceticism have not required such radical withdrawal from daily life in the world, but have instead called women and men to renounce wealth and privilege in order to say yes to other unusual possibilities for human living before God. The charming, chivalrous, well-to-do Giovanni Francesco di Pietro di Bernardone opened one such possibility when he took off his rich clothing and fashioned a holy life as Francis of Assisi. Elizabeth, queen of Hungary in the thirteenth century, explored another possibility when she spent her royal fortune, her personal comfort, and indeed her life on the care of the poor and those afflicted with leprosy. In the 1930s, Dorothy Day, taking on a life of voluntary poverty that balanced active practical charity and profound prayerfulness, founded a New York City house of hospitality that continues to serve the poor today. These Christians said a startling yes to the search and desire for personal holiness, for union with God. Their daily lives were ordinary, yet valiant in ways that built up their spiritual being for authentic and meaningful living for God and others.

These who did not withdraw, choosing instead paths of suffering service within the world, may trouble us just as much as those who renounced society altogether. They subordinated money and talent to introspection and prayer, ignored personal comfort to give lavishly to those in need, and spurned the advantages of affluence to find integrity and fulfillment in fidelity to the ordinary tasks of care for others. They lived out an intense and passionate love for God, not content simply to do good deeds but rather desiring and driven to do and be more in their whole being. Their passion and intensity may unnerve us because their holy lives call into question our society's demand for order, control, calculation, and propriety. So while Christian asceticism as a vigorous and robust no often leaves us feeling uneasy, Christian asceticism as a zealous and burning yes may alarm us even more.

CONTEMPORARY OBSTACLES
TO AN ANCIENT PRACTICE

Understanding just what it means to say yes or no is not easy, in part because our images and notions of asceticism carry a powerful negative charge. We take asceticism to be a way of negativity; we resist it as a practice that involves embracing what is harsh, grim, and severe and rejecting life's simplest daily pleasures. In this view, asceticism says nothing but no. Indeed, over the centuries, we Christians became so adept at saying and embodying no, so skilled at punishing ourselves, that we sometimes forgot why we were saying no. We forgot that the practice of asceticism ought to lead to closer union with God and bring about greater openness, compassion, and care for others. We forgot that though asceticism certainly includes turning away from something or someone, it also demands turning toward something or Someone. We allowed saying no to become an end in itself, rather than a means to an end.

Another difficulty in our practice of saying yes and saying no emerges from the very nature of contemporary culture. Ours is a time of seemingly unlimited choice. Contemporary culture craves novelty, variety, and multiplicity. Advertisements coax us to buy, to possess, and to accumulate more—but even worse, they convince us that in buying, possessing, and accumulating more, we ourselves actually become more. The latest compact disc player, television, automobile, or designer clothing is presented as the answer to sagging self-esteem, troubled relationships, and loneliness. Without the latest expensive belongings, we feel inferior and begin to believe that we are nothing. With them, we think more highly of ourselves and find our identity restored. But then there comes a jarring moment when we grasp sadly that what we thought was freedom of choice was only an illusion. Having said yes to the acquisition of so many material things, we are unable to say yes to the larger demands of the spirit. Slowly, perhaps even bitterly, we come to realize that we do not own our possessions, they own us.

When we begin to practice saying yes and saying no, however, we encounter still another difficulty. Even after we recognize that what is decisive in life is not what we have but who we are, we still are puzzled as to how this practice fits in a modern life. Christian

The endless cycle of idea and action,
Endless invention, endless experiment,
Brings knowledge of motion, but not of stillness;
Knowledge of speech, but not of silence;
Knowledge of words, and ignorance of the Word.
All our knowledge brings us nearer to our ignorance,
All our ignorance brings us nearer to death,
But nearness to death no nearer to God.
Where is the Life we have lost in living?
Where is the wisdom we have lost in knowledge?
Where is the knowledge we have lost in information?

T. S. Eliot, "Choruses from 'The Rock'"

asceticism is not spiritual boot camp, but neither is it effortless. The choices and decisions we make have consequences. When a student registers for a college course, she or he rules out the other courses offered at the same time. When, in marriage, a woman and a man say yes to each other, quite explicitly they are saying no to intimate sexual relationships with others. We teach our children that their choices have consequences. When television or sports or socializing begins to win the competition with school assignments, we talk with our children about the consequences a slump in grades could have on their future choices. When gentle persuasion fails, we may decide to enforce a loving no to television or sports or socializing for the sake of bringing about conditions that can contribute more constructively to the future. To say yes and no means taking on responsibilities and obligations. Saying yes and saying no are companions in the process of constituting a whole and holy life.

A WHOLE AND HOLY LIFE

A complicated and dynamic interior world belongs to every human person. It is here that we grapple with our experiences, struggling with questions and the responses we will make to them with our lives. We foresee, weigh, and consider the results of our actions, striving to

Our Physician brought from heaven remedies for every single moral fault. The medical art cures fevers with cold compresses, and chills by applying heat. Similarly Jesus prescribed qualities contrary to our sins: self-restraint to the undisciplined, generosity to the stingy, gentleness to the irritable, and humility to the proud.

GREGORY THE GREAT, "On Self-Renunciation"

understand how our decisions affect not only our personal future but also the future of society. A friend of mine puts it this way: "What you decide today, you are tomorrow." What we decide also shapes what the world will be.

It is not always easy to say no. Sometimes the most heartfelt and vigorous no languishes and withers because we are not sufficiently prepared for its full meaning and outcomes. In and of itself, "just say no" is never an adequate response, whether to drugs or to any other alternative that is immediately attractive but ultimately destructive. All too soon, our good intentions to change our behavior, to say no to drugs or alcohol or promiscuity, or to avoid persons and places that swamp our moral fortitude, begin to feel like deprivation and loss.

In order for a no to be effective, it must be placed in the larger context of a life-affirming yes. But saying yes is not always easy either. Sometimes, even as the yes forms on the tongue, we pull back. Every yes brings with it new duties, new tasks; every yes calls up the unsettling potential of change in our lives.

Sometimes, saying yes to one thing means giving up something else. The Gospels tell many stories of women and men who long to say yes to Jesus but hesitate. Although drawn by Jesus' distinctive wisdom and radical compassion, the timid and the proper are shy of his passion. These women and men hope that living a good life will be enough, and so, mistakenly, they confuse being good with being holy.

One such comes to Jesus. "Good Teacher," he asks, "what must I do to inherit eternal life?" He listens attentively to the reply: "You know the commandments: 'You shall not commit adultery; you shall not murder; you shall not steal; you shall not bear false witness; honor your father and mother.'" Perhaps the man's face is luminous; he has obeyed these laws since his youth, and now every fiber of his mind

*The alternative wisdom of Jesus sees the religious life as
a deepening relationship with the Spirit of God,
not as the life of requirements and rewards.*

MARCUS J. BORG, *Meeting Jesus Again for the First Time*

and heart tenses to hear the teacher's reply. Jesus sees this man and loves him. "Sell all that you own and distribute the money to the poor, and you will have treasure in heaven; then come," Jesus says. "Follow me." The man's face dims; perhaps his eyes widen and then glaze with disappointment. Jesus has invited him to a path that leads away from conventional goodness to a life that is more and more centered in God. Perhaps the man even grasps for the first time that his rigorous and conscientious commitment to laws, regulations, and boundaries is not a religion of living, dynamic love, but a system of rewards and punishments. To say yes would mean letting go of wealth, possessions, and even his comfortable self-image as a good religious person; to say yes would mean taking on a new way of being in the world. Jesus' invitation unnerves him, and he finds himself unable to surrender himself to such an extravagant God, too timid to walk such an unpredictable path (Luke 18:18–22).

The rich man is unable to say yes to Jesus, yes to a new and untried way of life. He is unable to affirm in his living the dependence on God and on other human beings that characterizes a holy and whole life. He is afraid of what the theologian Dorothee Soelle has called that "zone of liberation . . . in which the words 'mine' and 'yours' lose their meaning." His life is grounded in having, and he cannot risk saying yes to the more abundant life Jesus offers. His story challenges us to seek freedom from having in order to engage freedom for living. His story confronts us with the need to find ways to grow stronger in the practice of saying yes and saying no.

Learning when and how, to what, and to whom to give our yes or our no is a lifelong project. It is learning to live not merely in dull balance or tedious moderation but in passionate, disciplined choice and action. It is learning to find support and challenge, courage and correction, as we live out our choices. Sustaining and realizing our yes from day to day is only possible when negative and destructive

We can neither deceive God nor impose something on him.
We can only slowly forget God, and that would be terrible since
then we would slowly be forgetting ourselves as well.

DOROTHEE SOELLE AND FULBERT STEFFENSKY,
Not Just Yes and Amen: Christians with a Cause

behaviors are supplanted by positive and generative ones, when we redeem the routines of our daily lives, when we choose and carry out commitments that give and support life. Prayer, examination of conscience, and participation in small communities are three acts that can help us in this practice.

STRENGTHENING OUR YES AND OUR NO THROUGH PRAYER

Prayer is intimate conversation with God—real, demanding, loving, and engaged conversation between a real person and the real, living God. This conversation initiates, sustains, and augments a dynamic relationship full of risk and joy. We bring to this relationship the whole of who we are—history and culture, body and personality, affectivity and sensibilities, training and work. We bring to this relationship our very own memories, hopes, sorrows, disappointments, and achievements; we bring our very own deepest joys, most humiliating moments, and most excruciating pain. We bring our selves to the One who loves us most completely.

The language of prayer is the language of faith, of feeling, of love. Since each person who prays is unique, the tenor and content of each person's prayer will be unique. Prayer requires our attentiveness, our readiness, our active and watchful waiting to hear, to receive, to cooperate in what God imparts to us. For our conversations with God are never one-sided. "God is not a machine that we can insert a coin into and then expect to get whatever we want," say theologians Dorothee Soelle and Fulbert Steffensky. "Prayer changes the one who prays."

Oddly, many of us think that we need no practice in praying, that we should just know how to pray right from the beginning. I have benefited from mentors and friends who have nurtured me in ways of prayer. Now I offer these suggestions from my own experience, hoping they may prove useful to others in beginning or strengthening personal prayer:

- I choose a time for daily prayer (early morning, midafternoon, before supper, late in the evening). I resolve to keep to this time, even if I must put it in my appointment book.
- I find a place where I will not be disturbed. Sometimes it is helpful to close my eyes; sometimes it is helpful to look at an icon or picture or crucifix. Sometimes it is helpful to begin by reading the Scriptures. I settle myself in a posture that is somewhat, but not completely, comfortable.
- I take five or six deep breaths; I calm myself.
- I consciously place myself in the divine presence and address God. I speak words of love and praise, of joy and thanksgiving. I lift up the concerns or needs of the world, of those who are afflicted in any way, of those who are close to me. I ask for God's compassion and love, mercy and justice. As my own personal cares or joys surface, I place these before God and seek the divine will.
- If I find myself being distracted by thoughts or images, I will not cling to them or try to control them. As calmly as I can, I return to my conversation with God.
- For some minutes, I am quiet. I try to discover God's will for me; I listen to the stirrings of my heart.
- When the time for my prayer comes to a close, I offer thanks for God's care and compassion and mercy. For some few moments, I am quiet, gathering myself in order to rejoin the busyness of the day.

STRENGTHENING OUR YES AND OUR NO THROUGH EXAMINATION OF CONSCIENCE

Examination of conscience has been practiced by Christians for many centuries. It provides a structure for deliberate reflection on the daily choices and decisions we have actually made. Reflecting in this way, we can view the yes and the no we are actually saying and consider them in relation to our holistic choice for life. Many Christians conduct this examination in the context of personal prayer.

To examine the conscience is to ask oneself some hard questions: How do things stand between me and God? Where and how is my life growing? Who and what am I becoming? To what am I really saying yes with my life? Are my noes life-affirming ones? To answer such questions sufficiently, we must set aside time to reflect. What follows is a way of examining one's living, personal relationship with God that has been helpful to me.

- I find a quiet place. I calmly review the details of the day and thank God for all the good things that have happened. In this review, I may come upon some action or emotion or desire for which I cannot thank God.
- I thank God for these gifts and ask to see clearly and in hope how these gifts are helping me to grow more fully alive in my relationship with God.
- I review my decisions, choices, actions, omissions, attitudes, desires:

  What do these decisions, choices, actions, omissions, attitudes, desires indicate to me about my relationship with God, with myself, with others?

  What yeses and noes does my life in fact include?

  To what or to whom have I said yes or no this day, this week, this month, this year?

  What motivated me to say yes or no?

  What obstacles did I encounter?

  What specific conditions can assist me in sustaining my yes or my no?

  Do I understand that each choice I make influences the choices I can make in the future?

  Do I understand that in saying yes to every invitation or opportunity, every task or assignment, I limit the possibilities for my growth in other areas?

Am I afraid that saying no may require me to give up more than I had bargained for, or to grow in unfamiliar ways?

Do I have adequate spiritual nourishment or emotional support for the yes I seek to say?

What kind of person am I making of myself in my daily choices?

What kind of person do I hope to become?

Do I understand that my liberty, my ability to make and sustain my choices, is the very delicate and fragile possibility of orienting myself in life for eternal life?

- If there is a particular choice or decision that concerns me, I identify some supports to strengthen my resolve.
- I close my review by thanking God for this knowledge and for God's mercy and compassion.

STRENGTHENING OUR YES AND OUR NO THROUGH FAITH-SHARING GROUPS

In recent years, small group gatherings have played an increasingly important part in our contemporary search for spiritual growth. When an honest sharing of faith is at a group's center, it can provide a very helpful setting as we seek to be more deliberate in saying yes and saying no. Small faith-sharing groups can provide the support and challenge we need to examine and strengthen our lives with God.

Group structure may be as complex or as simple as the needs of the participants require. Here are some elements that group members might wish to consider:

- The number of members ought be small enough for effective group prayer, substantive faith-sharing, and sound knowledge of the other members. I have been most strengthened by groups of only three to seven.
- Hallmarks of these faith-sharing groups are gentleness, honesty, compassion, and humility. We must be willing—prudently, to be sure—to share the desires of our hearts with

other women and men who are seeking to say yes to life. We must be willing to hold another's welfare with as much concern as our own. When group partners challenge us to reconsider our yeses and noes, we must be open to hear and respond.

- The length, frequency, and schedule of group meetings will be determined by the goals of the members. Some groups will want to meet weekly, others biweekly, and still others once a month. In addition to their regular gatherings, some groups may want to arrange a structured retreat together once or twice a year. No matter what the group decides, keep to the schedule. Some of us will need to enter the meeting time in our appointment books. Each member should treat the meeting as a most important appointment, one not lightly canceled.

- The style of the group meeting will correspond to the goals of participants. Some groups may wish to meet weekly for a meal, followed by faith-sharing and prayer; other groups will want to meet after weekly worship, to practice keeping the Sabbath together. Some groups will incorporate Bible study. Still other groups may shape their faith-sharing around Christian social witness, with prayer, planning, implementation, and reflection on these communal acts of witness.

YES TO LIFE, NO TO DESTRUCTION

Daily personal prayer, examination of conscience, and participation in a faith-sharing group: these smaller practices can be of real benefit to us in sustaining the larger practice of saying yes to life, saying no to destruction. Together, they help us to understand, judge, and

I have set before you life and death, blessings and curses. Choose life so that you and your descendants may live.

DEUTERONOMY 30:19

evaluate our daily choices and decisions in light of their relation to our ultimate happiness, as individuals and as human beings in community. If we are to enhance and build up the capacities for a good, wholesome, and holy life, we must learn to say yes to what affirms and renews wholeness and life. And we must learn to say a related no to what induces and brings about destruction and ruin. In this practice, we are invited and challenged to make a fully conscious choice about who it is we are and who it is we shall become.

Chapter 6

KEEPING SABBATH

❧

Dorothy C. Bass

How often people today cry out in exasperation or despair, "I just don't have enough time!" There is so much to do: learn a living, fulfill a vocation, nurture relationships, care for dependents, get some exercise, clean the house. Moreover, we hope to maintain sanity while doing all this, and to keep growing as faithful and loving people at the same time. We are finite, and the demands seem too great, the time too short.

Those of us who feel time's pressure have lots of company in this society. In a surprise best-seller of 1991, *The Overworked American,* economist Juliet Schor reported that work hours and stress are up and sleep and family time are down for all classes of employed Americans. Wives working outside the home return to find a "second shift" of housework awaiting them. Husbands add overtime or second jobs to their schedules. Single parents stretch in so many directions that they sometimes feel they can't manage. Simultaneously, all are bombarded by messages that urge them to spend more (and so, ultimately, work more), to keep their homes cleaner (standards keep rising), and to improve themselves as lovers, investors, parents, or athletes. Supposedly to make all this possible, grocery stores stay open all night long, and entertainment options are available around the clock. We live, says Schor, in "an economy and society that are demanding too much from people."

What's a person to do? U.S. culture has some answers ready. "Quality time with your kids" is the answer for parents. An exercise machine that reduces stress and burns off fat in only twenty minutes, three times a week, is the answer for the overwrought and the overweight. "What you need is a good night's sleep or a vacation" is the answer one friend offers to another. Each of these answers has value. Yet our circumstances require a stronger response, and we are too caught up in the swirl of our lives to devise one.

In this situation, the historic practice of setting aside one day a week for rest and worship promises peace to those who embrace it. Whether we know the term *Sabbath* or not, we the harried citizens of late modernity yearn for the reality. We need Sabbath, even though we doubt that we have time for it.

As the new century dawns, the practice of Sabbath keeping may be a gift just waiting to be unwrapped, a confirmation that we are not without help in shaping the renewing ways of life for which we long. This practice stands at the heart of Judaism, as we shall see, but it is also available to Christians, in different form. For many of us, receiving this gift will require first discarding our image of Sabbath as a time of negative rules and restrictions, as a day of obligation (for Catholics) or a day without play (in memories of strict Protestant childhoods). Relocating our understanding of this day in the biblical stories of creation, exodus, and resurrection will be essential if we are to discover the gifts it offers.

Unwrapping this gift also requires supporting *underworked* Americans as they wonder what Sabbath keeping might mean for them. One of the cruelest features of the American economy, which asks too much of many people, is that it casts numerous others aside, leaving them without sufficient work. A Sabbath-keeping community, as we shall see, would be a community in which this injustice would not occur. When Sabbath comes, commerce halts, feasts are served, and all God's children play. The equal reliance of all people on the bounty and grace of God is gratefully acknowledged, and the goodness of weekday work is affirmed. Relationships that persist

Whatever is foreseen in joy
Must be lived out from day to day.
Vision held open in the dark
By our ten thousand days of work.
Harvest will fill the barn; for that
The hand must ache, the face must sweat.
And yet no leaf or grain is filled
By work of ours; the field is tilled
And left to grace. That we may reap,
Great work is done while we're asleep.
When we work well, a Sabbath mood
Rests on our day, and finds it good.

WENDELL BERRY, *Sabbaths*

throughout the week are changed in the process. As the great Jew-ish scholar Abraham Joshua Heschel said, "The Sabbath cannot sur-vive in exile, a lonely stranger among days of profanity."

WHAT IS SABBATH?

The way in which time is organized is a fundamental building block of any community. So basic is this that most of us take the pattern we are used to for granted, as if it were self-evident that time must be arranged in this way. For all the spiritual descendants of Abraham—Jews, Christians, Muslims—time flows in seven-day cycles. Other cultures move through time in different cycles, however. In most ancient societies, rest days followed lunar phases or rotated on some other pattern. During the French Revolution, anti-Christian leaders tried to weaken popular religious traditions by abolishing the seven-day week. The rhythms of the week subtly pattern the days and years of our lives, and they are filled with meaning.

The Sabbatarian pattern—six days of work, followed by one of rest—is woven deep into the fabric of the Bible. The very first story of Hebrew and Christian Scriptures climaxes on the seventh day, the very first time there was a seventh day. Having created everything,

Remember the Sabbath day, and keep it holy. Six days you shall labor and do all your work. But the seventh day is a Sabbath to the LORD your God; you shall not do any work—you, your son or your daughter, your male or female slave, your livestock, or the alien resident in your towns. For in six days the LORD made heaven and earth, the sea, and all that is in them, but rested the seventh day; therefore the LORD blessed the Sabbath day and consecrated it.

EXODUS 20:8–11

God rests, and blesses this day, and makes it holy. In this way, the Christian theologian Karl Barth has suggested, God declares as fully as possible just how very good creation is. Resting, God takes pleasure in what has been made; God has no regrets, no need to go on to create a still better world or a creature more wonderful than the man and woman. In the day of rest, God's free love toward humanity takes form as time shared with them.

Later, God teaches the people of Israel to share in the blessing of this day (Exodus 16). After bringing them out of Egyptian slavery into the wilderness, God sends them manna, commanding them to gather enough each morning for that day's food alone. Mistrusting, they gather more than they need, but it rots. On the sixth day, however, they are told to gather enough to last for two days. Miraculously, the extra does not rot, and those mistrustful ones who go out on the seventh morning to get more find none. God is teaching them, through their own hunger and nature's provisions, to keep the Sabbath, even before Moses receives the commandments on Sinai.

When those commandments come, the Sabbath commandment is the longest and in some ways the most puzzling. Unlike any of the others, it takes quite different forms in the two passages where the Ten Commandments appear. Both versions require the same behavior—work on six days, rest on one—but each gives a different reason. What is wonderful is that each reason arises from a fundamental truth about God's relationship to humanity.

The Exodus commandment to "remember" the Sabbath day is grounded in the story of creation. The human pattern of six days of work and one of rest follows God's pattern as Creator; God's people

PRACTICING OUR FAITH

Observe the Sabbath day and keep it holy, as the LORD *your God*
commanded you. Six days you shall labor and do all your work.
But the seventh day is a Sabbath to the LORD *your God; you shall*
not do any work—you, or your son or your daughter, or your male
or female slave, or your ox or your donkey, or any of your livestock,
or the resident alien in your towns, so that your male and female
slave may rest as well as you. Remember that you were a slave in the
land of Egypt, and the LORD *your God brought you out from there*
with a mighty hand and an outstretched arm; therefore the LORD
your God commanded you to keep the Sabbath day.

DEUTERONOMY 5:12–15

are to rest on one day because God did. In both work and rest, human beings are in the image of God. At the same time, they are not God but God's creatures, who must honor God by obeying this commandment.

In Deuteronomy, the commandment to "observe" the Sabbath day is tied to the experience of a people newly released from bondage. Slaves cannot take a day off; free people can. When they stop work every seventh day, the people will remember that the Lord brought them out of slavery, and they will see to it that no one within their own dominion, not even animals, will work without respite. Sabbath rest is a recurring testimony against the drudgery of slavery.

Together, these two renderings of the Sabbath commandment summarize the most fundamental stories and beliefs of the Hebrew Scriptures: creation and exodus, humanity in God's image and a people liberated from captivity. One emphasizes holiness, the other social justice. Sabbath crystallizes the Torah's portrait of who God is and what human beings are most fully meant to be.

THE SABBATH IN JUDAISM

As Sabbath crystallizes the Torah, so Sabbath—*Shabbat*—is the heart of Judaism. When Jews who have become inattentive to their religion wish to deepen their observance, rabbis tell them with one voice: you must begin by keeping *Shabbat*. But what does it mean to keep a day holy, to refrain from work, to honor God's creativity and imitate God's rest, to experience the end of bondage? This question has been on the minds of observant Jews, and in their hearts and actions, for millennia. Following Exodus 31, in which God makes the Sabbath the sign of an irrevocable covenant with the people of Israel, Jewish leaders have emphasized its special place in Jewish life and heard in its rhythm the structure that has kept Jewish identity alive amid terrible adversity. A saying affirms that "more than the Jews have kept *Shabbat, Shabbat* has kept the Jews."

Many centuries of debate and cultural change have shaped the law and liturgy of contemporary *Shabbat* observance, which varies considerably from one branch of Judaism to another. Infusing the practice as a whole, however, is a theology of creation and exodus, of holiness and liberation.

In observant Jewish homes, *Shabbat* begins each Friday night at sundown as a woman lights the Sabbath candles. It is a festive time; people dress up, the best tableware and food are presented, guests are welcomed. In some families, everyone turns toward the door, singing to greet *Shabbat,* which Jewish hymns personify as a loving bride who brings inner delight and as a beautiful queen who gives order and peace. Traditional prayers are prayers of thanks; indeed, mourning is suspended in *Shabbat* liturgies. Many families sing or read together after the meal. They will gather again the next evening for another meal at which they will bid farewell to the holy day. Finally, parents will bless their children and give them a bit of sweet spice so that the taste of Sabbath peace will linger on their tongues.

Jewish liturgy and law say both what should be done on *Shabbat* and what should not. What should not be done is "work." Defining exactly what that means is a long and continuing argument, but one classic answer is that work is whatever requires changing the natural, material world. All week long, human beings wrestle with the natural world, tilling and hammering and carrying and burning. On the Sabbath, however, Jews let it be. They celebrate it as it is and live in it in peace and gratitude. Humans are created too, after all, and in gratefully receiving the gift of the world, they learn to remember that it is not, finally, human effort that grows the grain and forges the steel. By extension, all activities associated with work or

*... Indeed, one can never truly know the inward feeling of the Sabbath
without the outward form. The Sabbath is not a theory to be
contemplated, a concept to be debated, or an idea to be toyed with.
It is a day, a day filled with hours and minutes and seconds,
all of which are hallowed by the wonderful pattern of living
that the nobility of the human spirit has fashioned over
the course of the centuries.*

SAMUEL H. DRESNER, *The Sabbath*

commerce are also prohibited. You are not even supposed to think about them.

What *should* be done? Specific religious duties do exist, including worship at synagogue and reading of the Torah. But the holiness of the Sabbath is also made manifest in the joy people expect to experience on that day. It is a good deed for married couples to have sexual intercourse on *Shabbat.* Taking a walk, resting, talking with loved ones, reading—these are good too.

To the eyes of outsiders, Jewish observance of the Sabbath can seem like a dreary set of restrictions, a set of laws that don't bear any good news. According to those who live each week shaped by *Shabbat,* however, it is a practice that powerfully alters their relationships to nature, work, God, and others. *Shabbat* is not just law and liturgy; it is also a shared way of life, a set of activities that becomes second nature, a round of custom and prayer that the youngest child or the oldest invalid can enter, a piece of time that opens space for God. Over and over, Jewish authors say of *Shabbat* what those who enter deeply into other religious practices also say: to experience its goodness, you must enter its activities. To find Sabbath peace, you must keep the Sabbath holy. "The real and the spiritual are one, like body and soul in a living person," writes Heschel. "It is for the law to clear the path; it is for the soul to sense the spirit."

CAN CHRISTIANS KEEP SABBATH?

Christians are fortunate when Jewish friends invite us to come to a meal on a Friday evening, to keep Sabbath with them. On our own, however, Christians cannot keep Sabbath as Jews do. We know God most fully not through the perpetual covenant God made with the Israelites at Sinai but through Jesus Christ. Yet we also honor the Mosaic commandments, and we stand in spiritual and historical kinship with the Jewish people, of whom Jesus was one. In an authentically Christian form of Sabbath keeping, we may affirm the grateful relationship to the Creator that Jews celebrate each Sabbath, and we may share the joyful liberation from drudgery first experienced by the slaves who left Egypt. But we add to these celebrations our weekly festival for the source of our greatest joy: Christ's victory over the powers of death. For Christians, this victory makes of each weekly day of rest and worship a celebration of Easter.

The first day of the week was special to Christians as an Easter day from the earliest days of their community. Sunday, the day on which the disciples had first encountered the risen Lord, became a day to gather, eat together, and rejoice. It was not in those years a day of rest, however; these gatherings happened after the work day was over, and for several decades, Jews who became Christians continued to observe *Shabbat* as well. But these were years when Sabbath observance was changing for Jews as well as for Christians. After the temple in Jerusalem was destroyed by the Romans in 70 C.E., the rabbis who reformulated Jewish practice for the new situation placed great emphasis on the Sabbath as a lasting sign of God's unique covenant with Israel. So Jewish observance was becoming more strict during this period. At the same time, Christianity was developing a separate identity from Judaism, and many people who were not Jewish were joining the church. Gradually, Christians of Jewish background stopped attending synagogue and observing Jewish law. Over the years, Sunday became their one-day-in-seven for both rest and worship.

The Gospels say that Jesus observed the Jewish Sabbath, though he ignored some laws that other teachers thought should restrict healing or eating in specific situations of need. "It is lawful to do good on the Sabbath," he says in Matthew's Gospel (12:12). Later, Christians continued to treasure the Sabbath commandment, along with the other nine commandments from Sinai. They also came to believe, however, that its meaning had changed within the new creation God began with Christ's death and resurrection. The holy day from now on, therefore, was not the seventh but the eighth, the day on which the future burst into the present. The appropriate response was to celebrate each Sunday with a feast of communion—one that looked back to Jesus' passion and resurrection and forward to the great banquet that would occur at the end of time. The result has been centuries of Sunday worship, usually crowned by the celebration of the Lord's Supper.

Building on this shared heritage, later groups of Christians shaped their Sabbath keeping in many different ways. The strict Sabbath observance of the New England Puritans, for example, gave rise to "blue laws" in many American cities and towns, which long influenced the structure of time in this society. More recently, Reformed churches of Dutch origin have anchored an American subculture within which Sundays are still filled with family visits and theological debate. On the other hand, some groups have been suspicious of Sabbatarianism so strict that it might seem legalistic ("If any where the day is made holy for the mere day's sake, then I order you to work on it, to ride on it, to feast on it, to do anything to remove this reproach from Christian liberty," Martin Luther declared) or have emphasized, like the Quakers, that all time is holy with God. Sunday mass has been and continues to be central to Roman Catholics. A few groups, including the Seventh-Day Adventists, have made Saturday observance central to their identity.

CAN WE KEEP SABBATH TODAY?

Even while the Bible, history, and the example of Judaism stir up a yearning for Sabbath within us, we are aware that taking on a Sabbath rhythm would not be easy—and pressures to work and spend are only part of the problem. Some other obstacles also make it difficult to retrieve this practice.

One is figuring out how to make Sunday special when it is no longer protected by legislation and custom. The arrangement of time by society as a whole is political, of course: how time is structured makes someone's life easier and someone's harder. Sunday first received special governmental recognition in 321, when the emperor Constantine decreed it a day of rest throughout the Roman Empire.

This spawned centuries of government-sponsored Sabbath keeping. In recent decades, however, the setting aside of Sunday as a special day has been losing force within American culture's politics of time. One reason is increasing sensitivity to religious diversity—a sensitivity pioneered by the Supreme Court in decisions that forced employers to respect the Sabbath practices of Jews and Adventists. Today, not only the laws but also the customs that once shielded Sunday from most commerce are disappearing, and Christians' day of worship and rest is not automatically "free" for church and family. Claiming its freedom will take effort and perhaps even sacrifice.

A second roadblock is the bad reputation many devout Christians have given to the day of rest and worship. In the centuries after Constantine, church attendance came to be required and profane activity to be banned on Sundays, though in fact these rules were often ignored. When religious reform swept through Europe in the sixteenth century, improving the people's use of their day of rest was a concern of Protestant and Catholic leaders alike. In the ensuing centuries, some Protestants worldwide not only required many hours of worship services each Sunday, but also made it virtually impossible for absentees to have any fun. Sabbath keepers were killjoys, it seemed. Little wonder that gloom still hangs over the Sunday memories of some who were children in more stringent times.

Today, economic forces are also nibbling away at the freedom of the day. In a vicious circle, people who spend more hours at weekday jobs need the other days for shopping, which prompts businesses to hire more Sunday workers, who join the growing percentage of the workforce who toil long, irregular hours, some trying desperately to make ends meet, others for the sake of more shopping. For millions of workers, long Sunday hours for rest and worship may be impossible within the current system. People who know the Sabbath pattern of creation, liberation, and resurrection nurture a dissatisfaction with this system, however, and can work for change. Keeping Sabbath, we grow in our longing for a system where all people have work at a living wage, and time for rest and worship too.

Will it be possible for twenty-first-century Christians who need Sabbath but also respect diversity, who need Sabbath but also yearn for joy, who need Sabbath but also struggle to make ends meet, to enter the practice of Sabbath keeping? Perhaps. But this can only happen as we help one another to develop new forms rooted in the enduring truths of creation, liberation, and resurrection.

Unwrapping the Gift of Sabbath Keeping

In our situation, Sabbath keeping will require a good deal of inventiveness! Tilden Edwards, an Episcopal priest who has explored this practice in real life as well as in a book, urges contemporary Christians to be flexible, embracing not a renewed Sabbatarianism as much as a pattern of "Sabbath time." He recommends a combination of Sunday worship and play with a regular rhythm of disciplined spiritual renewal during the week. Eugene Peterson, a Presbyterian minister, describes the "sabbaths" he and his wife observed every Monday, after their busiest day was over: a drive to the country, a psalm, a silent hike for several hours, a quiet evening at home. Pastors are not the only ones who must work on Sundays; others, too, sometimes need to find ways of keeping Sabbath on other days. Yet none of us should think that we can sustain Sabbath keeping, whenever it happens, all by ourselves. We need mutuality in this practice, which resists our ordinary patterns in so many ways. We need to help one another discover this gift.

Most often, Sundays will make the best Sabbaths, and not only because our schedules are relatively open on that day. Joining the assembly of Christians for the celebration of Word and Sacrament will remind us that Sabbath keeping is not about taking a day off but about being recalled to our knowledge of and gratitude for God's activity in creating the world, giving liberty to captives, and overcoming the powers of death. In addition, the friends with whom we worship can help us learn to rest and rejoice once the service is over.

What, besides churchgoing, is Christian Sabbath keeping? The answer must be tailored to specific circumstances and will vary considerably in different cultures and stages of life. It will be helpful in each circumstance to reflect carefully on both what is good and what is not.

What is not good on Sabbath, or in Sabbath time? We would do well to heed three millennia of Jewish reflection on the Sabbath

God of all glory,
on this first day you began creation,
bringing light out of darkness.
On this first day you began your new creation,
raising Jesus Christ out of the darkness of death.
On this Lord's day grant that we,
the people you have made your own by water and the Spirit,
may be joined with all your works
in praising you for your great glory.
Through Jesus Christ,
in union with the Holy Spirit,
we praise you now and forever.

PRAYER OF INVOCATION FOR SUNDAY WORSHIP,
Service for the Lord's Day [PRESBYTERIAN]

commandment. Not good are work and commerce and worry. To act as if the world cannot get along without our work for one day in seven is a startling display of pride that denies the sufficiency of our generous Maker. To refrain from working—not every day, but one in seven—opens the temporal space within which glad and grateful relationship with God and peaceful and appreciative relationship with nature and other people can grow. Refraining from work on a regular basis should also teach us not to demand excessive work from others. Commerce? Buying and spending are closely related to working too much; they depend on work, create the conditions for more work, and often *are* work. We could refrain from shopping on Sundays, making a choice that might complicate the weekly schedule at first but should soon become a refreshing habit. And worry? It may be difficult to banish cares from our minds altogether, but we can refrain from activities that we know will summon worry—activities like paying bills, preparing tax returns, and making lists of things to do in the coming week.

And what is good on a Christian Sabbath? Most important is joyful worship that restores us to communion with the risen Christ and our fellow members of his body, the church. For Christians, every Sunday is Easter Sunday, a time to gather together with song and prayer, to hear the Word proclaimed, and to recognize Christ in the breaking of the bread. It is a festival, a spring of souls, a day of freedom not only from work but also from condemnation. At times, worshiping communities lose sight of this: hymns drag, elders judge, children fidget, fancy clothes constrain, and the minutes tick slowly by. In other congregations, joyful prayer and song burst through the seams of the worship service, and hours pass before anyone is ready to leave. The contrast suggests that we all need to remember that Sunday worship is not just about "going to church"; it is about taking part in the activity by which God is shaping a new creation. It is a foretaste of the feast to come.

After worship, what many of us need most is time with loved ones—not useful time, for planning next week's schedules, but time "wasted" on the pleasure of being together, perhaps while sharing our enjoyment of art, nature, or athletics. For others, and for all of us at certain points in our lives, hours of solitude beckon, hours for sleep, reading, reflection, walking, and prayer. In addition, we might explore the long tradition of visiting the homebound or inviting lonely ones to our table on the Christian Sabbath, when the joy these occasions bring can be experienced apart from the pressures of other appointments.

Churches must be careful, however, not to devour Sabbath freedom with "religious" or charitable obligations. Filling Sunday afternoons with church committee meetings, for example, is a terrible violation of this freedom. And it is a violation that unfortunately seems to be increasing, precisely because of the pressures that Sabbath freedom specifically opposes. Of course, it is difficult to find time to meet during the week, but part of the point of Sabbath keeping is to cause shifts in weekday priorities. In many churches, it is the people on the committees who most need to be reminded to keep Sabbath! Resisting the temptation to meet on Sunday would help them to say to one another, "God intends rest and liberation for you during at least one seventh of your time." Eating, playing, and taking delight in nature and one another in the hours after worship would be wonderful ways for congregations or groups within them to keep Sabbath.

Sabbath, Our Good, and the Good of All

Puritan Sabbath keepers agreed that "good Sabbaths make good Christians." They meant that regular, disciplined attention to the spiritual life was the foundation of faithfulness. Another dimension of the saying opens up if we imagine a worshiping community helping one another to step off the treadmill of work-and-spend and into the circle of glad gratitude for the gifts of God. Taken this way, good Sabbaths make good Christians by regularly reminding us of God's creative, liberating, and redeeming presence, not only in words but also through a practice we do together in response to that presence. But even beyond this, there are other benefits of Sabbath keeping, and these could spill over to bless the whole world. With a change, the saying acquires an applicability that reaches beyond the spiritual life alone, and beyond the Sabbath practices of Jews or Christians. Imagine this: "Good Sabbaths make good societies."

The practice of keeping Sabbath bears much wisdom for people seeking ways through the crises of these times and the stresses of contemporary life. "The solution of mankind's most vexing problems will not be found in renouncing technical civilization, but in attaining some degree of independence from it," writes Heschel. Sabbath keeping teaches that independence. Refraining from work on a regular basis is a way of setting limits on behavior that is perilous for both human welfare and the welfare of the earth itself. Overworked Americans need rest, *and* they need to be reminded that they do not cause the grain to grow and that their greatest fulfillment does not come through the acquisition of material things. Moreover, the planet needs a rest from human plucking and burning and buying and selling. Perhaps, as Sabbath keepers, we will come to live and know these truths more fully, and thus to bring their wisdom to the common solution of humanity's problems.

A good Sabbath would also make a good society by balancing the claims of work and celebration, for workers and celebrants of all sorts. In prayers at the beginning and end of *Shabbat,* Jews thank God for the blessing of work. Not working on one day is tied to working on the other six; Sabbath affirms the value of work and interprets it as an important dimension of human identity. Sabbath keeping bears a longing that all human beings will have good work, as well as a longing that no one will be required to toil without respite.

Rest and worship. One day a week—not much, in a sense, but a good beginning. One day to resist the tyranny of too much or too little work and to celebrate with God and others, remembering thereby who we really are and what is really important. One day that, week after week, anchors a way of life that makes a difference every day.

Chapter 7

TESTIMONY

❧

Thomas Hoyt Jr.

Whe n I was a boy, my father took my sister and me with him to the prayer and testimony meeting each Wednesday night. He was the minister, and sometimes the three of us were the only ones there. But that didn't stop the service or hold back the Spirit. After we sang together and he prayed, it was time for my sister and me. "It is your time to pray," he would say, and I got on my knees and prayed. "Now sing your song." I would sing my little song. Next my sister would sing and pray. Then my father announced that it was time for the testimonies. And I would get up and say, "Thank God for what God has done for me, and I hope that you all will pray for me so that I will grow strong." On our way home at the end of the evening, he would say, "Didn't we have a good time tonight!" Yes, we surely did, in song, prayer, and testimony.

On those Wednesday evenings in the Trinity Christian Methodist Episcopal Church in Birmingham, Alabama, I was being nurtured in one of the most cherished practices of the Black Church: the practice of testimony. In different ways, testimony happens in every vital Christian community. It also happens, as we shall see, in the

Then I said, "Ah, Lord God! Truly I do not know how to speak,
for I am only a boy." But the Lord said to me, "Do not say,
'I am only a boy'; for you shall go to all to whom I send you,
and you shall speak whatever I command you, Do not be afraid
of them, for I am with you to deliver you, says the Lord." Then
the Lord put out his hand and touched my mouth; and the Lord
said to me, "Now I have put my words in your mouth."

JEREMIAH 1:6–9

midst of daily life and in the life of society. In testimony, people speak truthfully about what they have experienced and seen, offering it to the community for the edification of all.

The practice of testimony is one that people sorely need, particularly in a society where many voices sound yet where public speech that is honest and empowering is rare. No sooner is a political speech given than the "spin doctors" step in to bend its meaning. Talk show producers profit by laying the private confessions of others before millions of strangers. The pursuit of commercial gain drives the speech of advertising, which is present everywhere. Yet people without economic and political power often find that their voices are not heard at all. In this context, we need to consider what it means to testify. The Black Church's practice of testimony offers insights on matters that concern everyone who seeks a life that is truthful.

WHAT IS TESTIMONY?

We borrow from the world of courtrooms and trials when we talk about "testimony." Testimony occurs in particular settings—a courtroom or a church—where a community expects to hear the truth spoken. Witnesses—those making the testimony—must speak the truth as they have seen, heard, and experienced it. The practice of testimony requires that there be witnesses to testify and others to receive and evaluate their testimony. It is a deeply shared practice—one that is possible only in a community that recognizes that falsehood is strong, but that yearns nonetheless to know what is true and good.

False testimony is a lie in the heart of the witness.
This perverse intention is so fatal to the exercise of justice
and to the entire order of discourse that all codes of
morality place it very high in the scale of vices.

PAUL RICOEUR, "The Hermeneutics of Testimony"

Testimony is basic to human community. It appears in different forms, ranging across a spectrum from the highly technical procedures of the courtroom to the familiar exchanges of everyday life. We can learn something about the shape and significance of the practice from both ends of the spectrum. In courts of law, specific rules, customs, and traditions let witnesses know what it means to tell the truth, the whole truth, and nothing but the truth. Lies can result in grievous injustice, and they are severely punished. It is fascinating to note that there is a strong preference in the law for testimony that is spoken in person; the authority of a living witness has more weight than a tape or document. At the other end of the spectrum, testimony also happens in our most ordinary relationships at home, beginning very early in life. "What did you learn in school today?" parents ask—or more ominously, "Who broke the lamp?" If someone saw Johnny do it and steps forward to give an account, Johnny will be convicted. And testimony continues throughout life, until our last wills and testaments are witnessed by credible persons. Elsewhere, witnesses are summoned to give credible testimony at congressional hearings, and business entrepreneurs get witnesses to testify to the quality of their products in order to entice purchasers.

But what does all this "testimony" have to do with what took place at Trinity C.M.E.? The importance of the practice of testimony has appeared with great power within the religious arena among African American people. Looking at the particular shape of this practice among this people, we may see how its power can be reclaimed for the good of all people.

The testimony of ordinary persons in Sunday morning worship and weeknight prayer meetings is characteristic of worship in the "free church" tradition, where services are relatively informal and expressive. One classic praise testimony, popular in the contemporary Black Church, goes something like this: "Thank you, God, for waking me up this morning; for putting shoes on my feet, clothes on my back, and food on my table. Thank you, God, for health and strength and the activities of my limbs. Thank you that I awoke this morning clothed in my right mind."

In a world where bad news gets more attention than good, a testimony like this tells the truth. It also ties individuals to communities. Although only one person may be speaking at a time, that person's speech takes place within the context of other people's listening, expecting, and encouraging. In testimony, a believer describes what God has done in her life, in words both biblical and personal, and the hands of her friends clap in affirmation. Her individual speech thus becomes part of an affirmation that is shared.

TESTIMONY FROM MARGINAL LIVING

The testimony given by African Americans is derived from their experience of marginality in the American context. The fact that the African American experience in the United States has been on the margins since slavery is so well known that only a brief reminder is needed. A summary presents the overwhelming contours: the period of political disenfranchisement; military segregation and humiliation; exclusions from and restrictions in jobs and housing; segregation and discrimination in health care and social welfare; frequent injustice in the courts; and exclusions from voluntary, occupational, and professional associations, schools, and churches. Even though the civil rights movement brought relative justice and ended the universal system of apartheid, the black masses are still caught in a web of selective apartheid.

Even before coming to America, Africans were a religious people, with divinities, rituals, prayers, songs, codes of ethics, punishments, and rewards. Marginal existence in America gave birth to new experiences of fear, love, joy, hope, sorrow, guilt, loneliness, and struggle. Throughout their history and still today, these realities have shaped the lives of African American people. Out of all this, their testimonies have emerged.

Testimony that gives voice to these experiences has been central to the African American community since its beginning. Even before the African American churches became institutionalized, the people met in "brush arbors" where storytellers similar to the African *griots* and priests testified to God's goodness and helped them keep their heritage alive even in this strange land. Thus African American preachers became the embodiments and conveyors of the people's longings and hopes in the midst of pain. In secret communal meetings, they retold in their own words biblical stories they had heard in their captors' churches, reinterpreting them in the light of their own people's needs and experiences.

Thus the testimony of African Americans has been, and still is, verbalized in preaching, praying, singing, shouting, and storytelling. Their testimony has been shared in places where people could feel secure and free to worship as they pleased—places where they felt the Spirit and could commune with one another with handshakes and tears. And through the years, this has been therapeutic and salvific for the Black Church, as for other oppressed communities. Oppressed people, after all, cannot go to expensive psychiatrists. African Americans' therapy came on Sunday mornings and Wednesday nights, at worship services and prayer meetings where they could tell the community their hurts and pains in the context of praises to God for God's deliverance. In this way, times of testimony became times of catharsis and healing.

The testimony of the Black Church receives its power from the presence of the Holy Spirit. "There is no understanding of black worship apart from the presence of the Spirit who descends upon the gathered community, lighting a spiritual fire in their hearts," says theologian James Cone. "There is no understanding of black worship apart from the rhythm of song and sermon, the passion of prayer and testimony, the ecstasy of shout and conversion, as the people project their humanity in the togetherness of the Spirit."

TESTIMONY AND THE BIBLE

The Bible also undergirds the power of testimony among African Americans. The Bible itself provides many stories and images of testimony, from the creation to the prophets through the apostles and those who have waited in expectation of the end of history. A good example is the story of Peter's testimony in Jerusalem after the Holy Spirit fell upon the disciples and all the nations on Pentecost (Acts 2); the presence of the Spirit and the fact that all people are included make this story a particularly resonant one in the Black Church. The testimony of the apostle Paul is also treasured as a model. Titus, Paul told the Jerusalem Council (Galatians 2:1–10), was full of the Holy Spirit, even though he had not been circumcised as a Jew like the rest of them. Titus's faith was proof that God shows no partiality to race, gender, physical, or class distinctions. Biblical testimony, in these cases and many others, is a form in which the words of freedom are spoken and heard.

Moreover, the overall story of the Bible provides the framework for African Americans to perceive the activity of God in their own history. The stories African Americans learn in the Bible tell them how to look at their own story, what questions to raise, and even how to recognize an answer when it appears. Through hearing and reading the story of the Jews, African Americans come to understand their own story. Their great and powerful origins on the continent of Africa, enslavement, the suffering of their people, the protests of their prophets, and the present-day yearning for the full justice God has promised—all of these greatly resemble the biblical paradigm of the ancient Israelites, who testified to God as the One who had led them out of the house of bondage. Biblical stories, in sum, inspire African Americans with a similar view of their own history. The Bible's testimony provides a confession of what God has done in the history of another people, thus evoking testimony about what God has done in African American history and what God will do for their freedom.

The importance of the Bible in the African American experience joins the presence of the Spirit to shape the practice of testimony in this community. These two elements—Bible and Spirit—also appear in every other vital Christian community. The accents and styles may be different, but both are present wherever authentic Christian testimony is practiced. Such testimony comes to life within the context of a story larger than the witness's own personal experience—but this biblical story can also embrace and transform that experience. In this sense, Christian testimony is inspired by the same Spirit that animates all of life. Whether felt as a fire in the heart or as a gentle prompting to be honest, God's Spirit enlivens all true testimony and all true worship. Any time the gathered people "project their humanity in the togetherness of the Spirit," as James Cone puts it, they bear witness to God's transformative power in their midst.

PREACHING AS TESTIMONY

The preaching of sermons is a form of testimony that seems at first glance to separate one testifier—the preacher—from the rest. Within the shared practice of testimony, however, preacher and people work together. As Thomas G. Long has noted, the authority of the preacher derives not from rank, experience, intelligence, or even wisdom. It derives from the call of the community, which sends the preacher to the Word on behalf of them all. "So," says Long, "the preacher goes to the scripture, but not alone. The preacher goes on behalf of the faithful community and, in a sense, on behalf of the world."

Because preaching is such a shared practice, it demands a response. In many churches in the African American community, worshipers offer their responses out loud during the sermon itself, engaging in a pattern of call and response between preacher and congregation that can be inspiring for both. In these churches and all others, however, preachers also pray for responses of other sorts. An old joke tells about a pastor's first sermon in a new congregation. The congregation is very impressed and returns the next week eager to hear more, only to hear the preacher deliver the same sermon again. Well, they reason, the pastor is busy moving in and has had no time to

———— ∿ ————

I give thanks to my God always for you because of the grace of God
that has been given you in Christ Jesus, for in every way you have
been enriched in him, in speech and knowledge of every kind—just
as the testimony of Christ has been strengthened among you.

1 CORINTHIANS 1:4–6

[But] I do not count my life of any value to myself, if only I
may finish my course and the ministry that I received from
the Lord Jesus, to testify to the good news of God's grace.

THE APOSTLE PAUL IN ACTS 20:24

write a new one. The next week, however, when the preacher gives the same sermon for the third time, the elders of the church approach to ask what is going on. "I haven't preached a new sermon," the preacher replies, "because you haven't done what I told you to do in the first one yet!"

No doubt most preachers have felt this way. For indeed, testimony requires a response from those who receive it. Preaching is a witness intended to evoke other forms of witness. The practice of testimony through preaching opens up a space for others to add their own witness to the presence of God in the world. Such response can be seen in biblical accounts of preaching. For example, Jesus' own preaching and teaching were taken up by his closest followers after his death. Peter's testimony on Pentecost persuaded some three thousand persons to join the Christian community, where they "devoted themselves to the apostles' teaching and fellowship, to the breaking of bread and the prayers" (Acts 2:40–42).

The preacher is a witness who searches the Scriptures on behalf of the community and then returns to the community to speak what he or she has found. As Paul knew, this does not always mean that the preacher will pronounce what the community most wants to hear. The testimony of preaching is a prophetic testimony, one that makes compelling claims on both preacher and hearers.

Preaching is the practice of the whole church and not of the preacher alone. This reality both signals the importance of preaching and provides a note of grace during those painful times when preachers must speak for the community even though they themselves feel dry and alienated. In preaching, sustained by the Spirit and guided by the Bible, they can give useful testimony about truths larger than their own understanding and conviction. Just as a courtroom witness's limited experience in a large case can often provide an important piece of evidence that allows every other piece to fall

[O]n the Lord's Day . . . the people of God
celebrate a mock trial, in which the law is read, confession
and testimony obtained, and the verdict once again
given as it was once before all time.

RICHARD K. FENN, *Liturgies and Trials*

into place, so in a sermon, a preacher may speak the truth even though he has only glimpsed it as Moses glimpsed the promised land. "As your preacher this morning, it is only honest to say that I have never known fully that kind of life within the full, warm power of that faith for whose declaration I am an ordained minister," the Lutheran preacher Joseph Sittler once confessed from the pulpit. But "is the opulence of the grace of God to be measured by my inventory? Is the great catholic faith of nineteen centuries to be reduced to my interior dimensions? Are the arching lines of the gracious possible to be pulled down to the little spurts of my personal compass? Is the great heart of the reality of God to speak in only the broken accent that I can follow after? No. That ought not to be. Therefore, one is proper and right when he sometimes talks of things he doesn't know all about. In obedience to the bigness of the story which transcends his own apprehension, one may do this." Since testimony is the shared practice of the whole people of God, we may participate in it even when we do not have all the answers.

TESTIMONY IN SONG

If you would know the real life and history of a nation or people, study the testimony it makes in its songs. They tell of its thoughts, the bent of the mind of its people, and the overflowing of its heart. When life runs over, it is expressed in song. When the heart is too full of sorrow or joy for speech, it sings. This makes song one of the most precious forms of the practice of testimony.

When Miriam saw her people's enemies drowned in the Red Sea and her newly freed people safe on dry ground, her heart broke out in song as all the women danced, shaking tambourines. "Sing to the LORD, for he has triumphed gloriously," Miriam sang; "horse and rider he has thrown into the sea." She and the other maidens danced up and down the bank singing, "Pharaoh and his army were drowned in the sea" (Exodus 15:21). A slave-trader found Christ, received forgiveness for his sins, and broke forth in song: "Amazing Grace, how sweet the sound, that saved a wretch like me!" When the heart is overjoyed, it sings. A Baptist minister, having received a call to another church, was packing his household goods. His friends and parishioners, helping him pack, found tears running down their cheeks at the thought of losing their pastor. He felt the same about leaving those he loved. He found that he could not leave them, so he sat down and expressed himself in song: "Blessed be the tie that binds our hearts in Christian love."

Every people and nation practices testimony when it sings of its hopes and trials. The woodsman sings of the forest, the soldier of the battlefield, the farmer of the corn and the vine, the shepherd of the sheep. The songs that African American people have sung in history—spirituals, hymns, blues, jazz, gospel—have all helped them make sense of their lives in this country. Songs have been the vehicles of testimony, of telling the Spirit-filled truth, and they have been sung in confidence that God is present in both this life and the life to come. The spirituals of the slaves, for example, took seriously the idea that Jesus was going to prepare a place for them and would come back to receive them. All that they were denied on earth would be multiplied in heaven. They testified in song to the providence of God: "I got shoes, you got shoes, all of God's children got shoes; when we get to heaven, gonna put on our shoes and walk all over God's heaven." At the same time, they would pass by the master's room and sing softly, "Everybody's talkin' 'bout heaven ain't gwan there."

Heaven had a dual implication in the testimonies of slaves. It referred to life beyond life but also to a state in this life. Because of the risk involved in preaching liberation, the slave learned how to testify to God's liberation in the very presence of the slave master, singing, "Swing low, sweet chariot [underground railroad], coming for to carry me home [north to freedom]." When the slave masters forbade slaves to ordain ministers or to preach without the sanction of the "master," African American men and women still found ways to testify, to tell the story of God's liberation in song. The songs that African Americans sang in spirituals, and sing today in gospel music, are prayers, praises, and sermons, the testimony of a people before God.

TESTIMONY BEYOND WORDS

Testimony is made not only through speech and song. The philosopher Paul Ricoeur applies the term to "words, works, actions, and to lives which attest to an intention, an inspiration, an idea at the heart of experience and history which nonetheless transcends experience and history." There have been many witnesses—Sojourner Truth, Martin Luther King Jr., Mohandas Gandhi—who testified to "an idea at the heart of history" not only with their words, but with their bodies, their actions, their lives. Two of these three witnesses died violently in the process of making their testimony. "It is no coincidence," writes Thomas G. Long, "that the New Testament word for witness is *martyr*."

A quiet act of compassion can sometimes testify more powerfully to God's presence than a well-wrought sermon. Each day in our communities, persons reach out to others in trust and care. These persons bear witness to God's presence before the world. Think of the teachers who devote themselves to the growth and well-being of children. Think of the individuals who volunteer in soup kitchens and homeless shelters. Think of the countless times each day when kindness passes from one stranger to another or when someone speaks out to defend the powerless.

The rituals of Christian churches also offer nonverbal ways of practicing testimony. When we gather for Holy Communion, for example, we bear witness both to the story of Jesus' life and death and to its continuing power in our lives. When we wash a new Christian in the waters of baptism, we offer testimony to one another and to God that we are bound to one another and to Christians of every time and place. When we embrace one another in peace, we testify to the reconciliation God intends for all people. These and other rituals help us to learn the communal, shared practice of testimony.

TELLING THE TRUTH, TO
ONE ANOTHER AND TO GOD

Christian testimony has two dimensions. One is testimony to the church and the world, where witnesses tell others about the action of God. The other is testimony to God, where witnesses tell God the truth about themselves and others. These are ancient forms of Christian testimony, which find powerful expression in classic Christian texts like Saint Augustine's *Confessions,* written sixteen hundred years ago. In this great autobiography, Augustine tells the story of his life for two reasons: to confess the mercies of God to other people and to confess the truth about his own life to God.

The same pattern appears in the stories of conversion that have frequently been told in the testimony of the Black Church. These testimonies are directed to God as offerings of honor and praise. And they are also directed to other people, telling them the effects of God's power so that they, too, might know God's power in their lives. "I was on a downward road, no hat on my head, no shoes on my feet, no God on my side, no heaven in my view," the narrative of one former slave began. "Too mean to live and not fit to die. The handcuffs of hell on my hands, the shackles of damnation on my feet. But the Lord spoke peace to my dying soul, turned me around, cut loose my stammering tongue, sent me on my way. And ever since that day, I'm sometimes rising and sometimes falling but I made my vow to the Lord and I'll never turn back no more. I'm going to run on and see what the end's gonna be."

The power of testimony is to give voice to the faith that lets people run on to see what the end's gonna be. Stories like these, told in the context of oppression, are what the theologian Leonardo Boff calls "testimonies charged with hope." They keep alive the truth—a truth that society often does not honor. Life is stronger than death. People can change with God's help. God is worthy of our thanks and praise.

Long and rich participation in the practice of testimony has prepared African Americans to find a voice for justice in the face of oppression, a voice that rings out not only in church services but also in the world. Other people have also found truthful voices through the practice of testimony. This practice is an important part of the heal-

PRACTICING OUR FAITH

ing that is taking place all over the world through Alcoholics Anonymous as people stand up to tell painful truths about themselves to God and other people. The practice has also shaped the renewal of a church of the people in Latin America, where Archbishop Oscar Romero of El Salvador and thousands of other Christians have proclaimed the Gospel, urged the poor to speak of their lives in relation to its stories, and paid the martyr's price for doing so.

The practice of testimony requires a person to commit voice and body to the telling of the truth. It guards the integrity of personal and communal life, as much on the grand stage of history as in the small exchanges of home. Today, living in a world where falsehood is strong, we need to support one another as we rise to bear witness, speaking the truth about what we have seen and heard. When we do, we are also supported by another community, one that has inspired Christians since the earliest days: the "great cloud of witnesses" who have gone before us (Hebrews 12:1).

Chapter 8

DISCERNMENT

❧

Frank Rogers Jr.

Joyce, the middle-aged mother of four children, has been separated from her husband for a year and a half, ever since he abruptly announced that he was moving in with an assistant half his age. It has been like climbing out of a suffocating abyss, but now, after months of sleepless nights, her tentative attempts to recreate her life are taking hold. She has a steady job and a supportive network, the kids are settling into a routine, and she is discovering a personal strength that she never knew she had. And now, with the divorce almost complete, he wants to move back home. A committed Catholic, Joyce seeks counsel from her priest. Tormented by conflicting pulls, she desperately yearns to know what she should do. What does God want her to do? How can she know for sure? Please, how can she know?

As individuals and as communities, we are always facing decisions. Of course, many are seemingly simple and mundane—choosing a place to eat, for example, or deciding what to wear. Others, however, are complex and agonizing. For which vocation should I prepare? Whom should we choose as our leader? Should I switch jobs? Where do we cut to balance our budget? Even, Should this marriage be ended?

These are the decisions that make us cry out for guidance. Like the ancients who consulted the oracles at Delphi, we yearn for the clues that will direct us—a burning bush, a heavenly voice, a bright star, some sign, any sign, that will make clear to us which way we should go. So much is at stake, and we do not want to make a wrong step.

The yearning for divine guidance is heightened when we consider all of the colliding forces that storm around us. There are the conflicting promptings that wrestle within us, the tangled mix of self-deceptions and authentic impulses for life. Are the inclinations to stay in a marriage rooted in self-destructive guilt and a paralyzing fear of living free from abuse, or in commitment to fidelity and to faith in the healing Spirit of God? Are the inclinations to sever a marriage rooted in a chronic fear of intimacy or in a sober recognition that life sometimes flourishes more fully in the less painful of two painful realities?

And there are the conflicting pressures that come from outside of us. Do we listen to the friend who pleads with us to save our life by leaving a marriage or to the family member who pleads with us to stay with our spouse for the sake of the children? How do we assess advice to take care of ourselves when it emerges from a culture that also perpetuates forms of self-fulfillment that make marriage all too dispensable? The external influences of culture and even of friends are fallible, driven by mixtures of perceptiveness and deception, of freedom and addiction. What are we to do in the midst of this vertigo of uncertain insights and conflicting impulses? It is enough to leave one utterly confused.

Christians believe that we are not alone during such times. God is present, hoping and urging, in the midst of all the situations of life. As Christians, we believe that God is passionately involved in human affairs and intimately invested in all our questioning. Moreover, we believe that God's involvement in our lives has purpose and direction. God is seeking to bring healing and wholeness and reconciliation, transforming this broken world into that New Creation where there will be no more sadness or injustice or pain. Our decisions and our search for guidance take place in the active presence of a God who intimately cares about our life situations and who invites us to participate in the divine activities of healing and transformation.

There is that near you which will guide you.
O Wait for it and be sure that ye keep to it.

Isaac Pennington

Discernment is the intentional practice by which a community or an individual seeks, recognizes, and intentionally takes part in the activity of God in concrete situations. When we face decisions, we often feel that we are without help, and that we are completely on our own as we figure out how to sort things through. In fact, people have always faced difficult decisions, and over the centuries, Christian communities have developed insights and approaches that can guide us in our dilemmas today. The practice of discernment is one of these. It is a practice that can help Joyce, and us, make decisions in our often bewildering world.

Discerning the Spirit as an Individual

Virginia is trying to discern if she should move to another state for a job opportunity; Rebecca is trying to discern if God is calling her to some form of ministry; Bob is trying to discern if he should get married. All of us, at various times, find ourselves at crossroads where we seek guidance for some personal decision. We yearn to know the direction toward which God is inviting us.

Unfortunately, there is no method that guarantees that the ways of the Spirit will be discerned in any given situation. The Holy Spirit eludes capture by any formula. However, certain methods have been developed that help counter self-deception and heighten the possibility that God's Spirit can be known. Ignatius of Loyola (1491–1556), the Spanish founder of the Society of Jesus (Jesuits), offered one such method. Refined and practiced for centuries in Jesuit and other Catholic communities throughout the world, it has become a widely influential model.

Discernment, for Ignatius, always aims at enhancing one's participation in the work of God; it is always undertaken for the glory of God and the healing of the world. Therefore, several predispositions are vital for the practice to be followed with integrity:

- *A passionate commitment to follow God.* The guidance that we seek is toward that decision that will bring us into the fullest possible participation in the work of God in the world.
- *An attitude of indifference toward all other drives and desires.* If we are to align ourselves with God's purposes, we must first detach ourselves from our own desires for wealth, prestige, and security.
- *A deep sensitivity to the ways and being of God.* This sensitivity is cultivated through prayer, reading and meditating on the Scriptures, worship, and faithful acts of mercy and justice.

In the classic form of discernment developed by Ignatius, these three dispositions are especially fostered during a thirty-day retreat that involves sustained immersion in these activities. Because retreats of this length are not possible for everyone, experiences in Ignatian discernment that follow different rhythms have also been developed over the years.

If Joyce turned to the Ignatian practice of discernment in her quest for clarity, she would be guided through several steps of reflection. First, she would try to become aware of as many dimensions of the decision before her as possible. She would secure important information, consider all the possible consequences of her decision, solicit insight from confidants and significant others, weigh pros and cons, and perhaps even consult experts about dysfunctional relationships, midlife crises, and the effects of divorce on children. In as thorough a way as possible, she would want to develop a clear idea of what her choices entailed.

Second, she would devote a particular period of time—anywhere from a few days to several weeks—to considering the negative side, the decision she feels least inclined to choose. During this period, she would cease seesawing between the alternatives and seek to settle into what life would be like if this were her choice. She would frequently bring this alternative before God in prayer. In the context of this prayer, she would reflect deeply to surface all of the emotions, sensations, and thoughts that either attract her toward or repel her from this choice, even those stirrings that are most difficult to face.

She would seek to discern whether the sources of these various stirrings were divine, demonic, or neurotic. This difficult process re-

*It is characteristic of the evil spirit to harass with anxiety,
to afflict with sadness, to raise obstacles backed by fallacious
reasonings that disturb the soul. It is characteristic of the
good spirit, however, to give courage and strength,
consolations, tears, inspirations, and peace.*

IGNATIUS OF LOYOLA, *Spiritual Exercises*

quires painful honesty and self-awareness. It entails allowing our
thoughts and feelings to "echo down" into the depths of our being
and discerning if these movements have a life-giving source or a destructive one. For Ignatius, this is determined by the feelings of consolation or desolation that emerge. Essentially, feelings of consolation
are those that give rise to life, love, peace, joy, creativity, and communion. These are harmonious with the Spirit, even when painful.
Feelings of desolation are those that give rise to despair, confusion,
alienation, destructiveness, and discord. These are discordant with
the Spirit and do not have their source in God.

An additional layer of complexity is also present, however.
Sometimes self-deception blocks our understanding. Feelings of joy
and vitality associated with having an affair, for example, may seem
life-enhancing at first, though they actually have their roots in destructive impulses. Likewise, feelings that appear to be destructive at
first glance may have a deeper source in the Spirit of life. Sometimes
divisiveness is a painful step toward communion, conflict a path toward healing. In short, this process of echoing down to listen for the
deepest chords of our lives is complex, painful, and vulnerable to deception. As such, it requires patience, honesty, humility, and keen
sensitivity to the Spirit's music.

After Joyce has listened deeply to her heart and sifted through
all of her various impulses in relation to her "negative" option, she
would repeat the process for the same period of time with the other,
more positive option, the one to which she was originally more attracted. At the end of this period, she would reflect on the two
processes, weighing all of the information and comparing her various feelings to determine which choice gave rise to the deeper feelings of consolation. Relying on both her heart and her head, she

---

*By Christian discernment I understand the particular quest for the
will of God, not only to understand it but also to carry it out.*

JON SOBRINO, "Following Jesus as Discernment"

---

would then make a tentative decision and would spend some time
living with this, praying and reflecting on it as she sought confirmation from God that this was the right path. Such confirmation could
take the form of a deeply peaceful feeling that, even within the am-
biguities inherent in all of life, she had done the best that she could
to follow the way that resonated most fully with her understanding
and intuition of the Spirit.

Finally, Joyce would act in the direction that seemed most harmonious with the Spirit. Discernment is for action. To be sure, we
should be wary of acting when little light has emerged from the discernment process. If time permits, it is wisest to postpone action and
resume the process. However, discernment rarely yields absolute certainty, and action itself is part of the discernment process. Sometimes
our action reveals that a direction is misguided, in which case we
should repeat the discernment process. At other times, the direction
is confirmed.

DISCERNING THE SPIRIT IN COMMUNITIES

Decisions also constantly face groups of people, including religious
groups. Decisions of this kind may arise from global events—how
shall we respond faithfully to the outbreak of war?—or from such
local challenges as congregational conflict or a need to cut the budget. Sadly, the discourse surrounding these decisions often resembles
the hardened debate that takes place in sessions of the U.S. Congress
rather than the harmony of God's New Creation. Party interests, personality clashes, and power strategies take center stage, crowding out
genuine dialogue and respect.

The communal practice of discernment, in contrast, places
group decisions within the context of God's transforming activity. It

trusts that resolution based on something larger than self-interest and partisanship is possible. It orients the conversation and imagination of communities toward participation in God's activity by inviting members to share in the goal of that activity: the New Creation.

The early church clearly engaged in the practice of communal spiritual discernment. The Council of Jerusalem, for example, gathered to discern the Spirit's direction about the circumcision of gentile Christians (Acts 15). The Bible does not offer a formal process by which to structure the practice of discernment, but various groups of Christians have developed such forms over the centuries. One such group has been the Society of Friends (Quakers). For Quakers, the process of making and effecting decisions is shaped by a distinctive form of the practice of discernment: decision making by consensus.

Quakers believe that the Spirit of God is present within every person. Each person has, therefore, a fragment of God's wisdom which should be listened to and respected. The fullness of the Spirit's guidance is discerned when everyone's wisdom blends together to produce a decision that each person can affirm—in short, when consensus has been reached. Often, the solution is a higher synthesis of the various views, "a case where two and two make five."

This happened in the spring of 1967 in Jamestown, New York, after a visiting speaker in the Quaker meetinghouse called for an end to the Vietnam war. Vandals smeared ugly accusations on its white walls: "Treason! Traitors! There can be no compromise with Commies!"

In response, the local Quaker community called a "meeting." Among Quakers, there are "meetings for worship" and "meetings for business"; each begins in silence, to allow the Spirit to move through the community, leading each person out of narrow self-concern to an attitude that is receptive to the Spirit's promptings, both within the person's own consciousness and in the words of other community members. And so this meeting—a "business" meeting— began. The silence soon was broken, as one person after another spoke with deep feeling. As the group tried to decide what response to make to the vandalism, many different ideas were offered. It was evident that there was deep division between those who wanted to use the occasion to publicly condemn the vandals and their views and

Meetings for the transaction of business are conducted in the same expectant waiting for the guidance of the Spirit as is the meeting for worship. Periods of worship, especially at the beginning and the end, lift hearts and minds out of self-centered desires into an openness to seek the common good under the leadership of the Spirit of Christ.

Quaker Book of Discipline

those who wanted no publicity. Feeling ran high, and several times the clerk had to ask the meeting to do what Friends often do during a discernment process: settle back into silence.

Finally, someone suggested that the members of the community invite their friends and neighbors to join with them in repairing the damage. This would draw some publicity, of course, but it would be positive, not hostile to others. The idea was endorsed by the meeting, and an invitation was published in local papers. The next week, more than two hundred people joined the Quakers for a "paint-in," including some who disagreed with them about the war in Vietnam.

The process of communal discernment used in this case began in silence and moved through discussion and repeated silence toward consensus. The discussion stage of discernment often begins tentatively and gradually becomes more purposeful, until a direction begins to gain a wave of support. Members build on one another's ideas, endorsing and refining the rising consensus. If no such tide emerges after some time, the discussion is postponed. If competing directions emerge, the discussion continues until one seems to prevail. When consensus is slow in emerging, the discussion is punctuated with periods of silence where the members can listen for and become refocused on the Spirit.

Based on the conviction that the Spirit is one and therefore cannot offer conflicting direction, the Quaker practice requires that a full consensus be present before a decision is made. Ideally, this demand for consensus provides a check against monopoly by any subsection of the community. Each person must be heard, and everyone must adjust to the wisdom set forth by every other person.

The Jesuits also have a rich tradition of communal discernment. Its rhythm is different, however, incorporating times of individual prayer along the way. Unlike the Quakers, Ignatian communal discernment does not require full consensus. When it is determined that consensus will not emerge within the available time, the group can agree that the decision will be made by majority vote. Whether made by consensus or by vote, however, the decision still requires some confirmation before the community can conclude that it embodies God's leading. One important sign of confirmation is a peaceful conviction permeating the entire community—including those who dissented—that the decision is the one that will most allow the community to be faithful to God.

Both Ignatian and Quaker forms of communal discernment require a great deal from participants, who must intentionally try both to seek their own wisdom about God's direction for the community and to open themselves to the wisdom of the other participants. For the process to work, genuine dialogue must be present, and participants must develop inner freedom from captivity to their own certainties and ego needs. They must rise above dogmatism and the desire for control and esteem, laying these aside for the sake of finding God's leading through the whole community. The process is destroyed when voices are silenced, when honest listening is absent, when people push their own agendas, or when leaders wield their authority and power in ways that override the Spirit-led authority and power of the other participants.

WHEN DISCERNMENT DECEIVES AND WHEN IT DOESN'T

Spiritual discernment is a dangerous practice. It has extraordinary potential to be either prophetically subversive or grossly self-deceptive. A group or an individual is claiming for an experience or a decision the seemingly unaccountable authority of a self-confirming movement of the Holy Spirit. "God told us to become a sanctuary church . . . to fire the new pastor . . . to deny ordination to persons who are gay." "God told me to continue this affair . . . to enter ordained ministry . . . to discontinue chemotherapy." The claims appear self-authenticating and therefore not subject to any absolute external criteria. This is the beauty of discernment: faithful action becomes

*The discerning person can tell, for example, when prayer is
not genuine contact with God but a conversation with oneself;
when apparent humility is actually a twisted form of pride;
when a vision is really an hallucination and an ecstasy
a psychosomatic disturbance; when inspirations are projections
of suspect desires and when a vocation to celibacy is
more a flight from intimacy than a call from God.*

SANDRA SCHNEIDERS, "Spiritual Discernment
in the Dialogue of Saint Catherine of Siena"

more than blind obedience to external rules, as it is enlivened by the touch of the Spirit. But this is also its danger. The history of the church is littered with the stories of people who have claimed guidance from the Spirit when the prejudices of self-deception reigned instead.

From the earliest days of Judaism and Christianity, awareness of this danger has prompted faithful people to articulate criteria by which to judge the authenticity of claims regarding the Spirit. The Hebrew people had to distinguish time and again between true and false prophets (for example, Jeremiah 28:1–16). Likewise, the early church was admonished to test every spirit (1 John 4:1, 1 Thessalonians 5:19–21). The difficulty has been in establishing just what the criteria should be. The challenge is compounded when it is recognized that no external criteria can be considered absolute. For any given criteria proposed and exercised, abuses in application abound, and so do legitimate exceptions. Nevertheless, a number of normative criteria have been suggested to guide the discernment of authentic and unauthentic spiritual promptings:

• *Fidelity to Scripture and the tradition.* At the top of any list of criteria can be found the test of fidelity to the essential vision of the

*Beloved, do not believe every spirit, but test the spirits to see
whether they are from God; for many false prophets
have gone out into the world.*

1 JOHN 4:1

Your word is a lamp to my feet and a light to my path.

Psalm 119:105

sacred writings and teachings that constitute the faith tradition. The Israelites were strictly admonished to ignore any prophet or visionary who taught a god other than Yahweh as known through the Torah (Deuteronomy 13:2–6). Later, the apostle Paul warned against those who taught a different gospel, even if they were angels (Galatians 1:6–9). Applying this guideline is more complex than simply citing biblical passages, however. It requires us to know Scripture as a whole, and to continue searching it with the guidance of the Spirit.

• *Fruit of the Spirit.* Another indication of the authenticity of spiritual discernment is the degree to which the outcome nurtures the fruit of the Spirit in a person or community (Galatians 5:22–23). Usually, the virtue of love is given priority (1 Corinthians 13). We can deceive ourselves about the presence of these virtues, to be sure, but over time we are likely to notice their absence.

• *Inner authority and peace.* One indication of the work of the Spirit is a deep sense of peace and calm certainty about the prompting of the Spirit. Such inner authority is distinct from dogmatism because it is humble, serene, and open to correction.

• *Communal harmony.* The Spirit works toward reconciliation and harmony among people. The presence of this harmony is an indication of the Spirit's presence (John 17:23, Acts 4:32, 1 Corinthians 3:1–3). Again, however, there is no easy rule. Sometimes the Spirit's prophetic work is divisive rather than unitive, at least for a time, as when it leads us to protest injustice. In addition, there are forms of superficial placidness that actually entail a "tyranny of the majority," violating true harmony.

ᘯ

The fruit of the Spirit is love, joy, peace, patience, kindness, generosity, faithfulness, gentleness, and self-control.

Galatians 5:22–23

- *Enhancement rather than extinction of life.* The Spirit is a Spirit of life and wholeness and health. Experiences and promptings of the Spirit should contribute to personal empowerment, heightened selfhood, intrapsychic wholeness, and relational health. Insights that disempower, diminish creativity, fragment the psyche, or contribute to relational dysfunctionality are suspect.

- *Integrity in the process of discernment.* A final indication that an experience or prompting is of the Spirit is the degree to which the person or community has engaged in a discernment process with integrity. To be sure, the Spirit blows where it will, and even the most diligent discernment does not yield any guarantee of the Spirit's presence. Nevertheless, a person or community's action is more suspect to the extent that it ignores or violates dimensions of the practice of discernment. When groups or individuals have refused to consider various alternatives, failed to heed advice, avoided issues of faith, and suppressed deep emotions, their decisions are suspect.

None of these criteria is absolute; each of them is open to distortion and exception. In the end, spiritual discernment depends on faith. We do our best within the forms we have, but we ever depend on the mysterious emergence of the Spirit who resonates and persuades and, always, comes as a gift.

THE PROMISE IN THE PRACTICE OF DISCERNMENT TODAY

New applications of the practice of discernment are emerging all over the world today. This is partly due to the influence of liberation theology, which emerged in Latin America among Christians seeking to involve marginalized people in faithful action for change. In "base Christian communities," they meet to reflect on the neighborhoods and society within which they live, to interpret their lives by reading and reflecting on the Bible, and to act together in faithful response to God.

One such group is made up of middle-aged mothers living in the barrio of East Los Angeles. "I am very afraid for myself and my children; what are we going to do?" asked Lupe at one of their meetings. All agreed that they shared her fear; in their own front yards, they had seen beatings and shootings, drug sales and muggings. As was their habit, they turned to the Bible for help. The assigned text that evening was the story of Jesus calming the storm (Mark 4:35–41). They mused over the disciples' fear, and their own.

"I think that the sea is the barrio at night," one finally said, "and the wind is the gang kids with their drugs and their guns. If we had faith, we wouldn't be afraid of walking past them, or to ask them not to disturb us." But what would faith like this look like in their barrio-sea? That night, they formed a Campaign for Peace. They all agreed to sit on their porches at the same time that week; and when that time came, the astonished gang members grew uncomfortable and decided to go somewhere else. With this success behind them, the women next organized a procession through the neighborhood, and then a work party to paint over graffiti, and a community meal for all, including members of the gangs. As a result, there was a thaw in that neighborhood: some gang members helped with the painting, a few began attending Sunday Eucharist, and the rest at least moved away.

Through a process of discernment, these women found ways uniquely suited to their own situation to participate in the creative and redemptive activity of God. They were alert to the social context within which they sought to be faithful, and attentive to the Word as they encountered it in the Bible. They discerned and acted, and in the acting discerned new forms of action. The process in which they engaged was supple and practical, imaginative but down-to-earth.

The practice of discernment makes intentional a process of reflection on and participation with God's Spirit as the fundamental context in which we live and make choices. It is embedded in a variety of forms, all of which aim to check deception and nurture openness to the New Creation. The methods are easy. The practice, however, is challenging, painful, and complex. Unjust power is exposed; personal agendas are demoted; fears are confronted; interests are threatened; lines of authority shift. The practice probes deep into the inner motives of persons and communities. And yet the practice bears a promise. In exposing the obstacles that fear and selfishness put in the way of freedom, it opens avenues through which a healing

Spirit may move. And in providing an opportunity to imagine solutions we did not anticipate at the beginning, it helps us to find better paths toward the future.

In a world of relational rupture, gang violence, cultural intolerance, and rampant self-deception, this practice helps us to discover ways to live that heal and bring life rather than contribute to the pain around us. The practice bears a promise. We cannot count on complete certainty; we will continue to stumble, and even sometimes to flee from the insights we gain. Even so, in this practice, we encounter precious opportunities to cooperate with other people and to be alert to the activity of God. As we listen for the steps of God's Spirit in our midst, and as we seek ways to attune our own steps to these, we will find ourselves taking part, not only with God but also with one another, in the healing of the world.

Chapter 9

SHAPING COMMUNITIES

❧

Larry Rasmussen

The perennial Christian strategy, someone has said, is to gather the folks, break the bread, and tell the stories.

It is as simple, and as disarming, as that. But within that simplicity lie complex questions. What shape ought the gathering to take? Do some sit in carefully designated spaces and the rest elsewhere? And who breaks the bread? Do all, or only some? For that matter, who tells the stories? Do all take a turn, or do people speak as the Spirit prompts? Are some interpretations and interpreters more authoritative than others? On what grounds? The apostle Paul, teacher of community, urged the Corinthians to judge all bread breaking and storytelling and congregating by whether it was "done for building up" the community. But that was not sufficient to answer all the questions in this fledgling church. Should prophets speak in tongues if no interpreters were present? Should women speak? Must all who speak acknowledge the authority of Paul? (1 Corinthians 14:26–40).

Apparently, the program of gathering the folks, breaking the bread, and telling the stories is more complicated than it first seems.

There are varieties of gifts, different roles, real tensions, significant conflicts. The ordering of community can give shape to the gifts of its members and provide space for the successful negotiating of conflict. The lack of good ordering can prevent gifts from being shared and allow tensions to fester.

The shaping of communities is the practice by which we agree to be reliable personally and organizationally. This practice takes on life through roles and rituals, laws and agreements—indeed, through the whole assortment of shared commitments and institutional arrangements that order common life. In one sense, then, shaping communities is not just a single practice of its own. It is the practice that provides the choreography for all the other practices of a community or society.

CONSTITUTING A WAY OF LIFE

Christian congregations require governance, as Paul knew so well. And so does society at large. Indeed, the issue of shaping communities may be *the* issue confronting society today, only one instance of which is congregational gathering. After all, how *do* we order life together in a world with a nasty tendency to fall apart? Who gets to make the decisions about how we assemble and for what purposes, about dividing life's basic goods ("bread"), and about writing the standard account of what is going on and why (*the* "stories")? In whose hands does effective power reside? What kind is it? How is it used, and to what ends? Who benefits and who pays? Who frames the issues and directs the kind of attention they get? How does information flow, and who orchestrates the responses people make, as well as the environment within which they act? These are the issues of community governance.

Governance is a crucial part of our life together for at least two reasons. One reason is simple: life is a mess. It is not *only* a mess, but it is a mess. Some of it is a mess all the time, all of it is a mess some of the time, and disordered houses do not stand. Just as our bodies do poorly without food, bodies politic do poorly without governance. Communities, in order to *be* communities, must be ordered, cared for, led. The other reason is equally vital: governance is necessary for the positive flourishing of life. Proper ordering, as any gardener, cook, orchestra conductor, or housekeeper can tell you, is basic to good living. Sheer randomness is not the highest state of being. Thriving, not to say surviving, requires the creative ordering of freedom.

The particular shape that any community takes is already a creation and reflection of its way of life. As gifts are received, roles assigned, conflicts handled, and practices lived in certain ways, a community lives out its own way of being in the world. Through governance, a way of life is constituted (as in *Constitution*). The practice of governance is the soil in which all the practices of a community are rooted and nourished. Coordinating a community's practices through good governance helps to make its way of life clear, visible, and viable.

COMMUNITY GOVERNANCE AND LEADERSHIP

Good governance requires good leadership. Good leaders bring different people with different knowledge and gifts together for joint performance, and they do so in a way that draws out the strengths of people while rendering the weaknesses as irrelevant as possible. Leaders are thus choreographers of a sort. They help people identify the challenges they face and untangle the issues entailed in them, and they do so in a way that gives people work appropriate to their skills and on a scale and at a pace they can tolerate. When it is well done, such choreography generates homegrown leadership around identified challenges and makes for creative rather than destructive responses to common problems. Good leaders also clarify the purpose, values, and goals of a group, and thereby help to set its tone and create its ethos.

Because we inhabit a curious historical moment, our need for creative governance is particularly acute. We are not confident that the past is a reliable guide that can simply be extended into the future. Yet we cannot tell what may emerge to take its place. Ours is thus one of those proverbial "times between times." We lurch from crisis to crisis, and at the same time have to work out more viable ways of living together on largely untested turf. A moment like this cries out for leadership, not least because the scale and interdependence of our

*Some years ago a famous novelist died. Among his papers was
found a list of suggested plots for future stories, the most prominently
underscored being this one: "A widely separated family inherits a
house in which they have to live together." This is the great new
problem of mankind. We have inherited a large house, a great
"world house" in which we have to live together—black and
white, Easterner and Westerner, Gentile and Jew, Catholic and
Protestant, Moslem and Hindu—a family unduly separated in
ideas, culture and interest, who, because we can never again live
apart, must learn somehow to live with each other in peace.*

MARTIN LUTHER KING JR.,
Where Do We Go from Here: Chaos or Community?

problems are out of sync with the capacities of our institutions to address them adequately.

The practice of shaping communities, while always necessary, takes on a certain urgency in such moments, when it has to stretch toward the creative in the very moment it faces mounting constraints. Social experimentation becomes unavoidable in a time like this. But good outcomes do not. To negotiate such a season even reasonably well requires able leadership and high levels of citizen participation.

A case involving a copper plant near Tacoma, Washington, provides a helpful example, Ronald Heifetz reports in his book *Leadership Without Easy Answers*. William Ruckelshaus, head of the U.S. Environmental Protection Agency (EPA) in 1983, had to resolve a serious conflict: the copper plant was a major polluter in the Northwest, but it was also an important employer, with an annual payroll of $23 million. Jobs, the local economy, and health were at issue, and under the Clean Air Act of 1970, Ruckelshaus and the EPA had the authority to decide the plant's fate. But Ruckelshaus declined to use this authority and instead insisted on a process that would involve the community at large in the decision. He explained why with a quote from Thomas Jefferson: "If we think [the people] not enlightened enough to exercise their control with a wholesome discretion, the remedy is not to take it from them, but to inform their discretion."

PRACTICING OUR FAITH

Going beyond the law's requirement for hearings, the EPA organized a series of public workshops that included plant workers, union representatives, local citizen organizations, and environmental groups. This format provided participants with education about plant emissions, incidence of disease, and the local economic implications of various possible courses of action, as well as time for prepared testimony and open deliberation. What the community eventually decided was not in the minds of Ruckelshaus, local EPA officials, or the citizens themselves when the process started. The collective decision was that Tacoma's economy needed to diversify and that this process must include retraining for present plant workers. The community had decided for itself what it wanted for the future.

Heifetz comments that Ruckelshaus's adept leadership rested on several principles. First, Ruckelshaus identified the gap between the reality people faced and their aspirations—their "adaptive challenge." He helpfully kept attention focused on the issues created by this gap throughout the process. Second, in facing this adaptive challenge, Ruckelshaus helped regulate the level of distress that inevitably emerged as difficult issues were confronted. He did this by providing a structure that let the people educate one another (and the EPA) in the course of a well-paced deliberative process. Third, he had devised a strategy that shifted responsibility for describing the problem and devising solutions from the EPA to the primary stakeholders themselves—namely, community members. Within the boundaries of the law, authority and trust were thus largely relocated to the community, as was responsibility for creative actions.

THE COMMUNITY OF JESUS

Christians look to Jesus as an example of leadership and to the early Christian communities as places of exemplary participation. The narratives about Jesus provide models for life-giving governance, but often in surprising ways. The practices of governance Jesus commended did not match the prevailing versions and evidently were not supposed to. Rather than shaping his followers into the usual hierarchy of power, Jesus constituted his community around power turned upside down.

A dispute also arose among them as to which one of them
was to be regarded as the greatest. But he said to them, "The
kings of the Gentiles lord it over them; and those in authority
over them are called benefactors. But not so with you; rather
the greatest among you must become like the youngest, and
the leader like one who serves. For who is greater, the one
who is at the table or the one who serves? Is it not the one
at the table? But I am among you as one who serves."

LUKE 22:24–27 (COMPARE MATTHEW 20:25–28, MARK 10:42–45)

Consider a passage that appears in the Gospels of Matthew, Mark, and Luke. It is very near the end of Jesus' life, and the disciples are arguing. "Which of us will be the greatest?" they ask, jockeying for position. Jesus tells them that the shape of authority in his community is different from what they assume. His is an upside-down kingdom whose ways contrast with those of "kings" and "benefactors." In his reign, he tells them, status distinctions are reversed.

What happens when we turn to the early Christian communities? Is the upside-down instruction of Jesus reflected in the communities that took his name and told his story as their own passion? No single or even dominant model of community governance seems to exist among first Christians. The practice of ordination, for example, is simply not a New Testament issue, although the ordering of gifts and effective forms of good leadership most certainly are. Paul's churches, for example, have local leaders, who may well have been the owners of the houses where Christians met to worship. Yet there is no common governance form across the Pauline communities. Paul often names community workers and gives thanks for them in many places, and they apparently are called to preside by the community. Judging from his letters, however, not a one bears a title or wears a badge. We can only conclude that uniform governance practices did not exist.

Both Jesus' own radical pattern for shaping communities and the great variety of governance forms adopted by early Christian communities make it difficult to give Christian governance a label that fully describes it. However, Heifetz, who has studied leadership across several cultures, offers a phrase that can be useful for describing the varieties of early Christian governance: "creative deviance on the front line." It is deviance because it does not accept standard forms of ordering life as normative, even when they are dominant. It is creative because it seeks a positive alternative form. It is on the front line because it lives in the tension between our own time—what the apostle Paul called "this present age"—and another yet to come. We could also call this governance style "community democracy" if it is clear that such a style depends on shifting leadership, high levels of member participation, the capacity of its organizers and troublemakers to see through the dominant ways of doing things, and a collective ability to offer alternatives.

The practice of community governance as community democracy and creative deviance on the front line was born in Judaism. Both the Jesus movement and the first Christian communities were Jewish, with deep Hebrew roots. Even when Christianity grew among Gentiles and broke from Judaism, its Scriptures, its form of church organization, its sacraments, and the God it believed in all derived from Jewish Christianity. It embraced Judaism's sense of a covenant relationship with the one God, who had heard the cries of the Israelites in slavery and responded to their suffering. And it embraced the imperatives of Israel's community practices first fashioned in Sinai. These were imperatives to redress social inequities, protect the vulnerable, keep the power of privilege in check and under critique, steward the gifts of earth as a God-given trust held in common, extend hospitality to the stranger and sojourner, and consider the enemy's welfare on the same terms as one's own.

The Gospel materials reflect practices that display this Jewish heritage as Jesus and his movement embodied it. Discipleship (joining the way of Jesus) is decidedly egalitarian. People who are routinely excluded elsewhere are included here. Pride of rank is rejected and has no place. Followers are to teach all they have learned to all who will hear, but no particular deference is given scribes as teachers. Rather than being offered front-row seats at Jesus' gatherings, disciples are invited to enter more resolutely the way of service, even suffering. Some speak of Jesus as King, but he himself refuses the title. His position is more like that of a prophet—without favorites, without secure establishment, without honor or privilege, and without followers who possess any of these. Foxes and birds often have better housing.

At the same time, some formal practices of Judaism, such as ritual cleanliness, and some informal ones, like social barriers related to class, gender, and ethnicity, are largely disregarded in community practices around Jesus as leader of a radical Jewish renewal movement. His teachings on wealth and poverty continue the prophetic challenge to pursue justice, especially for the poor, as the foundation of social life itself. Exorcisms, healing, and feeding ministries mean freedom from common bondages and a discovery of people's own dignity and powers for day-to-day survival and life in God. The last are first. The least are subjects of attention and honor, and carriers of gifts and responsibilities. Leaders are community servants, like Jesus himself.

The fact that Jesus did not hold any office and was neither king nor priest was crucial. The "body" of people gathered around his body was made up of ordinary people, distinguished from one another not by status but only by their varied gifts and contributions, the variety of services they rendered one another in their common life. Because of this, the theologian James Mackey has argued, the whole idea and experience of the Body of Christ—a name for the church since its earliest days—implies a profound "democratization" of power. It makes room for the exercise of a variety of ways to care for one another and the world. This radical inclusivity has its source in Jesus.

Jesus' own source was God and a life utterly centered in God. But it was the God of the Jewish community and its practices—practices that empowered the Jews to be a vanguard people, a witness to the nations, and a foretaste of things to come for all creation. Differently said, a people practicing creative deviance on the front line.

Feminist moral theology is utopian, as all good
theology is, in that it envisages a society, a world,
a cosmos, in which there are no excluded ones.

BEVERLY WILDUNG HARRISON, *Making the Connections*

THE CHURCH AS ALTERNATIVE COMMUNITY

The earliest Christian communities were such a people. They were "a new humanity," part of a new world order, a "third race" (beyond Jews and Gentiles) transcending ethnicity and nations, and the "first fruits" of a new age coming to birth in the midst of a dying one. In all these self-understandings, the communities identified themselves as an alternative way of ordering life together. This shows up in their governing practices as they deviate from and reimagine prevailing arrangements. Both men and women are chosen as local leaders (Romans 16:1–15). Conflicts are handled by gatherings of councils that try to work toward consensus (Acts 15). Room is always declared, if not always permitted, for the unplanned eruptions of the Spirit in the gathered assembly and for the exercise of gifts, as validated both by direct experience of the Spirit and community deliberation (1 Corinthians 14). And at this early stage of community democracy, liturgy is the collective work of all Christians, service belongs to each, and the title of minister is one they all share. Special gifts of community members—"charisms"—are there for the sake of building up the Body of Christ as community.

But this is not the whole story. New Testament letters are also full of tensions. Communities lived uneasily between loose democratic governance (some of it fueled by the expectation that the world would soon end) and a tighter order that came to be focused on the bishop's office in each city. Ambivalence was always present: should Christians accept and adapt the existing versions of governance in the wider society, or ought these be rejected outright as Caesar's rather than God's? By the fourth century, however, governance and leadership of a certain kind triumphed, largely because Christianity gained status as a universal imperial faith in an empire walking the edges of disintegration. To state it without nuance: stability won out over change, hierarchy prevailed over egalitarianism, male-held office triumphed over gender equality, power was more centralized than dispersed, and social, political, and economic privilege lodged with the few rather than the many.

Even so, the radical impulses that run from the origins of the people of Israel through the movement around Jesus and its extension in the communities of first followers never lost their hold. Through the centuries, renewal movements that hark back to the Gospels and earliest Christianity itself have appeared again and again. In the Middle Ages, monasteries, convents, and religious orders such as the one founded by Saint Francis of Assisi spoke in these tones. In the sixteenth century, Martin Luther preached that all the baptized are members of the priesthood of all believers and lifted up daily work as a holy calling. Later, many other movements, including Baptists, Quakers, Mennonites, Methodists, and Congregationalists, had their origins in this kind of renewal. Today, renewal of this kind continues among Catholic, Orthodox, and Protestant Christians around the world. It can be seen, for example, in the base Christian communities of Latin America, the house churches of Asia or Eastern Europe, and the renewed strength of lay ministry in the churches of the United States.

When such renewal comes, common qualities surface again and again. These qualities are in tension with governance and leadership dynamics of a more orderly sort, where power is concentrated along clear lines of authority and function. The qualities that make for community democracy and creative deviance include these:

- A sense of divine power as the power for peoplehood
- A basic equality that dignifies the varied gifts of varied members
- Forms of address that tend more toward "brother" and "sister" than titles
- A sharing of resources with a view to need
- An effort to cross social boundaries for a more inclusive community
- An uneasy relationship to every dominant order, every "Caesar"
- An empowerment of all members, either as laity or within a new religious order
- A conviction that somehow all this is good news and a vanguard example for the wider world

Authority and *servanthood* are words that are used in these communities. But in comparison with their use in society at large, they are wholly reimagined and recast. In a community of equals, their mean-

ing is reordered. And in this community, members come to understand another word of Jesus: "I do not call you servants any longer . . .
but I have called you friends" (John 15:15).

THEN AND NOW: OUR ADAPTIVE CHALLENGE

Where does this Christian vision of the practice of community governance leave us as we face the complex issues of ordering community and society today? What does the experience of the origins of
Israel, of Jewish and Gentile Christianity, and of periodic Christian
renewal offer for our own efforts at governance and leadership?

Our own historical season at the end of the second millennium
of the Common Era bears an eerie resemblance to the time when
Christianity began on the three continents of the Mediterranean
basin. Like that time, ours is a "Hellenistic" era—diverse, cosmo-
politan, multilingual, multiracial, multicultural, multireligious, frag-
mented, eclectic, riddled by extremes of all kinds, and more than a
little violent. We often feel dislocated and off-center, just as people
did then. In the world of early Christianity, the solidity of empire was
giving way, and new configurations were in the making, many of
them bedeviled by chaos and confusion. Almost everyone worried
about moral degradation. Not a few sought new, saving communities and ways of life, whereas others simply could not conceive that
the Roman Empire would ever come to an end.

What the first Christians offered such an age was not only a
common loyalty but also a certain way of leaning into a turbulent
world with their own particular practices. True enough, they could
not make up their minds about many things they deemed important.
Full agreement was definitely not their strong suit! But they had a
faith full of feeling, energy, conviction, and the willingness to experiment imaginatively with inherited practices, traditions, symbols, and
stories. They related all this to real human needs and—perhaps most
important of all—offered a place of high participation to community
members from all ranks and with diverse gifts. They adapted governance practices and traditions they knew, but they also initiated
new ones when, in their judgment, these kept faith with the way of
Christ and made for the upbuilding of community in the Spirit.

Theirs was the spirit of an anticipatory community that could give present form to a hoped-for future through a range of adaptable practices. These were Spirit-led people shaping the specifics of community order as they went. Their way of life was created and amended out of life together in worship and in shared participation in other practices, in light of the great reversals of Jesus.

None of this means these communities were beyond corruption or even entirely right for their time and place. These were ordinary people who displayed the petty, ugly side of all human communities. There is no need to romanticize them; we need to learn from them, not copy them. Indeed, their own example instructs us to test the spirits in our time, as did they in theirs. When we do, we will surely find significant differences between our situation and theirs. Yet "creative deviance on the front line" and "community democracy" are a powerful legacy and process, which need to be interpreted and renewed in every age. And not least in a turbulent, searching age such as our own.

SETTING THE TABLE OF COMMUNITY

But what are the steps we need to take today in the choreography of shaping communities? How should we now gather the people, break the bread, and tell the stories?

The rites, sacraments, and patterns of the gathered congregation provide a focus for thinking about how community is ordered among us. Take the eucharistic table, for example. Decisions on who gets to sit at the table, in what places, and in accord with what table manners are reflective of the order of a community—in the church, but also in the wider social order. So are choices about who cooks, who serves, who cleans up, who breaks the bread, and who initiates and steers the conversation. Which bodies are present at the table and which are absent matters immensely, as does their health or lack of it. One does not need to be a keen student of society to realize that table fellowship itself is a reliable map of economic well-being and discrimination, political order and differentiation, and social hierarchy and caste. Table governance shapes communities. The practice is distilled in how we take, bless, break, and give bread to one another.

*Just as social systems organize themselves in relation
to a structure of authority, focusing attention at the
head of the table, our social commentators do so as well.
Leadership may more often emerge from the foot of the table,
but that is not where we spend most of our time looking.*

RONALD HEIFETZ, *Leadership Without Easy Answers*

We can adapt and create governance and leadership practices, then, by answering questions like these: Do our practices welcome all to the table? Are the discriminating distinctions drawn between people in society considered of no account here, and how do we show that in the way we regulate our life together? Are the guests in turn called to be the hosts? Are means created and encouraged by which each participant can find gifts for meeting the hungers of the world? Are children as well as adults, and old as well as young, welcome participants? Does the organization of general community life—and not only the celebration of Eucharist—encourage leadership to emerge from the foot of the table? Do the ways in which we organize life together ask for participation that nurtures significant levels of personal commitment and responsibility, on a scale and in ways people can handle?

Consider one concrete example as but a glimpse of innumerable possibilities for the creative shaping of communities. Imagine yourself sitting, as I did, amid a congregation deliberating "business": what our response to recent neighborhood safety and security problems should be; who would represent the congregation in a community coalition trying to secure low-income, occupant-owned housing; what changes in the congregational budget were necessary because of unexpected expenses; and when the annual congregational retreat should take place and who would plan it. Different issues brought different responses in the meeting, from heated argument and disagreement to shared laughter and common insight. Somewhere in the midst of free-flowing exchange, the pastor quietly lifted the cloth from the vessels on the small table to the side of the meeting's presider, prayed the eucharistic prayer, asked one of the musicians to lead a simple chant, and gave the loaf to the person closest with the words, "The body of Christ, broken for you." Then the cup and "The blood of Christ, shed for you." Each fed the next, repeating the salvatory and orienting words while looking directly into the eyes of the neighbor they had just argued and laughed with. A song followed, then everyone went back to deliberating what was to be done and who would do it. Yet these were not exactly the same persons and community as before. For one thing, the sharing in the sacrament oriented their discussion anew. They sought actions commensurate with this action.

To think outward from the Eucharist about shaping communities is only one example of what can be done with any and all of the focal practices of congregational gathering—baptism, confirmation, remembrance of the saints, and all the festivals of the liturgical year. These can become fertile places for discernment together about how the life-giving way of life that we seek needs to be ordered.

What links the church's example of "creative deviance on the front line" with examples like that of Ruckelshaus and the EPA is a patterning for cooperation made possible by a guiding vision. A model of governance that forces everyone to do the same thing is rejected. Multiple experiments are encouraged, and leadership emerges from the foot and sides of the table as well as the head. Innovation arises from the diversity of members, just as unity issues from joint action.

The shaping of communities where good governance and able leadership can emerge is less a single practice than a continuing process by which all the other practices described in this volume are oriented to the upbuilding of community. The key, besides some imagination, is high levels of personal involvement and commitment wed to mutually shaped community leadership. By embodying these in its own life, the church can help society at large to find its way amid the adaptive challenges of this historical moment—and all as part of a certain steady rhythm that gathers people to tell stories and break bread together.

Chapter 10

FORGIVENESS

❧

L. Gregory Jones

What is involved in the practice of forgiving someone—or indeed, being forgiven ourselves? Almost all of us sense the importance of forgiveness, aware as we are of situations and relationships where there has been a breach, or where unresolved conflicts cause harm year after year. Knowing these, we yearn for resolution, for ways of moving toward a future that is free of brokenness. But thinking about forgiveness—to say nothing of finding the courage to practice it—can be difficult.

The very notion of forgiveness conjures up many painful images in our minds. Merely to consider this practice causes us to think about horrifying evil: slavery in the United States, or the Holocaust in Nazi Germany, or individual acts of rape, child abuse, and domestic violence. It is difficult even to comprehend the depths of pain and suffering in such situations. No wonder, then, that we are unsure whether forgiveness can make a difference—and if so, how.

Thinking about forgiveness also causes us to consider the smaller, day-to-day struggles involved in living with others at home, in church, or in the workplace. These struggles involve annoyances that seem petty but that nonetheless can sow the seeds of bitterness, as well as specific conflicts that sometimes fester into large and painful wounds. In these situations, it may be easier to understand that forgiveness is the right response than to be able to give or receive forgiveness, or even to want to do so.

Most of us would admit that sometimes we just don't want to forgive someone or ask them for forgiveness, even when we know we should. The "should" may be based in our deepest beliefs; whenever we pray the Lord's Prayer, after all, we ask God to "forgive us our trespasses as we forgive those who trespass against us." Or the "should" may arise from our wish for peace, from our yearning for relationship restored. Even so, we just don't feel able to forgive, or to ask for forgiveness; the wounds are too raw, or we sense that the other person is unwilling to repent or to grant us the forgiveness we seek. And sometimes we simply prefer to let the conflict fester. Church council records from sixteenth-century Switzerland tell of a man who pretended that he could not remember the Lord's Prayer because he knew that if he said it he would have to forgive the merchant who had cheated him. This was something he had no intention of doing!

Many of us believe in the importance of forgiveness and long to find ways of making it more central to our life together. Yet we wonder whether and how this can happen. On paper, forgiveness is great. The problem comes when we try to take it off the page and live it out in our actual relations with one another. Can we do this?

THE PRACTICE OF FORGIVENESS: A WHOLE WAY OF LIFE

It may help to begin by recognizing that forgiveness is not simply a one-time action or an isolated feeling or thought. Rather, the Christian practice of forgiveness involves us in a whole way of life, a way that is shaped by an ever-deepening friendship with God and with other people. The practice of forgiveness is not only, or even primarily, a way of dealing with guilt. Instead, its central goal is to reconcile, to restore communion—with God, with one another, and with the whole creation.

The practice of forgiveness calls us willingly to do things with and for one another so that communion can be restored. Forgiveness

*So to live a "forgiven" life is not simply to live in a
happy consciousness of having been absolved. Forgiveness
is precisely the deep and abiding sense of what relation—
with God or with other human beings—can and should be; and
so it is itself a stimulus, an irritant, necessarily provoking protest
at impoverished versions of social and personal relations.*

Rowan Williams, *Resurrection*

works through our ongoing willingness to *give up* certain claims against one another, to *give the truth* when we assess our relationships with one another, and to *give gifts* of ourselves by making innovative gestures that offer a future not bound by the past. Being forgiven requires an ongoing willingness to honor a new claim that has been made on us, to speak with a new truthfulness, and to live in a new way with one another.

Conflict and brokenness can take many different forms, of course. Therefore the specific words, gestures, and actions that foster reconciliation in one case may not work in others. Yet the overall problem of conflict and brokenness—this sense that, though we are intended to live in community, we invariably hurt and are hurt by one another—is all of one piece. It is a problem we encounter in every part of life. Thus forgiveness does not happen piecemeal; it involves us in a whole way of life. It involves us as participants in the activity by which God is making all things new.

In this sense, then, the practice of forgiveness is not effective until we transform it from something that is great on paper into a way of life that we live in our relations with one another. But how do we overcome obstacles to embodying forgiveness in our lives? How can we understand better what Christian forgiveness involves? How can we go about practicing it in our life together?

Facing the Obstacles to Forgiveness

One reason we find it difficult to embody forgiveness is that most of us have fresh experiences of situations where forgiveness did not happen.

How is it, we wonder, that people can regularly speak of the power of love, and of the desire for forgiving or being forgiven, and yet be so consumed by hatred, so driven by a thirst for revenge, or so willing simply to settle for a chilling apathy? How do we account for the cycles of violence and abuse in our families and our communities? And how do we explain our fascination with violence and hatred, not only in our relations with others but also in movies, television shows, and games? How should we understand the loveless indifference that afflicts many relationships, where people rest content with low-grade bitterness rather than struggling to transcend it? Why do we allow conflicts to fester?

Part of the problem is that we are often less sure of what and whom we love than we are of what and whom we hate. Indeed, we too often stake our identity on being against some person or group. We define ourselves against those who are strange to us, hoping perhaps to overcome our own uncertainty and vulnerability by defining them as less than human. Or we define ourselves against those from whom we have become estranged, whom we perhaps once loved but now see as enemies or threats to our well-being.

As a result, we allow feelings of hatred or bitterness to define and consume our lives, even to our own destruction. The story of two shopkeepers illustrates this. Their shops were across the street from each other, and whatever one did, the other would try to match and, if possible, exceed. One night, an angel of the Lord came to the first shopkeeper and said, "The Lord has sent me to you with the promise that you may have one wish that, no matter how extravagant, will be granted to you. There is only one catch: whatever you receive, your rival shopkeeper will receive twofold. What is your wish?" The first shopkeeper, thinking of his rival, responded: "My wish is that you would strike me blind in one eye."

———————— ✺ ————————

Love is the only force capable of transforming an enemy into
a friend. We never get rid of an enemy by meeting hate with hate;
we get rid of an enemy by getting rid of enmity. By its very nature,
hate destroys and tears down; by its very nature, love creates and
builds up. Love transforms with redemptive power.

MARTIN LUTHER KING JR., *Strength to Love*

————————————————

Such self-destructiveness in the service of seeing someone else "get theirs" creates vicious circles. A different kind of vicious circle can run on indifference. For example, we may decide to compensate for our spouse's continual failure to acknowledge our needs by beginning to ignore his or hers. By contrast, the prospect of forgiveness requires that we take the risk of offering words, gestures, and actions that break the pattern of lovelessness for the sake of reconciliation.

What kinds of words, gestures, and actions? Perhaps words of gratitude such as "Thanks for your kindness in doing this," or words of explicit forgiveness or contrition such as "I forgive you, let's work this out" and "I'm sorry, please forgive me." Perhaps a gesture such as a handshake—originally a sign that one is not carrying a weapon in the right hand. Perhaps a gesture of actually filling out a "bill of forgiveness" to give to another person, ritually signifying the transaction that has been communicated between the two persons. Or perhaps the offering and receiving of food as a sign of hospitality; it is not easy to eat your enemy's food, because so much is at stake. In these acts, the participants on each side offer something of themselves to the other, and the possibility of a new relationship begins to emerge.

There are also times, however, when bitterness and hatred seem justified, and the words, gestures, and actions of forgiveness appear remote. This is particularly the case in situations where people have been or continue to be afflicted and oppressed by totalitarian political regimes, domestic abuse, racial bigotry, or countless other grievous wrongs. In such situations, bitterness and anger may be righteous, lending energy to appropriate resistance and insistent action for change. Even here, though, the danger is that righteous indignation can all too easily corrode into an inability to love.

Regardless of the sources of our hatred, our bitterness, or our loveless indifference, we must undertake the difficult process of unlearning these habits of feeling. There are ways to respond to frustration that are more edifying than letting grievances fester or exploding with hate, and adults need to learn them as much as small children do. Sometimes we can find forgiveness by walking in the shoes of another person or by helping each other see how much we depend on mutual forgiveness. In situations where we feel powerless, we may find the courage to practice forgiveness by discovering that we have the power to forgive. My children learn what it means not to insist on one's own way when I tell them that I have been wrong and seek forgiveness from them.

THE DANCE OF FORGIVENESS

All this suggests that we need the support, encouragement, and discerning help of others as we learn how to practice forgiveness in every aspect of our lives. Learning the alternative life-way of forgiveness takes time and involves hard work. It happens as we live into this practice and all the others in this book and discover that our thoughts and desires are changing. It happens as we are transformed by walking in this way of life with other people, in response to God's active presence among us.

The process of forgiveness begins as we venture forth, either on our own or through the invitation of others, to learn the steps of this beautiful, if sometimes awkward, dance. The steps, which follow, can be identified separately to help us in rehearsal. In the performance of the dance, however, they are integrally interrelated.

- *We become willing to speak truthfully and patiently about the conflicts that have arisen.* This is not easy, and there may not even be agreement about what has happened. Therefore, we need not only truthfulness but also patience, the virtue the ancient theologian Tertullian called "the mother of mercy." When we try to be patient and truthful, we can discern more clearly what is going on.

- *We acknowledge both the existence of anger and bitterness and a desire to overcome them.* Whether these emotions are our own or belong to the other party, it does no good to deny them. Besides, anger can be a sign of life, of passion; we should be more troubled by those whose passion is hidden or, worse, extinguished. Even so, we can learn to overcome and let go of anger and bitterness as we begin to live differently through practices that transform hatred into love.

- *We summon up a concern for the well-being of the other as a child of God.* Sometimes our partner in the dance of forgiveness is a total stranger; at other times, he or she is an intimate from whom we have become estranged. Either way, seeing the ones on whom our bitterness focuses as children of God challenges our tendency to perceive them simply as enemies, rivals, or threats. Now they are potential friends in God. It was this ability to see enemies as potential friends that enabled Abraham Lincoln to speak a kind word about the South during the Civil War, at a moment when feelings were most bitter. Asked by a shocked bystander how he could do this, Lincoln said, "Madam, do I not destroy my enemies when I make them my friends?"

- *We recognize our own complicity in conflict, remember that we have been forgiven in the past, and take the step of repentance.* This does not mean ignoring differences between victims and victimizers; people need to be held accountable for their actions, and some people need to repent and ask forgiveness while those who have been victimized struggle to forgive. Even so, in all but the most extreme cases, we also need to recognize and resist our temptation to blame others while exonerating ourselves. All too often, we see the specks in other people's eyes while not noticing the log in our own (Matthew 7:1–5).

- *We make a commitment to struggle to change whatever caused and continues to perpetuate our conflicts.* Forgiveness does not merely refer backward to the absolution of guilt; it also looks forward to the restoration of community. Forgiveness ought to usher in repentance and change; it ought to inspire prophetic protest wherever people's lives are being diminished or destroyed. Forgiveness and justice are closely related.

- *We confess our yearning for the possibility of reconciliation.* Sometimes a situation is so painful that reconciliation may seem impossible. At such times, prayer and struggle may be the only imaginable options. However, continuing to maintain reconciliation as the goal—even if this is "hoping against hope" for reconciliation in this life—is important because it reminds us that God promises to make all things new.

The "ministry of reconciliation" that shapes the Christian way of life is "from God, who reconciled us to himself through Christ," the apostle Paul wrote to the church in Corinth. "In Christ God was reconciling the world to himself, not counting their trespasses against them, and entrusting the message of reconciliation to us" (2 Corinthians 5:16–21). If we are to grow in the practice of forgiving one another, we need also to come to a better understanding of the shape of Christian forgiveness, of God's practice in forgiving us.

THE SHAPE OF GOD'S FORGIVENESS

Forgiveness begins with God's love, as that love works toward reconciliation amid the sin and evil that mar God's good creation. Forgiveness aims to restore us to communion with God, with one another, and with the whole creation. Accepting this forgiveness is costly, for it requires that we acknowledge the truth of human sin and experience its effects. But the only way to evade the cost of forgiveness is to deny that we need it. When someone responds to an offense with vengeance, insisting that "I never forgive," a wise Christian might reply, "Then, my friend, I hope you never sin."

As Christians understand our world and our lives, we are all complicit in sin, whether through loveless indifference or horrifying evil. In the midst of tragic brokenness, God's forgiveness aims to heal people's lives and re-create communion. The healing that comes with God's forgiveness strengthens us to be involved in other practices that are witness to God's forgiving, re-creating activity for the world. As the French theologian Christian Duquoc says, forgiveness is "an invitation to the imagination." It is not "forgetfulness of the past"; rather, it is "the risk of a future other than the one imposed by the past or by memory."

Christian Scripture testifies to God's forgiveness in both the Old and the New Testaments. Israel knows a gracious, forgiving God even in the midst of its betrayals of the covenant with God and of the Israelites' sins against one another (see Exodus 33–34, Psalm 51, Hosea 11). As Christians, we see God's forgiveness embodied most fully in the life, death, and resurrection of Jesus of Nazareth. Why is it, we wonder, that the One who comes as a baby on Christmas and embodies God's forgiving love for all of humanity could nonetheless be nailed to a cross? In becoming human, Jesus becomes vulnerable to the world of human beings. He becomes vulnerable not only to the human capacity to touch and celebrate, but also to the many ways in which people diminish, betray, oppress, and abandon one another. Even though he is vulnerable to these, he does not allow himself to be defined by them. Instead, he breaks apart the cycles of destruction, not just for himself but also for us, thereby offering us new ways of living together.

Jesus calls disciples also to embody forgiveness as a way of life where people are drawn into communion with God and one another. He does so particularly in his table fellowship with tax collectors and those identified as "sinners." When Jesus is attacked for such associations (Luke 15:2), he responds by telling the parables of the lost sheep, the lost coin, and the lost sons, stories of the radically inclusive nature of God's reign. Each of these parables, and particularly the parable of the prodigal and the ungrateful sons (Luke 15:11–32), are stories about God's practice of forgiveness.

As Jesus' ministry progresses, however, he faces even more persistent and threatening attacks, and ultimately he is led to the cross. He is crucified by human beings, yet in spite of our unjust judgment, Jesus absorbs our sin and evil without passing them on. And in the resurrection, God vindicates the ministry of Jesus, showing that God's forgiving and reconciling love, God's desire for communion, overcomes human sin and evil even at its worst. The risen Christ returns with a judgment that does not condemn but that offers forgiveness and new life.

Jesus in his ministry gives forgiveness a human, physical form, showing us a way of life that we are called to imitate. Similarly, his cross and resurrection provide the context for us to receive God's forgiveness and to forgive others in God's name. Our worship of the risen Christ sets the context for us to find new ways of coping with the sorts of conflicts and tragedies that can all too easily destroy us and others.

In this context, indeed, we find help in taking the actions that make forgiveness real among us, as the following true story illustrates. A twelve-year-old boy named John was playing one day with the nine-year-old girl who lived next door. Her name was Marie. Unfortunately, they found a loaded pistol in a dresser drawer and before long their make-believe game turned into a tragic nightmare and little Marie was dead. Everyone in the small town attended the funeral of the little girl—everyone except John, who could not face anyone and refused to talk to anyone.

The morning after the funeral, Marie's older brother went next door to talk to John. "John, come with me," he said. "I want to take you to school." John refused, saying, "I never want to see anyone again. I wish it was me who was dead." The brother insisted and finally persuaded John to go with him. The brother talked with the school principal and asked him to call a special assembly. Five hundred and eighty students filed into the gymnasium. Marie's brother stood before them and said, "A terrible thing has happened; my little sister was accidentally shot by one of your fellow classmates. This is one of those tragedies that mars life. Now I want you all to know that my family and John's family have been to church together this morning and we shared in Holy Communion." Then he called John next to him, put his arm around his shoulders, and continued: "This boy's future depends much on us. My family has forgiven John because we love him. Marie would want that. And I ask you to love and forgive him, too." Then he hugged John, and they wept together.

To be sure, this is as much the beginning as it is the end of the story. Marie's family will need to continue to struggle to embody this love and forgiveness each and every day of their lives. And John will undoubtedly continue to struggle to accept this love and forgiveness each and every day of his life. Yet Marie's brother sought John out when he most needed it and risked his own feelings of grief to offer a judgment of grace to John. Beyond that, he also offered a public witness to others, calling the whole community to practice forgiveness. The pattern of Christ's own ministry, death, and resurrection provided a context within which Marie's brother was able to offer specific words, gestures, and actions. In this way, the possibilities for a community dealing with a great and painful brokenness were transformed.

For us, as for Marie's family, God's forgiveness occurs when real human behavior is transformed by grace. When this happens, our own practice of forgiveness becomes what the British theologian Nicholas Lash calls "the outcome, in the Spirit, of God's utterance in the life and death of Christ." The ongoing presence of the Holy Spirit—as consoler and critic, as comforter, judge, and guide—empowers us as we discern specific ways to embody Christ's forgiveness in the world. With our imaginations stimulated by real-life stories of forgiveness, and with our conversation and habits shaped in ways that invite innovative gestures of forgiving love, we find that we can enter this beautiful practice, in spite of its difficulties.

*According to Gustavo Gutierrez, to recognize one's
own sin implies also the will to restore broken friendship
and leads to asking for forgiveness and reconciliation.
The capacity for forgiveness itself creates community.*

ELSA TAMEZ, *The Amnesty of Grace*

Christian forgiveness is not confined to churches; indeed, God's forgiveness also appears as the Holy Spirit works in the world. Whenever we see people who refuse to submit to, and thus to reproduce, the effects of sin and evil, we see glimpses of the Spirit's work of forgiving and making new. So, for example, in postapartheid South Africa, a national commission on "guilt and reconciliation" has been established as a means of avoiding the reproduction of violence, vengeance, and conflict while nonetheless taking seriously people's responsibilities for their actions. Similar processes, where vengeance is renounced even though accountability is required, happen in less dramatic ways all over the world.

We understand the world and our own lives better as we come to understand the nature and purpose of God's forgiving and reconciling love. But how can we help this to make a greater difference in the world? That is, how can we go about practicing forgiveness in our life together?

BUILDING COMMUNITIES OF FORGIVENESS

In order to participate in the practice of forgiveness, we need to unlearn those things that divide and destroy communion, including our own habits of thought, feeling, and action. We need to learn to see and live as forgiven and forgiving people. The brothers and sisters with whom we seek to live truthfully in Christian community can especially help us to do this. In worship, we offer prayers of confession for our sin, say or hear affirmations of pardon, and extend to one another the reconciling hand or kiss of peace. In addition, historic rituals of the church—including, for Roman Catholics, the sacrament of reconciliation—help to form us in confession, repentance, and new life.

*So then, putting away falsehood, let all of us speak the truth to
our neighbors, for we are members of one another. Be angry but
do not sin; do not let the sun go down on your anger, and do not
make room for the devil. . . . Put away from you all bitterness
and wrath and anger and wrangling and slander, together
with all malice, and be kind to one another, tenderhearted,
forgiving one another, as God in Christ has forgiven you.*

EPHESIANS 4:25–32

We need one another in order to learn to tell the truth about
our lives, both in praise and in penitence. We also need to unlearn
those ways of talking with one another that confuse, dominate, and
control, and to learn patterns of redemptive speech and silence that
build up communities where people are supported in the practice of
forgiveness. Sometimes this means simply refusing to speak rather
than lashing out at someone; being truthful does not mean saying
everything we think, nor does it mean saying it judgmentally. Sometimes there is a redemptive silence to be offered through bodily presence when perhaps there is nothing much to be said. Yet we also need
to cultivate redemptive patterns of speech, both in our discerning
judgment and in the ways in which we offer or receive forgiveness.
The book of Ephesians urges us to "speak the truth" with one another, but only within a passage that closes with instructions to forgive one another as Christ forgives us (4:25–32).

Yet even a forgiving community has boundaries. In one of Jesus'
parables, a servant who has been forgiven by his master shows no
mercy to a fellow servant, and as a result is sent away to be punished
(Matthew 18:23–35). Exclusion, however, ought to be seen as only
temporary; it can be approved only within the context of hope that
fellowship will be restored. Even when people have made themselves
"enemies" by their unwillingness to repent, we are not allowed to de-
monize them; rather, we are called to love them (Matthew 5:44). Just
as Jesus reached out to Gentiles and tax collectors, seeking to bring
them back into the fold of God's covenant of grace, so also are we
called to continue to reach out to and love even our enemies.

PRACTICING OUR FAITH

This does not mean that we must love them at close range, however. Sometimes reconciliation requires separation, particularly in abusive or oppressive situations where proximity threatens our very identities in relation to God. But it also requires the struggle to learn to wish enemies well even when we cannot be in their presence, and even when they are impenitent, and even when we are appropriately angry. Boundaries are legitimate. Permanent hopeless barriers are not.

The practice of forgiveness also calls us to develop habits by which to unlearn sin and learn holy living. Doing something on seventy times seven occasions, after all, would begin to weave it into the patterns of our lives (Matthew 18:21–22). Our broken ways can become habitual, and our forgiveness needs to become habitual too. Just as learning a craft requires the apprentice to learn what to do in particular situations and to develop patterns of right thinking, feeling, and acting that extend throughout life, so also does learning forgiveness.

Learning to live as forgiven and forgiving people is a lifelong task, open to the young child as well as to the aged adult. None of us is finished with learning the practice, and none of us is without the ability to teach some aspect of it to others. We learn forgiveness in communities of mutual support and challenge, communities where we can struggle to grow day by day in our ability to trust one another and bear one another's burdens (Galatians 6:2). At the same time, we need to be aware that forgiveness can be abused. When isolated from faithful patterns of mutual discernment, mutual confession, and ongoing repentance as a vocation for every member of a community, the language of forgiveness can be manipulated to protect the powerful or to make conflict even worse than it was before. Honest, sturdy communities guard against such abuse.

Then Peter came and said to him, "Lord, if another member of the church sins against me, how often should I forgive? As many as seven times?" Jesus said to him, "Not seven times, but, I tell you, seventy times seven."

Matthew 18:21–22

Practicing Forgiveness by Worshiping Together

To learn the practice of forgiveness is to get in the habit of embodying forgiveness as we make our way through the world. Christians are strengthened in this by the central rituals of our faith. Baptism initiates us into God's forgiveness and sets us on the lifelong journey of living into God's promises. Eucharist recalls the power of Christ's self-offering, re-members the Body of Christ as the community shares the eucharistic meal, and anticipates the fullness of the messianic banquet at which God's reconciling work will be complete.

Prayer, which undergirds all the practices of Christian life, is also a ready help. Sometimes we can pray on behalf of others who are not yet ready to ask or offer forgiveness in their own prayers. At other times, we pray for ourselves. In neither case is there a promise that prayer will work quickly! The British author C. S. Lewis realized this and made the following note in his journal: "Last week, while at prayer, I suddenly discovered—or felt as if I did—that I had really forgiven someone I have been trying to forgive for over thirty years. Trying, and praying that I might." These things require patience. Sometimes forgiveness is a gift we recognize only retrospectively after months, perhaps years, of struggle. Yet at other times, and in other ways, practicing forgiveness can produce dramatic transformations in our imaginations and the psychological, social, and political horizons of our lives.

Even when a particular situation seems so intractable that we cannot imagine that forgiveness will ever be possible, we can still pray and, in the praying, remember the startling promises of God. The liberation theologian Jon Sobrino tells of a prayer offered in the 1980s in a refuge in San Salvador, where dozens of people were seeking shelter from the violence of war. It was All Souls' Day, and these refugees longed to visit the cemeteries and place flowers on the graves of their loved ones, but they could not. So instead they put cards on the altar, each one bearing the name of a loved one killed amid the violence and repression of El Salvador. Flowers were painted around each name. One card, however, bore no flowers, only words: "Our dead enemies. May God forgive them and convert them."

Worship and prayer prepare us to reclaim and imagine the gift and the task of practicing forgiveness. They remind us of God's redemptive activity, stimulate our imagination, and call us forth to a renewed commitment to embody God's forgiveness throughout our lives. So do stories such as Marie's and John's and the example of other faithful Christians through the centuries and around the world. Watching them, we learn to discern more clearly what it means to practice forgiveness and to join in the ministry of reconciliation that God has entrusted to us—and, discerning, to live into the wholeness of a forgiven and forgiving way of life.

Chapter 11

HEALING

John Koenig

Though we sometimes try to deny it, illness, injury, and psychological distress dog virtually every step of our daily walk through life. They grip us and the people we love with pain, touching every thought and motion by their presence, often briefly but sometimes for years on end. They dilute our sense of control, undermining our certainties and building up our resentment of the limits they impose. Sometimes we even feel defined by our maladies and those of the people we love. We become a "man with a withered hand," a "woman who has been suffering hemorrhages for twelve years," or a "woman whose little daughter has an unclean spirit" (Mark 3:1; 5:25; 7:25). We yearn for the touch that will make us whole, or we yearn to be able to offer this touch of wholeness to someone we know.

We live in a society that defines healing as an activity that takes place largely between patients and their physicians or nurses. Christians understand the practice of healing as something much larger than this. The central image for us is not *cure* but *wholeness*. Drawing on our Jewish heritage, we envision human wholeness chiefly in terms of right relationships with God and our neighbors. We believe that what Jews call *Shalom*—an all-embracing peace that spells the end of meaningless suffering—is the ultimate reality. And we believe in the resurrection of the body, which will embrace in new life both the psychological and the strictly physical dimensions of our being. The first fruits of this resurrection, Jesus himself, promised to be with us forever and to share the benefits of his victory over death in very concrete ways, even now.

In this vision, healing is an indispensable part of the coming wholeness that God intends for all creation. This means that the practice of healing is a central part of the reconciling activity of God in the world. "Salvation means healing," wrote the theologian Paul Tillich, "and healing is an element in the work for salvation." Healing events are daily signs of the divine mercy that is surging through our world and guiding it toward its final perfection. This is true whether they take place by the sharing of chicken soup, the performance of delicate surgery, or the laying on of hands in a service of worship.

For Christians, it is particularly the One we name as Messiah who in his many acts of healing discloses God's passionate love for our flesh and blood. Moreover, from the earliest days of the church, believers have insisted that everyone baptized into Jesus' name is called to share in the spreading of that very specific compassion. When we act in communion with God to bring about healing, or when we ourselves receive it, we participate directly in the divine restoration of the material order. The complete health that God desires for our psyches and spirits—our so-called "religious" well-being—cannot be separated from our physical selves. It is as embodied beings that we must begin to find wholeness for ourselves and our societies.

❧

Peter said, "I have no silver or gold, but what I have I give you;
in the name of Jesus Christ of Nazareth, stand up and walk."
And he took him by the right hand and raised him up; and
immediately his feet and ankles were made strong.

Acts 3:6–7

The Paradox of the
Christian Practice of Healing

When we are very ill, we are brought to the place where life and death meet. For Christians, this place is the cross. Yet in the central mystery of our faith, the cross is also a prelude to new life.

Transformation occurs when we experience our illness in this context. Even though we are hurting desperately, we also feel that an unanticipated peace and strength are ours. This paradoxical experience may come and go over the months; it is not one we can control, or achieve in a specific number of simple steps. Nor does it depend on renouncing the quest for the strength offered by modern medicine. Rather, it is a coming to terms, a reframing of what is important, an opportunity to let go of the frivolous or misguided patterns that structured our lives when we were "healthy." No one would choose illness for this reason, but many would testify that illness brought them closer to God and to loved ones and made them feel, oddly, more alive than ever before. As one man put it, "Chronic illness can become an academy for the abundant life."

Once, as I ministered at the altar during a special time of intercession and laying on of hands, a parishioner named Tom approached my station. I knew that Tom had cardiac problems and was struggling with addiction; this was the prayer request he had made before, and what I expected him to request that night. But now Tom asked for something else. "And would you please pray also for my sister Maggie, who is dying of cancer?" Somehow Tom's simple request overwhelmed me. Sorrow and fatigue gripped me, and I broke into tears. Everyone's need was so much greater than I had imagined. This last petition seemed just too much, too heavy to bear. When I

What about the fact that not everyone who receives prayer is healed? . . . The most straightforward answer to this perplexing question is "I don't know." I wish—desperately so—that every single person who sought Healing Prayer were instantaneously and totally healed. But it simply does not happen that way.

Richard Foster, *Prayer: Finding the Heart's True Home*

---

started to cry, Tom did too. But then, putting my hands on his shoulders, I suddenly began to speak bold words over him. They flowed out like fresh water, washing away the tears. To this day, I believe that the prayer I offered was not really my own. No magic occurred: Maggie died soon afterward, and Tom continued to grapple with the pain in his life. But a few months later, I discovered that his conviction was like my own: some new kind of health had come to birth in each of us that night. Strangely, in the very expression of our grief, God's love had welled up in our bodies and minds to renew us.

Religious talk about "healing" is commonplace among Christians around the world. But some of us shy away from it, suspicious that many "faith cures" are phony and confident that modern medicine holds the only approach to healing worth mentioning. It is time to broaden our view. In the context of both the contemporary anxiety about health care and the age-old human need for healing, we need to reflect on the wide range of healing events that have always taken place in the life of the Christian community, and on those that are also happening right now. Healing might well be a Christian practice that is ripe for retrieval today. Understanding this practice in the life of the Christian community over the centuries and in some faithfully creative congregations today can help us to appropriate it more fully.

CHRISTIAN HEALING IN HISTORY AND TODAY

In early Christian communities and for roughly the first three centuries of the church's life, Christians regarded healing by prayer and the laying on of hands as a normal part of the church's mission. Early histories tell many stories of miraculous cures. In subsequent periods, however, ecclesiastical records grow quieter about healing by spiritual means. During the high Middle Ages, for example, as great wars and plagues swept over Europe, little is recorded about healings effected by means of prayer. Perhaps in response to difficult times, church practice emphasized preparation for death. The Protestant reformers of the sixteenth and seventeenth centuries typically understood biblical healing as a set of practices vital to the church's founding but no longer important or necessary in its daily life. In the eighteenth and nineteenth centuries, many church people, influenced by the Enlightenment, came to think of spiritual realities as altogether separate from bodily ones. As a result, matters of physical health were relegated to the domain of science.

Even when expectations for healing through spiritual means were at a relatively low ebb, however, many Christians exercised great compassion in caring for the sick and injured. During the medieval period, for example, the zeal of religious orders in caring for the sick led to the founding of a large number of hospitals. In the eighteenth century, efforts by British Methodists to reform social institutions—schools, workhouses, prisons, orphanages—directly improved the physical health of thousands of people. By the early nineteenth century, medical missionaries were being sent out from many Western churches on the presupposition that making the Gospel known must include opportunities for physical healing. Later in the same century, North American proponents of the social gospel urged churches to shape their agendas on the basis of faith in God's will to redeem the whole material order, including the economic dimensions of human life. All of these activities reflected Christian efforts to participate in the divine activity of bringing wholeness to all creation. Like hospitals, social welfare agencies, medical missionaries, and economic and environmental activists today, believers of past eras participated in the practice of healing.

But what about our own time? Christians today fulfill our call to be healers in many different ways. We serve as medical personnel in hospitals, clinics, and research facilities, and we offer psychotherapy as a part of our care for one another. Well-trained religious chaplains now serve in most American hospitals, addressing the emotional aspects of illness and healing with skill and compassion. We belong to organizations that promote programs of wholeness and healing for the environment and try also to care for it appropriately in our daily lives. Some of us offer healing to one another in recovery groups like Alcoholics Anonymous and Adult Children of Alcoholics. We serve in hospices, many of them begun under Christian initiative, and we are involved in reclaiming the value of therapeutic touch. Some churches are actively involved in providing long-term care to people living with AIDS.

Today, however, uncertainty about the economic structure of health care brings special anxieties to almost everyone participating in the practice of healing. Increasingly, we see healing defined in terms of anonymous lab reports and generic treatment plans. More than ever, physicians and nurses find themselves pressured into the roles of bureaucrat, politician, and accountant. For many of us, medical professionals and patients alike, the question "Whither healing?" is now taking on a special urgency.

Within this context, the Christian community needs to draw more deeply on its tradition of healing, for the sake of individuals and society alike. In spite of the discomfort that some modern people feel with spiritual healing, it is important for Christians to offer the full range of our historic practice of healing to those who search for wholeness in this troubled time. Creative ministries in congregations can suggest some ways ahead.

CONGREGATIONAL MINISTRIES OF HEALING

St. Luke's Episcopal Church in Darien, Connecticut, has developed the practice of healing in ways that bring the power and insight of the Gospels into a modern suburban setting. This mainline congregation—appropriately named for the evangelist thought to have been a physician—has been sponsoring healing services since the 1960s. Every Wednesday for nearly thirty years, groups of worshipers have gathered for Eucharist, intercessory prayer, anointing with oil, and the laying on of hands. The services were initiated by clergy, but over the years some laypeople have undertaken sustained programs of study and prayer in small groups to prepare for commissioning as ministers of healing. Gradually, the idea emerged of offering courses in this practice to others, and St. Luke's School of Christian Healing was born, open to people of all denominations.

"At the beginning," relates Avery Brooke, well-known author in the field of spirituality and one of the original group members, "none of us wanted to admit that *God* was performing the healings which occurred in our prayer and study sessions. As sophisticated people, we preferred more secular explanations: psychosomatic mending, relaxation from stress, that sort of thing." Moreover, these laypeople thought it would be presumptuous to claim a vocation as a healer. But then, Brooke recalls, "we began to think in terms of

*Are any among you sick? They should call for the elders
of the church and have them pray over them, anointing
them with oil in the name of the Lord. The prayer of
faith will save the sick, and the Lord will raise them up;
and anyone who has committed sins will be forgiven.*

JAMES 5:14–15

obedience to our baptismal vows, and some of us could not escape the conviction that we were being called to a task that has always been central to the church's ministry, even when it goes unnoticed. We needed to learn to get ourselves and our concern for results out of the way and just let God act through us. Recalling the scripture, we began to lay hands on one another, praying in the name of Jesus."

The particular New Testament text to which Brooke alludes is found in the Epistle of James and seems to be the earliest recorded attempt on the church's part to carry on Jesus' healing ministry within a kind of liturgy. For members of St. Luke's and for increasing numbers of Christians today, the words of James prove valuable in offering straightforward convictions about the therapeutic quality of the church's life, as well as mandates relating to the actual practice of healing.

Although leaders of the healing teams at St. Luke's have chosen not to quantify the results of their ministry, they are willing, when questioned, to narrate dramatic instances of physical or psychological recuperation, as well as slow improvements in general health despite chronic illness, and more rapid than usual recoveries after surgery. Yet as one member puts it, the group's strongest conviction remains that "when we pray for healing *something always happens,* even if it isn't what we asked, [and] it is not the individual praying who is doing the healing, but God's power working through us."

A very different form of the Christian practice of healing has developed at another large mainline congregation, Grace Lutheran Church in River Forest, Illinois. Here, small groups gather regularly to share stories, support, and prayer. One group consists of people suffering from chronic diseases and another of health care professionals. Both groups were born when clergy and parishioners alike

Christianity roots its healing ministry in the good soil of the Church
as a community of ordinary people who come together to do things
with God's help that they could not do in their own strength.

UNA KROLL, *In Touch with Healing*

realized that they had permitted healing activities to become separate from congregational life. Grace Church's special calling in this situation, they sensed, was to provide a space in which the realms of faith and healing could be reconnected, as they were in the early days of Christianity.

Stephen Schmidt, a college professor who suffers from Crohn's disease—a debilitating inflammation of the digestive tract—describes the chronic disease group as "a place where simple Christians grapple with profound truth." For the members of this group, there is no lively hope of getting well in the usual sense of that term, so they have reconceived health and healing as experienced realities *within* the reality of illness. For Schmidt, such healing comes primarily through a mutual bearing of emotional burdens and a deep bonding within the group, which offer new experiences of Christian faith and love. Prayer and Scripture readings play a role in each meeting, but the most effective mediators of God's grace seem to be personal exchanges between members. The experience of the group, says Schmidt, "recapitulates the insight that the most profound words of healing are spoken by unlettered saints of suffering." Those who have had a good month can support those whose month has been difficult and painful; and when a member dies, those who remain can work through their feelings of grief and anger, for that member and for themselves. No ordained ministers belong to the group, yet Schmidt believes that these fellow sufferers become, in truth, priests for one another. "Here Christians meet in need and mutual grace. Here we absolve each other . . . here the word of life is spoken . . . here the Scriptures are read and listened to . . . here the sacrament of the Eucharist is offered by the gift of one or another as bread of life, and here we practice priesthood without ecclesial office, but with faith and love."

In both Darien and River Forest, congregations have acted with wisdom and perseverance to make the practice of healing available to those who suffer. Unlike St. Luke's, Grace Church does not offer regular worship services that are explicitly devoted to prayer and the laying on of hands. Yet both parishes are clearly striving to fulfill their vocations as healing communities. In doing so, they are taking their cue from Jesus' commission to his first disciples to heal the sick (Matthew 10:1; Mark 6:7; Luke 9:1–2), as well as the conviction of early church members that whenever they preached the good news of God's kingdom, the power of Jesus would be present to heal (Acts 3:1–10; 4:30; 9:32–43). Both congregations, St. Luke's and Grace, are building on this ancient tradition in the conviction that their members will be formed, by Christ, to offer and receive healing as a normal, everyday part of their life together.

In these two churches, an urgent need for healing—a need that exists in every congregation—was met by a set of concrete activities that made God's healing presence palpable. "Throughout the centuries," writes Sister Kathleen Popko, reflecting on the mission of Catholic hospitals, "the church's mission has been to create the human conditions where one can experience God, particularly in those moments of vulnerability and brokenness. The church's members and institutions collectively strive to respond as Christ would, by bringing to bear the support and concern of the community, by being a sign of God's presence, and by revealing that even suffering and death have meaning in the Christian perspective." It is through the hands, voices, ears, and compassion of the broken people with whom we work and pray that God's healing presence touches our lives and makes a difference.

HEALERS

When we embody God's healing presence to others through touch, concern, or liturgy, we take part in God's activity of healing the world. This is something we want to offer to others, almost as much as we want to be healed ourselves. And it is one of the basic things we do with and for one another. It happens as one spouse helps another through cancer, as a friend prepares special foods and offers fervent prayers, or as a parent comforts a child with a fever.

*The church's story of healing leaves an impression of
lost opportunities. Theology and practice did not support and
enrich each other as they should. At times, both departed from
the biblical heritage. Still the gift of healing persisted.*

TILDA NORBERG AND ROBERT WEBBER, *Stretch Out Your Hand*

Yet some of us are also called to vocations of healing in a more specific sense. And these individuals face many obstacles in the present situation, even beyond the pressures, inherent in their art, that have been known by healers over the centuries. The shape of our health care system is driving painful wedges between those trained in the healing arts and those who require their talents. Corporate insistence on containing costs makes it hard for physicians and nurses to care for patients in ways that attend to the spirit as well as the body. Mistakes are often punished severely, and it is difficult to find avenues for dealing with the failure and guilt that are inescapable parts of this work.

Such concerns shape another group at Grace Lutheran Church: the health professionals group. When ministers sent an initial invitation to church members in this category, they discovered a widespread feeling that the congregation had thus far failed believers by not providing emotional and spiritual support for the almost daily crises they had to face in fighting off death for their patients. On the other hand, members expressed gratitude for the safe place granted them in this group. Because of it, they felt a new freedom to tell stories about God's presence in their working lives and to confess their feelings of inadequacy.

Gradually, as they began to open themselves to one another with more honesty, it also dawned on them that their desire to reach out for help had often come to expression through regular involvement in a wide range of church activities. As physician Douglas Anderson writes, each of these healers realized that "one of the main sources of preventive and restorative therapy was participation in congregational life and worship." For him, singing provided a special tonic to strengthen his own work as a healer. "During a festival concert at Grace Church, in the course of which I had the opportunity to sing

PRACTICING OUR FAITH

Vaughan Williams's *Five Mystical Songs,* I witnessed and experienced a powerful dimension of congregational healing. As I sang the words of the mystical poet George Herbert, 'O let thy blessed spirit bear a part and make up our defects with its sweet art,' perceptions of separateness from the self, of freedom and well-being washed over me. With the self removed from the center of attention, I was able to focus on God's spirit. The invitation 'Come to me, all who labor and are heavy laden, and I will give you rest' (Matthew 11:28), was accepted and experienced as a physical reality in the lives of many congregation members present at that service." Here is a caregiver finding union with God's renewing Spirit, not simply as an individual but also in company with his needy fellow worshipers. Here is healing in the midst of the congregation.

TOWARD AN INTEGRATED PRACTICE OF HEALING

Illness and injury come in many forms. And the flow of information in contemporary society brings this sad fact to consciousness with disturbing frequency, making us aware of our vulnerability and need in spite of modern medical advances. Nearly every week brings word of some new environmental hazard, form of violence, or other pathology that threatens our well-being. Poverty undermines the health of millions of people in our country and billions around the world. And the Holocaust and other genocidal wars in this century make us see that our practice of healing must oppose powers that can only be described as demonic. The twentieth century will be regarded as a time that cried out for new forms of healing.

In the midst of this need, a number of us are asking ourselves whether we have not lost sight of, or at least failed to exercise in their fullness, some of the foundational gifts for healing known to the earliest

ﭏ

Jesus called the twelve and began to send them out two by two, and gave them authority over the unclean spirits. . . . They cast out many demons, and anointed with oil many who were sick and cured them.

MARK 6:7, 13

church. In part, we feel this way because of a painful realization that our so-called therapeutic culture has not brought us the abundance of life promised by Jesus (John 10:10). But there may be another reason that we feel we are not taking full advantage of the healing resources offered by our heritage. As we learn more and more about the rich mercies of the God who bestows gifts for healing, it becomes harder to keep our expectations low. Today, most of us are likely to be acquainted with members of our own churches and of neighboring congregations who identify themselves as charismatics or pentecostals. It is becoming increasingly clear that as a group, such Christians and the healing practices they advocate are not alien to the fullness of the church's tradition.

A quiet openness to the healing gifts of the Spirit is found in the ministry of Tilda Norberg, a United Methodist pastor authorized by her bishop to serve the church as a Gestalt therapist, spiritual healer, and teacher. Her ministry includes not only one-on-one and group therapy sessions but also workshops for clergy, medical personnel, and laypeople who wish to become more deeply involved in Christian healing. In training healing teams, she strives to forge integration between congregational life, therapeutic and medical practice, and social ministry. A short credo shapes her work:

- The healing ministry of Jesus is still continuing in the community of faith.
- Healing includes the whole person—spiritual, physical, and emotional.
- God wills our wholeness and is actively involved in our growth.

Much of Norberg's work is done with people who have been abused. One way to find healing is to renounce the crippling falsehoods—the myths and lies and stereotypes—that have become entangled with their bodies and emotions and thus continue to shape their lives. Norberg addresses this need with what she calls "liturgies of lies and truthfulness." In these rituals, fellow believers, embodying the Church of Jesus Christ, surround those who have suffered abuse, name the lies out loud, and proclaim the truth of God's love. For example, the following words were part of a eucharistic liturgy, spoken to a woman who long ago suffered in a Japanese concen-

Silence, Lord, the unclean spirit
in our mind and in our heart;
speak your word that when we hear it,
all our demons shall depart.
Clear our thought and calm our feeling;
still the fractured, warring soul.
By the power of your healing,
make us faithful, true, and whole.

Thomas H. Troeger, "Silence! Frenzied, Unclean Spirit"

tration camp and came away from those early years of her life convinced that God cared nothing about the terrors she had experienced: "Kathy, you decided as a child that God forgot about you. That is a lie. God never forgot about you. We in this church believe Jesus wept with you in that camp. . . . Jesus helped you survive."

Tilda Norberg emphasizes, wisely, that such liturgies are no quick fix. Yet she has learned from experience that in combination with other therapies and regular participation in Christian congregations, they can help to turn people's lives around. Healing, she notes, is "not just fixing up things that are wrong. Real health, from a Christian point of view, is coming to the fullness of your vocation as a child of God. It means becoming Christ-like."

THE FUTURE OF CHRISTIAN HEALING

Drawing on the various glimpses just provided, we can perhaps begin to discern which forms of healing are likely to play important roles for North American Christians as we enter the twenty-first century. How can we participate in God's practice of bringing *Shalom* to the ill and injured? Here are some of the concrete forms this practice is likely to take in our time:

- Christians will continue to contribute to and draw on contemporary medicine, though with increasing emphasis on interaction between medical professionals and congregations, and between treatment and faith.

- Congregations are also likely to become more involved in promoting behaviors that enhance health, particularly as the average age of members increases. As many Christian groups have testified for decades, abstaining from harmful substances and developing wholesome physical habits are two ways of participating in the advent of *Shalom*. Parish nurses are already helping this to happen in thousands of U.S. congregations.

- We will become more deeply engaged in efforts to make systems of health care accessible to all people and sensitive to the importance of good relationships between healers and patients. These priorities can be pursued through public policy debates; they will also shape administrative policies in the numerous hospitals and other institutions of healing that exist under church supervision.

- Increasing numbers of believers will find settings that combine traditional medical care with intentional prayers for health, especially in small groups and healing services.

- The practice of intercessory prayer and various kinds of touching or anointing, often in conjunction with the sharing of Christ's body and blood in the Eucharist, will be found in more North American churches than ever before, extending the sacramental understanding of healing that has already emerged in many places.

- Healing through gifts of the Spirit in the name of Jesus will mark a growing number of ministries, whether or not they are identified as charismatic or pentecostal.

The Christian community bears rich resources for a people in need of healing. Particularly in this time of anxiety and distress about health care, the diverse healing ministries of the church need to become a more integrated, more normal, and more public feature of our mission. To the extent that this occurs, we can speak of an institutional recovery, or at least a new appropriation, of something that lies at the very heart of our earliest tradition. "Jesus went throughout Galilee, teaching in their synagogues and proclaiming the good news of the kingdom and curing every disease and every sickness among the people" (Matthew 4:23). For us, as for our Master, preaching, teaching, and healing must combine to form a seamless garment.

Chapter 12

DYING WELL

❧

Amy Plantinga Pauw

Death is an inevitable part of life. There is no getting around it. This is a frightening prospect, for the specter of death destroys any illusion that we are in full control of our lives or that we are our own makers and keepers. Most of us will experience the death of someone we love dearly, and all of us must face our own. How is it, then, that some people are able to die with the assurance that death is not the final word? How is it that some are able to face the death of a loved one trusting that love is stronger than death?

The Christian answer is that we belong in life and in death to God, whose love is stronger than death. This answer is not merely

---

Even though I walk through the valley of the shadow of death, I fear no evil; for you are with me; your rod and your staff—they comfort me.

PSALM 23:4

---

a matter of interior, personal conviction. It takes concrete form through the patterned life of the Christian community, molding the way we live as well as the way we die. In the weekly rhythm of the Christian life, the community gathers to celebrate the resurrection, God's final victory over death. Every year, during the season of Lent, it focuses on Christ's death on the cross. And in other rhythms, too, the church surrounds those enduring the pain, fear, and grief of death with visible, tangible signs of assurance and hope. Through impromptu conversations and well-planned funerals, through singing, prayer, and anointing with oil, through gifts of flowers and food, the Christian community acts out its beliefs.

Those who face death experience the living presence of God through the living presence of the community that cherishes and mourns them. And the community members who cherish and mourn these deaths are at the same time preparing themselves for the deaths that will surely come to them someday. "The church has made it possible for me to face and accept death, and to hope that death does not destroy life," writes theologian William M. Shea. "The church has made it possible for me to believe that God's love is stronger than death." In the Christian practice of dying well, Christian people do things with and for one another in response to God's strong love, translating into concrete acts our belief in the resurrection of Christ, and of ourselves.

WISDOM AND CARE FOR OUR TIME

Death stands in a continuum with other significant life passages, each of which is linked to certain Christian practices. Unlike baptism, confirmation, and marriage, however, death is universal. Death "comes equally to us all," the pastor and poet John Donne declared, "and makes us all equal when it comes." Moreover, this final and momentous life passage is the one that most often leads us to confront fundamental questions about the moral and religious significance of our lives. Impending death often drives us to seek the reconciliation with others we may have been avoiding for years. It infuses our reflections on mortality and suffering, healing and hope, with new urgency. Here, at the very edges of life, the practices of the community can proclaim what we most need to hear: that even in death, we are not alone.

This is a radical assertion in a society that often isolates death and dying from the flow of daily life, unlike almost every other society in history. In modern Western society, the two institutions that have had the most influence on how people face death—hospitals and funeral homes—have altered the communal practices that once surrounded this life passage. As a result, contemporary people are especially in need of the wisdom and care that the Christian practice of dying well can offer.

We live in a culture in which the process of dying has largely been handed over to a medical establishment reluctant to admit the limits of its life-preserving powers. The modern West is an anomaly in this regard: most ages and cultures have lived much closer to the fact of human mortality. As we live longer and tend increasingly to die in hospitals of chronic diseases, the "rescue credo" of modern medicine often interferes with our chances of dying well.

Religious convictions about the power of divine love beyond death, argued the ethicist Paul Ramsey, can provide the courage needed to recognize the limits of modern medical care. Maybe only faith in God can provide the basis for "a conscionable category of 'ceasing to oppose death,' making room for caring for the dying." Contemporary Christians acknowledge what people in other times and cultures have never forgotten: that there are other kinds of hope to offer to dying persons besides the hope of elusive and high-risk physical cures. Today, many medical professionals are also seeking new avenues in curing and caring for the terminally ill, as Christian caregivers join with other concerned people to shift the focus away from the disease and back to the person. Hospice care is a growing response to this need.

Likewise, the formal acknowledgment of death and response to grief have largely been handed over to funeral homes. No longer simply providers of custodial services for the corpse, funeral homes now place ads in the yellow pages promising sympathy, care, and peace of mind "when you need us most." We may deplore the lucrative services funeral homes have developed to meet these needs—for example, the beautification of the corpse and the use of elaborate metal caskets. But we must also notice that mourners are attracted to these services because of a genuine void in modern Western society. People yearn for communal practices that pay tribute to the dead and bring comfort to the bereaved.

Here, too, the fertile ground of Christian practice concerning death and dying may yield new fruit. The church is a community of memory in a way that the workplace and the neighborhood, much less the funeral home, are not. In worship, we regularly offer prayers of thanksgiving for the lives of those who now rest in God's mercy. As we do so, the names and faces of a few dear ones are on the minds and hearts of each worshiper. At the same time, these prayers are larger than our personal memories, and the worshiping community will continue to offer them long after our own dear ones, or even we ourselves, are remembered by name. Moreover, the Christian community can offer a depth of spiritual and practical support for the sorrowing that the funeral home can never match. Dying in its embrace, we are confident that after we die, the church will gather to celebrate our life and mourn our passing, and confident that the community will care for our family through prayers, visits, and generous hospitality.

THE MANY FACES OF DEATH

The circumstances of human death vary enormously, and it is impossible to consider all of them. But we must acknowledge that Christian practices hold no magic formula for transforming premature, tragic, or unjust deaths into good deaths. We will not all die peacefully of old age, and when a life is cut short—by accident, suicide, childhood disease, or violence—Christians view it as an evil. And beyond the terrible deaths of individuals are the horrors of mass death. The twentieth century is certainly not the first century to witness them, but we have seen perhaps more than our share. The forced march of the Armenians, the Nazi death camps, the famines in Biafra, the Cambodian killing fields, and the murders of "the disappeared" in Latin America—all display cruelty beyond our ken. One source of special anguish in these kinds of death is that the victims are usually denied participation in the practices that make dying well possible. They die too young, too suddenly, too far removed from loved ones.

What does dying well mean for those who suffer "bad deaths" and for the loved ones they leave behind? Here the fact that dying well is not an individual practice but a shared one is especially significant. Death marks the end only of physical life; an individual's presence, however, extends beyond death as one's life is remembered and absorbed redemptively into the community that remains. The extent to which it is possible for the bereaved to find redemptive significance in the "bad death" of a loved one depends in large part on the practices of the community to which they belong. And the knowledge that one's life will continue to matter to the community even after one's death can be a powerful source of comfort for individuals living under the threat of sudden or violent death.

The history of Christian practices surrounding the passage of death spans almost two millennia. Christians have ministered to the dying and the dead in times of severe persecution as well as times of strong alliance with reigning powers, in times of ecclesiastical corruption and times of church reform, in times of communal cohesiveness and times of urban isolation and fragmentation. An enduring and irreducible complexity seems to underlie Christian responses to the reality of death in its many forms, in many different circumstances and cultural, political, and ecclesiastical contexts. *When Christian practices are healthy, dying well embraces both lament and hope, and both a sense of divine judgment and an awareness of divine mercy.* The joining together of these diverse components reflects the variety of biblical attitudes toward death, as well as centuries of Christian theological and experiential wisdom. Each component is associated with certain shared activities of the community.

LAMENT

The early church inherited the Jewish community's practice of using the Bible's psalms of lament to mourn the death of the faithful. That death evokes despair and anger is not a discovery of twentieth-century psychology; it is at the heart of the practice of lament. Psalms of lament bring before God the raw intensity of the emotions evoked

For my soul is full of troubles,
and my life draws near to Sheol.
I am counted among those who go down to the Pit;
I am like those who have no help,
like those forsaken among the dead,
like the slain that lie in the grave,
like those whom you remember no more,
for they are cut off from your hand.

You have put me in the depths of the Pit,
in the regions dark and deep.
Your wrath lies heavy upon me,
and you overwhelm me with all your waves.

PSALM 88:3–7

by death. When we pray these psalms, we expose our emotions instead of hiding them, as some Christians do when they mistakenly imagine that God will be offended by their bitterness and outrage. Jesus himself experienced great anguish in the face of death, and according to tradition, cried the bitter lament of Psalm 22 from the cross: "My God, my God, why have you forsaken me?" (Matthew 27:46). When we lament, we acknowledge the truth that God does not remove all the pain and torment of dying, either for the sufferer or for the community.

Lament needs to be an integral part of Christian practice in response to death and dying, precisely because we value so highly God's gift of earthly life. The treasured promise of Romans 8:38–39 that not even death can separate us from the love of God in Christ Jesus does not erase the fact that death does separate us from those we love on earth. Death is an irrevocable, wrenching loss for those the dead leave behind. But it is also a loss for those who die—a loss of the parts of creation they took delight in, the relationships they held most dear, and the possibilities they envisioned for the future. Particularly in the case of premature or tragic deaths, it is appropriate for Christians to adopt or develop rituals and liturgies of lament to remember those who died. Hope of everlasting life with God does not undercut Christian gratitude and concern for this life, nor deny the place of lament in Christian responses to death.

Lament must, however, be balanced by hope and thanksgiving. We are of the earth, created both good and finite. Like the flowers and the grass, we eventually wither and fade, but we may still enjoy seasons of vivid and luxuriant bloom. The approach of death can be a time of thanksgiving for all of God's good gifts during our earthly life. Christian funerals are also a time to remember the accomplishments and good efforts of the dead and to thank God for who they were and what they meant to those around them. Funerals provide a time to celebrate the gifts and the legacy of those who have died.

In addition, however, mortal life is also a place of great vulnerability and often tremendous suffering. And so Christian funerals also express hope for life beyond death, mirroring the hope that often sustains Christians before they die. In the obituary for an eighty-six-year-old man, his family celebrated the fact that "his forty-year struggle with depression has ended, and his perfect enjoyment of the beauty of God has begun." In a paradoxical way, Christians can speak about death in terms of gain as well as loss. We believe that true human fulfillment occurs only beyond this life, though our capacity to imagine life on the other side of death is a bit like a caterpillar's grasp of life on the other side of the cocoon. The fundamental Christian conviction is that, far from separating us from the love of God, death marks the point at which temporal obstacles to our experience of that love pass away. Indeed, the accounts of early Christian funerals reflect an almost defiant sense of confidence and joy. Participants in funeral processions wore white garments, sang psalms of praise, carried palm branches, and burned incense as a witness to the resurrection. Christians carried out these celebrations in the daytime as a bold, public display of hope for life beyond death. Christian funerals are always a time to celebrate both the gift of temporal life and the hope for life with God beyond death.

Yet Christian hope for life beyond death is a hope that has passed through the furnace of suffering and death. Christians affirm the good news of Easter only in the wake of the anguish of Good Friday. Our hope for everlasting life permits no evasion of death's hard reality. Jesus' response to the grieving Martha has remained one of the favorite scriptural texts for Christian funerals: "I am the resurrection and the

For I am convinced that neither death, nor life, nor angels, nor
rulers, nor things present, nor things to come, nor powers, nor height,
nor depth, nor anything else in all creation, will be able to separate
us from the love of God in Christ Jesus our Lord.

ROMANS 8:38–39

life. Those who believe in me, even though they die, will live" (John 11:25). But in this Gospel story, Jesus proceeds to weep with Martha and her sister Mary over the death of their brother Lazarus. Indeed, even the resurrection does not erase from Christ's hands and feet the wounds of the crucifixion. Sharing the meal of Eucharist at Christian funerals is deeply appropriate, because in this sacrament, both Christ's brokenness and God's promise of new life are made vividly present.

The cross, an instrument of death, is always at the center of Christian hope. Because of this, the practice of dying well has a paradoxical quality. On the one hand, as followers of Jesus Christ, we are not to save death and dying for the end of our lives. Life in Christ requires dying now. Those who hope in God as the redeemer from death must enter into the vulnerable, suffering love that leads to the cross. The entire Christian life draws us into an ongoing "death," in which we die to everything that thwarts God's intentions for life, peace, and joy. As John Calvin summarized it, "Man dies to himself that he may begin to live to God." Christians testify to hope for everlasting life with God by dying in the present to all that stands in its way. Sometimes, indeed, this leads to the premature physical death of martyrdom, as it did for early Christians who died in passive endurance for the sake of the faith and for such recent martyrs as Martin Luther King Jr. and Oscar Romero, who died in active struggles for justice.

On the other hand, Christian hope also requires a restless protest against death. Death from natural causes at an advanced age or as a release from severe suffering is something to be grateful for. But the gratitude is for the gift of a long life or for the merciful end of suffering. Death, though part of our natural condition, is not something with which Christians can be fully at peace. This is one of the places where Christian practices regarding death and dying do not fit well with contemporary cultural attitudes. Some recent self-help literature insists that there is nothing sad, frightening, or destructive about our own death; it is simply a final opportunity for personal growth or a "friendly companion on life's journey" as we finally merge with the larger rhythms of the cosmos.

Christians find comfort instead in the confidence that God is actively working against the powers of death in all creation. "When the writer of Revelation spoke of the coming of the day of shalom, he did not say that on that day we would live at peace with death," notes the philosopher Nicholas Wolterstorff. "He said that on that day 'There will be no more death or mourning or crying or pain, for the old order of things has passed away.'" In its power to separate and alienate, death is part of the old order. Christians who hope for the coming of God's new reign must nurture resistance to the powers of death in this world.

This facet of Christian hope is seen in the protest against unjust death that forms an integral part of some Latin American worship services. The names of the deceased are read off one by one, and at each name the congregation exclaims, *Presente!* Parents, children, relatives, and friends lifted up in this way have often died brutally and tragically. Yet the Christian worshipers refuse to accept violent death as the last word on them. As part of the "great cloud of witnesses" (Hebrews 12:1), they are declared present to the living community through God's gift of life that triumphs even over the last enemy, death.

ת

Out of the daily suffering of poor women and out of the lives surrendered in the struggle against the causes of this situation of death, people are living a renewed paschal experience. The experience of death, war, abduction, rape, and abandonment enables them to experience more profoundly the meaning of the Lord's resurrection. . . . Hope in the resurrection in no way means escape from the present reality but, rather, it means a deeper involvement in the struggle against death.

LUZ BEATRIZ ARELLANO,
"Women's Experience of God in Emerging Spirituality"

This ritual of hope in the face of brutal and unjust deaths is also done for the sake of the living. God desires a world in which peace and justice embrace. Christian hope responds as we struggle to prevent these kinds of horrible deaths in the future. This struggle on behalf of the living is at the same time an act of hope on behalf of the dead. It is the hope that their lives, and even the apparent absurdity of their deaths, will yield a new resolve to establish justice on earth.

JUDGMENT

The complementary themes of human hope and lament are mirrored by the themes of divine mercy and judgment. These themes reflect the complexity of the Christian tradition's view of death. On the one hand, we understand death as a natural part of our finitude as creatures whose days are numbered. On the other hand, we also believe that death is intertwined with our sinfulness, with the human rejection of God's loving and life-giving intentions. Though Scripture is ambiguous about how sin originates and spreads, it is clear that sin is deadly. Left unchecked, sin pollutes, distorts, and finally destroys us. The writings of the apostle Paul in particular forged strong bonds between death and human sin in Christian reflection. Though the Bible also supports other understandings of death, Paul's notion that "death spread to all because all have sinned" (Romans 5:12) was dominant throughout most of Christian history.

Fear of God's wrath—God's harsh judgment of our sinful lives—shaped the Christian experience of death for many centuries, and it continues as a powerful motive in some Christian communities today. Scenes of the Last Judgment, carved by artists on the doors of

~~~

I have been shocked by the number of Christian men and women who come to their deathbeds knowing nothing about the God of love and mercy. They have known instead the Judge of impossible standards, and they have been, naturally enough, afraid to meet that God.

Eve Kavenaugh, "Prayer of the Flesh"

PRACTICING OUR FAITH

medieval cathedrals or presented in the books and films of contemporary Christian fundamentalists, depict the agony of those condemned to eternal fires. Fortunately, this kind of fear has given way in many Christian communities today to an understanding of divine judgment that does not deny divine love. The modern weakening of the link between death and God's wrath helps us to affirm the naturalness of death and to overcome simple formulas that claimed to understand the mysteries of God's judgment and mercy. In death and in life, we rely on God's grace, for others and for ourselves.

Still, Christians do insist that sin leads to death in a myriad of ways, and that no passage in our lives is free from sin, including death. We have lived fallen lives, and we will die fallen deaths. This means that we need to acknowledge God's judgment and seek God's forgiveness in our dying as well as in our living. Where possible, dying Christians need to seek human forgiveness as well. Confessing our sins and asking for forgiveness are regular rhythms in the Christian life. But death, as the final life passage, infuses these regular practices with a heightened urgency and significance. Though speaking of "sin" is uncomfortable for many modern people, the sense that we need forgiveness at the end of life is in our bones. This is what dying people yearn for—the opportunity to heal a breach with a sister, or to say to a son the words of love that were always so hard to speak when he was growing up. When families gather at the bedside of one who will soon die, these are the words they say: "I am sorry that I hurt you. I love you. Please forgive me." And "I understand. I forgive you. I love you too. Be at peace." In this way, we participate, however haltingly, in the reconciliation God is working in the world.

The practices of the medieval period, an age of short and unpredictable life expectancy, embodied profound insight into the fear death evokes, as well as the desire of the dying to settle accounts with God and others. The ritual of anointing with oil, used in earlier times for physical as well as spiritual healing, became a tangible way to prepare the dying soul for entrance into heaven. This provided a concrete assurance of forgiveness to people for whom words could often no longer convey meaning. Likewise, offering prayers and masses on behalf of the dead expressed concern for the bereaved and affirmed the communion of all the saints, both living and dead. In the sixteenth century, however, financial corruptions that had grown up around these rituals led Protestant reformers to repudiate them altogether. Even though this represented an important witness against manipulating the fear of death for the sake of wealth and power, the reform left Protestant Christians without adequate ways of allaying fears of God's wrath.

One of the many gains of the modern movements in Christian ecumenism and liturgical renewal has been a new willingness to set aside old theological and institutional animosities and learn from the practices of other communions. Catholic liturgies have placed renewed emphasis on the Christian funeral as a celebration of the paschal mystery of Christ's own death and resurrection. Many Protestant communions have adopted rituals of prayer for the dead and anointing for the sick. The significant convergence between the Catholic and Protestant practices of dying well is a hopeful sign for the future of the Christian community.

MERCY

Divine judgment and divine mercy, though complementary, do not have equal weight in Christian reflections on death. Judgment is the counterpoint in death's rhythm; its notes are always secondary to the dominant theme of divine mercy. We worship a God who "does not deal with us according to our sins, nor repay us according to our iniquities," but whose steadfast love is as great "as the heavens are high above the earth" (Psalm 103:10–11). This rhythm is reflected in healthy Christian communities as well. Anointing the sick with oil and praying for the dead acknowledge the reality of divine judgment against sin and the human need for forgiveness. But these practices do not invite us to judge the dying and the deceased in God's place. Instead, they call us to acknowledge God's mercy toward the dying and to embody it through our words and actions. The fundamental way of expressing our thanks for the divine mercy that sustains us is to be instruments of that divine mercy to others.

Caring presence is the most basic way of making divine mercy actively present to a person who is dying. We need divine mercy mediated to us at every point of our lives, of course. But our need for it is especially great during the passage of death, when both our phys-

Precious Lord, take my hand, Lead me on, help me stand;
I am tired, I am weak, I am worn;
Through the storm, through the night, Lead me on to the light;
Take my hand, precious Lord, lead me home.
When my way grows drear, Precious Lord, linger near,
When my life is almost gone,
Hear my cry, hear my call, Hold my hand lest I fall;
Take my hand, precious Lord, lead me home.

THOMAS A. DORSEY, "Precious Lord, Take My Hand"

ical and emotional resources ebb. An important way in which Christians incarnate the mercy of Jesus Christ is by loving care for the body. Dying for most of us will be a messy, painful business; we cannot expect to die well in a biological sense. But skilled and compassionate ministry to the bodily needs of dying persons can give them a profound sense of God's merciful presence. Eve Kavenaugh, a nurse who works with terminally ill patients, recognizes these deep interconnections between body and spirit. She sees her work as an opportunity to express God's mercy to the dying "by faithful and loving care of the body, which becomes increasingly more difficult to care for and often repulsive. If I remain loving and faithful to that task until the end, the patient has a new and life-giving experience of God."

A phrase from the ministry to persons living with AIDS captures the importance of physical presence in caring for the dying. At the terrible last stages of the disease, family and friends embrace the dying person with a "care-giving surround." Christian communities

ↄ2

Drawing on medieval Celtic practices, the musician Therese
Schroeder-Sheker ministers to dying patients in hospital, hospice,
and home settings in Missoula, Montana. Through music, she and
the singers and harpists who intern with her seek to transform
deathbeds into sanctuaries of palliative care and spiritual presence.

can likewise embody divine mercy by a care-giving surround that aims at physical comfort and companionship for all who face death.

The Christian activity of caring presence also requires loving support of the person's spirit. Serenity and trust in God do not come easily to those whose minds are ravaged by disease and pain. Christians who continue to radiate faith and love of God through a prolonged period of dying are grace-filled teachers to the rest of the community. But dying well is not to be seen primarily as something that a dying individual achieves. A serene death is not an accomplishment by which a person must prove his or her spiritual maturity, and a difficult death is not a cause for despair.

During the last pain-racked weeks of a grandmother whose faith had long been an inspiration in her community, serenity seemed far away. Her face did not show the feelings of acceptance and calm that her loved ones so longed to see there. In some ways, they realized, she was like a baby at baptism: others must claim God's promises on her behalf. And so that is what they did at her deathbed, speaking the prayers and singing the hymns when she was too weak to do so herself. It comforted them, in the end, when she managed to let them know of her gratitude—to them, for sharing their faith, and to God, for a life of many blessings. But even if this acknowledgment had been beyond her, they would have held her in this embrace, as her parents and sponsors had done some seventy years before. Like our birth into Christian faith, our dying well draws strength from the faith of the entire community. We live by grace, and we also die by grace.

In Life and in Death, We Are God's

Some years ago, Eric Wolterstorff died in a mountaineering accident at the age of twenty-five. His father Nicholas has written about this tragedy in a book treasured by many people who have experienced similar losses. At the funeral, he reports, the community's actions and symbols spoke as much as the words. The cloth placed over the coffin was "simple but wonderfully beautiful," and near it burned a candle, symbolizing resurrection. The opening words recalled Eric's baptism. The music was "glorious." Together, the gathered people

We do not live to ourselves, and we do not die to ourselves.
If we live, we live to the Lord, and if we die, we die to the
Lord; so then, whether we live or whether we die, we are
the Lord's. For to this end Christ died and lived again, so
that he might be Lord of both the dead and the living.

ROMANS 14:7–9

celebrated the Eucharist, "that sacrament of God's participation in our brokenness." They "came forward successively in groups, standing in circles around the coffin, passing the signs of Christ's brokenness to each other." The funeral did not console him for Eric's absence, Wolterstorff writes. But it did do something else. "It sank deep into me the realization that my son's death is not all there is."

A Christian funeral like this one has its deepest meaning for people who have been nurtured by basic Christian convictions during the course of their lives. The same is true of the other acts of prayer and concern with which the Christian community surrounds us as we near the end of our days. Their power "cannot be instantaneously transmitted to the sick person waiting upon death whose flesh already is ravaged and mind is tormented by disease," the theologian Vigen Guroian points out. "The meaning for living and dying that faith provides must be owned by the person over a lifetime." The Christian practices surrounding the passage of death echo the regular rhythms of worship and fellowship in the Christian life. Dying well grows out of the Christian community's attempts to live well before God in the present.

Dying well involves participation in complex, difficult, communal practices. But like all Christian practices, it rests on the promise that there is a divine ground beneath us in all the passages of our lives. If we manage to live well or die well, it is because we are not our own, either as individuals or as a human race. This recognition humbles us; but it also gives us hope that in our failures as well as in our successes, we belong to God. With the assurance that not even death will separate us from God's love, we can dare to nurture the Christian practices that will help each of us to embody God's mercy to one another while we live and then, when it is time, to die well.

Chapter 13

SINGING OUR LIVES

꼭

Don E. Saliers

For several years, my family and I lived in an urban housing development where our daughters, then quite young, learned to sing a set of ritual songs. First, the kids would gather in circles and teach one another, clapping and singing. Then someone might bring some jumping ropes, and the singing children would circle around two who turned the ropes. One after another, they would slip inside the whirling rope for a few hop-dancing steps before darting away. "Miss Mary Mack, Mack, Mack—all dressed in black, black, black!" they sang, rhythmically accenting the rhyming words.

That dancing, singing image has come back to me many times in the course of working with churches on matters of worship. That circle of song and movement, with its delight and physical energy, its formal, ritual character marked by surprising improvisation, remains for me an image of vitality and delight in being alive: shared music making that the human body remembers—a kind of natural language of praise.

Singing is discovered and invented, it is born at times
when there is no other possible way for people to express
themselves—at the grave, for example, when four or five
people with untrained, clumsy voices sing words that are
greater and smaller than their faith and their experience.

HUUB OOSTERHUIS, *Prayers, Poems and Songs*

This is but one reminder of the fact that human beings have always sung at play and at work, on festive and solemn occasions, in joy and in grief. Whether around campfires or in recital halls, on the playground or in churches and synagogues, the act of singing has expressed human feelings and the sense of being in the world, of being alive. If music is the language of the soul made audible, then human voices, raised in concert in human gatherings, are primary instruments of the soul.

Music also conveys common memories, with powerful associations. Any who participated in the civil rights struggle of the sixties will always hear the courage and the promise in "We Shall Overcome." A whole generation of Americans who lived through World War II can never forget Kate Smith's voice singing "God Bless America." African American spirituals—"Go Down, Moses," "Walk Together Children," "Sometimes I Feel like a Motherless Child"—came into being to express the suffering and hope that one people shares. Now, through association, songs like these also touch much wider circles of people.

The act of singing together is deeply and indelibly human. When we sing, words are given greater range and power than when we speak. Something is shared in singing that goes beyond the words alone. Among Christians, this something has taken shape over many centuries in a practice that expresses our deepest yearning and dearest joy: the practice of singing our lives.

SOMETHING IN US INSISTS ON SONG

There is something about human beings that needs to make music, something that insists on song. Every culture sings about the world it experiences, in its own distinctive sound. In fact, we come to know about a people by listening to what they sing and bring to expression in their music. What we sing and how we sing reveals much of who we are, and entering into another's song and music making provides a gateway into their world, which might be much different from our own. Sharing our song with others who do not know us is sharing a gift, akin to the sharing of food at a common table.

What is it that prompts the song? What is it in human life that cannot keep from singing? It begins with and in our bodies. The heart beats, we breathe in and out, we move from one place to another, we make sounds—even from our first cry as a newborn. "The world resounds with the joyful cry, 'I am!'" said the composer Scriabin. The very elemental rhythms of human life itself—heartbeats racing with excitement, the stamping of feet, the clapping of hands in delight, the baby sounds becoming after a time little chains of words—all these show the origins of music and song in the body. Music is not merely the language of the soul, but also of the body. It is life's language embodied.

If the body is the basic instrument and our physical being the elemental rhythm and sound maker, then the prompting of music and song is found in our social life, our life together. I can still hear from my own childhood the music of parents calling as my friends and I played late into the twilight: "Ma-ry, John-ny, time to come ho-ome." Always the chantlike falling minor third. Isn't it remarkable that the parental call sounds similar in so many cultures?

But the communal character of song doesn't stop there. Other rhythms and melodies emerge as well. Some of them are deeply rooted not in play but in work, whether forced or voluntary. Planting

———— ꙮ ————

My life flows on in endless song
above earth's lamentations;
I hear the real though far off hymn
that hails a new creation.
No storm can shake my inmost calm
while to that rock I'm clinging;
while love is Lord o'er heaven and earth
how can I keep from singing?

TRADITIONAL QUAKER HYMN

———————————

Singing Our Lives

the crops, harvesting, working on the chain gang—these, too, have generated song. Armies sounding brave drum and pipe, or with ambiguous valor singing of blood and earth and "fatherland," or marching off to war singing in every language some equivalent of "When Johnnie Comes Marching Home Again," stir the patriot's heart. The dirges of women crying out of loss when Johnnie or Dietrich or Maria does not return are also heard in every culture. And songs arise from those enslaved, singing of freedom and release: "My Lord, What a Mornin' When the Stars Begin to Fall." All these are songs of the body and the soul.

But there is more. Singing is also a pleasure and a delight. The sheer magic of ordered sound captivates every culture, from simple song flutes to ample orchestras. The range of sounds from voices and varied instruments creates its own special world of enjoyment. Children love music games and can often be heard making up songs. Listening to someone sing and play the songs of love is something we cultivate as a pleasure. Even folks who say they can't sing, or who have been told that they shouldn't, still whistle or hum tunes at work or when no one is around. Thus even the "unmusical" have a secret solidarity with the music of earth.

Whether in the idiom of folk song or in the highly complex language of the opera or the concert hall, human beings are brought together in the pleasure of music. However humble or sophisticated, singing together is an act of freedom. This is why tyrants, sensing the binding power of music, suppress the poets and the musicians as well as the political writers who threaten their control of mind and heart.

Whatever people can say with passion and in heightened speech they will end up singing in some form. When our language is used to move beyond the mere giving of information, we come to the threshold of song. When life is deeply felt or perceived, music gives shape and voice to the very pattern of our experienced world, through pitch, rhythm, and intensity, through lyrics and harmony. The tensions, resolutions, moods, convictions, and playfulness of everyday life are translated into the patterns of sound. But so also are the deepest mysteries of love and death, of loss and recovery of the sense of life. So the act of singing together of life lived and felt binds heart and mind with ordered sound.

FAITH IS BORN AND LIVES IN SONG

Given all this, it is not surprising that music and song are so closely linked with the praise of divinity. As Saint Augustine observed long ago, whoever sings "prays twice," in music as well as words. From its very origin, the Christian community sang. In the New Testament, Paul's letters are punctuated by doxologies, hymn fragments, and references to the practice of singing in worshiping assemblies. In writing to the church at Colossae, he joins singing to teaching and admonition, wisdom and the Word (Colossians 3:16).

The Christian church was born singing the songs of ancient Israel, the synagogue, and the Greco-Roman world. Psalms and canticles formed the heart of prayer and the music of the earliest Christian assemblies. Luke's Gospel barely gets through the second chapter without bursting into song four times: Mary sings that her soul magnifies the Lord, Zechariah sings blessing to the Lord of Israel, the angels near Bethlehem sing "Glory to God in the highest," and old Simeon sings his farewell song of peace. Each of these songs became regular parts of Christian daily prayer within the first two centuries. Saint Augustine, writing in the fourth century, could observe: "Apart from those moments when the scriptures are being read or a sermon is preached, when the bishop is praying aloud or the deacon is speaking the intention of the litany of community prayer, is there any time when the faithful assembled are not singing?"

Christians still sing these songs from Luke's Gospel, as well as many other songs both old and new. One recent hymn, Fred Pratt

ᨊ
_____

When in our music God is glorified,
and adoration leaves no room for pride,
it is as though the whole creation cried
Alleluia!
So has the church in liturgy and song,
in faith and love, through centuries of wrong,
borne witness to the truth in every tongue,
Alleluia!

FRED PRATT GREEN, "When in Our Music God Is Glorified"
_____

Let the word of Christ dwell in you richly; teach and admonish
one another in all wisdom; and with gratitude in your hearts sing
psalms, hymns, and spiritual songs to God.

COLOSSIANS 3:16

Green's "When in Our Music God Is Glorified," expresses what is at stake when we lift our voices to God. Singing this hymn, we affirm what is true but unspoken in all good hymn singing: we sing not alone, but in union with the whole creation and with our brothers and sisters through the ages.

The gathering of a Christian community to sing praises to God seems such a simple act, and it has been going on for nearly two millennia. But we should not take this practice for granted. It needs to be learned and nurtured and taught. And it needs to keep developing, as it has done through the centuries and continues to do today.

WHAT IS YOUR FAVORITE HYMN?

I once asked a circle of about twenty women in a South Carolina congregation to name some of their favorite hymns. Their replies were not surprising: "Amazing Grace," "Blessed Assurance," "How Great Thou Art," "Standing on the Promises," "In the Garden." Then I asked how they had learned these hymns. This question brought forth a wonderful set of unexpected stories. For nearly two hours, these women, most of them well into their seventies, spoke of their memories. They remembered the sounds of their grandfather's or grandmother's voice, the squeak of the parlor organ, or the comforting feeling of leaning on their mother's shoulder while the family sang. They remembered Sunday night and Wednesday night prayer meetings, Sunday School assemblies, summer camps, and family singing at holiday time. Hymns had deep associations for them. As they told me these things, they revealed the deep body memories and profound associations they had with both the words and the music. These hymns and songs were in their bone marrow.

Toward the end of our conversation, however, several women began to say how much they also liked some of the "new songs" in the United Methodist Hymnal. One commented on how "Hymn of Promise" (Natalie Sleeth's resurrection hymn) had changed her attitude toward singing at funerals. Another said how much she enjoyed "Jesus' Hands Were Kind Hands," especially when the children sang it in worship. Another said that she loved hearing the choir and congregation sing "When in Our Music God Is Glorified" and the refrain to "Lift High the Cross," even though she could not sing them well herself. None of these hymns had been in the familiar hymnals they had used for decades, but the women embraced them nonetheless, responding to the new alongside the "oldies and goldies" they had learned in childhood.

Over the course of a lifetime, singing had shaped these women's faith. The words they sang in all those different situations went deep into their souls. Yet what they had developed was not only a memory of the old but also an openness to the new. The tunes they knew by heart had remarkable powers of association. Even though the number of their "favorites" was relatively small, the women were surprisingly open to learning new hymns—often because there were affinities in melody, harmony, and words with the older ones already known and loved.

It is sometimes thought that the theology of a hymn—what it teaches and expresses about our relationship to God—is contained solely in the words. Talking with these women, however, it was clear that far more than the words were at stake. Over time, participation in the practice of lifting their voices to God had worked in subtle and complex ways to shape basic attitudes, affections, and ways of regarding themselves, their neighbors, and God. They left me with little doubt that what they believed represented far more than intellectual agreement with the message in the words. Their music was "by heart," in the heart, and sung from the heart. Through the practice of singing, the dispositions and beliefs expressed in the words of the hymns—gratitude, trust, sadness, joy, hope—had become knit into their bodies, as integral parts of the theology by which they lived.

This knitting of an embodied theology happens whenever Christian congregations sing, even though they do so in a great variety of ways from one culture to another. It has been happening since the earliest Christians extemporized variations of praise to God in the new images of Jesus' teaching and ministry, and above all in images of the mystery of his death and resurrection. The trinitarian character of faith was sung long before it was put into the language of doctrinal theology. Indeed, the church's theology was embodied in its liturgical and singing practices before more formal theology developed.

HYMNING THE WORLD TO GOD

Hymn singing, far from being an ornament or decoration to Christian worship and the life of faith, is intrinsic to worship and faith experience. Indeed, in certain Protestant churches, the singing of hymns seems to be the most important part of the liturgy, the people's shared work of worship. For people in this tradition, this is the specific form of the larger human practice of singing that most deeply touches their spirits.

What is a hymn, and what do hymns do in Christian worship and life? Saint Augustine's simple definition of a hymn—a song with praise addressed to God—is still a good place to begin. Hymns can also express other dimensions of our lives before God, such as lament or dedication, giving us words as they teach us God's Word. The classical hymn is a particular musical form, consisting of a number of stanzas sung to the same melodic line. Because this structure is less free than a simple chant tone or a plainsong melody, hymns cannot serve every liturgical function. They are especially suitable as congregational song, for their rhymed stanzas and formal structure make them sung poetry, expressive of the people's praise, affirmation, and devotion. Thus they enter the memory, encoding religious experience, commingling belief with affection and depth of emotion.

The history of Christian hymnody contains a wondrous variety of developments, in both poetry and music. In every age of renewal, however, the Psalms have provided a foundation for both the people's sung prayer in the liturgical assembly and the composition of hymns. The Hebrew Psalter was the musical heritage of Jesus, and then of his early followers. At the conclusion of the Last Supper, Christ and the disciples sang a hymn that was probably drawn from

It is not you that sings, it is the church that is singing, and you,
as a member . . . may share in its song. Thus all singing together
that is right must serve to widen our spiritual horizon, make us
see our little company as a member of the great Christian church
on earth, and help us willingly and gladly to join our singing,
be it feeble or good, to the song of the church.

DIETRICH BONHOEFFER, *Life Together*

the Psalms (Matthew 26:30). Again, a stanza of Fred Pratt Green's "When in Our Music God Is Glorified" helps us remember and participate in this singing: "And did not Jesus sing a hymn that night, when utmost evil strove against the light? Then let us sing, for whom he won the fight: Alleluia!"

Today, the church worldwide is experiencing an extraordinary explosion of hymn writing. The most imaginative and challenging forms of the Word in contemporary hymnody are, I think, grounded in the acknowledgment of God in praise. They hymn the world to God, proclaiming God in the vocative of address. Jaroslav Vajda's "God of the Sparrow, God of the Whale" exemplifies how powerful these sung texts can be: on the one hand, faithful to the Word in Scripture; on the other, breaking into contemporary consciousness with imaginative boldness:

> God of the sparrow God of the whale
> God of the swirling stars
>> How does the creature say Awe
>> How does the creature say Praise
> God of the earth-quake God of the storm
> God of the trumpet blast
>> How does the creature say Woe
>> How does the creature say Save
> God of the rainbow God of the cross
> God of the empty grave
>> How does the creature say Grace
>> How does the creature say Thanks
> God of the hungry God of the sick

God of the prodigal
> How does the creature say Care
> How does the creature say Life

God of the neighbor God of the foe
God of the pruning hook
> How does the creature say Love
> How does the creature say Peace

God of the ages God near at hand
God of the loving heart
> How do your children say Joy
> How do your children say Home

This text, intentionally without punctuation, plays on the ambiguity of question and declaration. The power of this hymn lies in its bringing together five central biblical stories or prophetic images, converging in the last image of the loving, ever-living God of the ages. The cumulative affect and effect are to take the assembly ever more deeply into the Creator/creature relationship, finally to be at home with God.

Other churches among the varied families within the Christian tradition rely less on hymns than on other elements in the song of faith and sacred music. In many churches, worshipers chant greetings, psalms, and prayers, shaping through these notes the ongoing dialogue between worshipers and the divine. Creativity is erupting here as well. It is a time when old and new take shape together as people rediscover the wide range of biblical song: canticles, prophetic utterances, acclamations, and early Christian hymn fragments such as "Awake, O sleeper, and arise from the dead, And Christ shall give you light" (Ephesians 5:14), or the earliest hymn still sung, the *phos hilaron* ("O gracious light").

Occasionally, in all this singing, the songs of earth and heaven meet. These are times and places when the significance of singing together is suddenly revealed, whether inside or outside church. One such occasion occurred for me in 1985, during an ecumenical gathering at the Orthodox Center outside Geneva, Switzerland. Among those participating in the liturgy of Holy Week and Easter were several from behind the Iron Curtain—from Romania, Russia, East

Germany, and Czechoslovakia, as well as from Ethiopia and several English-speaking countries. We were invited to attend the great Easter Vigil in one of the several churches grouped together there, which included a French-speaking Greek Orthodox, a Russian Orthodox, and the small expatriate Romanian congregation I chose to attend. Shortly after midnight, as each liturgy concluded, we poured out of our respective church buildings into the chill, starry night, singing in several languages, "Christ is risen!" while the bells sounded the Easter morning air. It was as though we stood—from so many different cultures, languages, and liturgical traditions—at the very center of the cosmos, singing and receiving the song in which heaven and earth had embraced. Members of the Atlanta Symphony Orchestra and Chorus told me later that they, too, had experienced such a moment, in a stirring performance of Beethoven's Ninth Symphony in East Berlin shortly before the Wall fell. At the end, the hall erupted in applause and tears, and conductor Robert Shaw raised his fist in triumph and freedom, prefiguring the joy that would envelop the city in just a few months' time.

FINDING OUR VOICES

How do people learn to sing such hymns, psalms, and spiritual songs? The vast majority of Christians have learned the way the vast majority of any human community learns: by rote. They have listened over and over, learning by both habit and conscious memorization. This is the way of all preliterate cultures, and certainly the way we learn music as very young children. But with the advent of musical notation, and eventually of hymn books for the congregation, people also learned by note. With musical literacy has come an enormously expanded range of what can be sung, especially in those traditions that place the hymnal or songbook alongside the Bible as central to devotion and corporate worship.

More recently still, learning to sing has used electronic means—recordings and tapes—which now exert a massive influence on how and what we sing everywhere, including the church. The Christian music sections of record stores are part of the enormous recorded

Sing to the Lord a new song,
God's praise in the assembly of the faithful.
Let Israel be glad in its Maker;...
Let them praise God's name with dancing,
Making melody to God with tambourine and lyre.

PSALM 149:1–3

music industry which is, for good and for ill, shaping a new generation's listening and singing practices. The style of such singers as Mahalia Jackson, Aretha Franklin, and Amy Grant has greatly influenced how worshiping congregations "hear" religious song. Moreover, many congregations have begun to do away with hymnals, using instead simple "praise choruses" that can be sung to user-friendly tunes taught by rote, with words projected onto a wall or screen.

Changes and differences in how worshiping congregations learn to sing together have resulted in a vast array of styles and texts and musical forms. These developments raise important questions for the practice of Christian worship and song—questions that will be struggled with for the foreseeable future. How much should the surrounding culture—popular or elite—influence both the style and the content of praise, lamentation, prophetic vision, and thanksgiving? What creative tensions need to be preserved between what has become part of the "tradition" and the ever-emerging "contemporary" forms of music and poetry? Or, more pointedly, what does Saturday night have to do with Sunday morning? And what do the singing practices of our Sunday (and other) Christian gatherings have to do with life every day?

SING SUNDAY, SING LIFE

How closely to follow changing cultural sensibilities in singing the Christian faith is only one of the issues that ties the practice of hymn singing to life outside the sanctuary. Another is the power of music to sound prophecy—to ring out in opposition to injustice. Perhaps the greatest of the proclamatory prophetic hymns is James Weldon Johnson's "Lift Every Voice and Sing," written in 1921 as testimony to the powerful, graced experience of God discovered by African American people in the midst of their suffering. The hymn draws on biblical images of Exodus as it tells the story of slavery and struggle, sweeping singers into a music that makes "earth and heaven ring with the harmonies of liberty":

> Sing a song full of the faith that the dark past has taught us,
> Sing a song full of the hope that the present has brought us;
> Facing the rising sun of our new day begun,
> Let us march on, till victory is won.

In church and in other places of African American empowerment, this hymn can indeed "resound loud as the rolling sea."

Sometimes the singing that proclaims justice is quieter, though not therefore less powerful. The power of such song shines forth in a heartrending story of terror and faith from El Salvador, a story told by survivors of a mass rape and murder that took place in 1981 in the little town of El Mozote. One of the youngest victims did not weep or scream as she was assaulted. Instead, she sang hymns and simple spiritual songs, stopping only when she had breathed for the last time. The soldiers were stupefied; then they wondered and grew afraid. Through the horror of El Mozote appears the uncanny power of the song of faith—enough to bring fear to men of hideous intent. One thinks of the humble evangelical church community in which that young girl learned to sing in innocence. Her practice of singing to God became a martyr's witness against evil. Now, I am sure, she sings with the heavenly host, while her song continues to haunt the violent in El Salvador and wherever her story is told and her hymns are sung.

Few of us will ever be taken to a place where our songs will be wrung from us in a martyr's witness against evil. But we must know cries of protest and resistance as well as shouts of joy if we are to have a music that is true and good. When our songs do not sound the depths of lamentation, when they ignore the tragedies of life, our hymns of praise will ring hollow.

They began playing something Cass did not recognize,
something very slow, and more like the blues than a hymn.
Then it began to be more tense and more bitter and more
swift. The people in the chapel hummed low in their throats
and tapped their feet. Then the girl stepped forward ...
threw back her head and ... that voice rang out again:

O, that great getting-up morning,
Fare thee well, fare thee well!

Reverend Foster, standing on a height behind her,
raised both hands and mingled his voice with hers:

We'll be coming from every nation,
Fare thee well, fare thee well!

The chapel joined them. . . .

JAMES BALDWIN, *Another Country*

SHARING THE SACRED POWER OF SONG

In our present North American cultural context, the singing assemblies in our churches and synagogues are among the very few remaining places where words and music actually form human beings in a communal identity. The phenomenon of public singing at civic events has shriveled to an occasional "Happy Birthday" or "Take Me Out to the Ball Game," or perhaps a weak effort at the national anthem. But when people meet to worship, public singing still offers formation in a shared identity. This identity flows out of an ancient story that continues to take on new life, in words and tunes that speak today. It gives voice to individual people in praise, lament, and need, but it does not leave them isolated, surrounding them instead with a great choir.

Communal singing outside the churches can also do this, and it surely has something to teach those of us who gather in church to sing on behalf of the world to the Creator and Redeemer of all things. I recall a benefit concert given by two singer-songwriters, the Indigo Girls. The crowd of four thousand, who knew the words by heart from listening to their music, stood together singing antiphonally the words to "Prince of Darkness": "My place is of the sun, and this place is of the dark." The song kept moving back and forth along the edges of dark and light, of moral evil and a sense of the good. And I found myself caught up in their ringing affirmation of the side of light and healing. These, too, are hymns and songs from the earth: cries and whispers and intimations of what the church may politely neglect or reject. The new hymn writers for a generation yet unborn are listening both to these words and to the language of the ancient psalms and canticles that speak of God. Theirs too will be a language of the human heart at full stretch, singing of life in its whole range to the Source of all life, sounding earth and heaven.

The rich and complex practice of singing our lives takes many forms, some of them only now coming into being. One thing can be said of them all, however: where people sing of God, an embodied theology—a way of living and thinking about life in relationship to God—is formed and expressed. Through this practice, music lends its power to all the other practices that shape and express who we are. Singing, we embrace our loved ones with music as they are baptized or confirmed or married. We sing as we help one another find the courage to die well and as we praise God each Sabbath for creation, liberation, and resurrection. Singing, we give testimony of our beliefs, we shape communities by rhythm and pitch, and we welcome Mary and Joseph to the stable on Christmas Eve.

John Wesley, a preacher who promoted hymn singing in the Methodist movement he founded, was right: hymns are a "body of practical divinity," a sung theology. At a time when many outside the churches wonder about what those "believers" sing in their worship gatherings, those in—and outside—the church need to reawaken to the liberating, healing, prophetic voice that may yet transform human life.

Chapter 14

GROWING IN THE PRACTICES OF FAITH

❧

Dorothy C. Bass and Craig Dykstra

A sk people to discuss a practice in the concreteness of their own lives, and you will find it hard to stop the conversation. What would it really mean to practice forgiveness in this situation? What is your favorite hymn? What no does our family have to say in order to say an important yes? Do we live in a society that honors the human body? How should I discern the right thing to do? Have you known anyone who died well?

During the past few years, the authors of this book have had many conversations that started with questions like these. Ask about practices, we have found, and stories tumble out. Tears and laughter erupt. Connections get made. People talk, and people listen. We offer this book to a larger circle of readers in the hope of encouraging many similar conversations.

But our aim is not only to foster good conversations, as nourishing as those are. Our deepest and dearest purpose is to contribute to the search that is going on all around us for a life-giving way of life. We hope that talk about practices can make a difference in the way people walk with one another and with God.

In this final chapter, we offer some suggestions about how that might happen. It is a little awkward to do this, because we know that each reader comes to these practices from a unique situation. Some may feel trapped in practices that are stifling, others isolated from shared patterns of life, and others fairly comfortable with the way things are right now. Readers may be attracted to certain practices but doubtful that it would be possible to enter them, for any number of reasons. We warn you, therefore, that accepting our invitation to consider these practices will require you to think and act creatively within your own situation.

And yet—mark this well—this is not something you can do alone, no matter how unique you think your situation is. Whoever seeks to participate in practices structured in response to God must do so in the company of other people. We simply cannot walk with confidence and hope, in these and other difficult matters, all by ourselves. Our perseverance will falter, and our insights will be too limited.

Being together with other people who share our concerns is indispensable. But even this is only part of the answer. A specific group of people will, to be sure, have some ideas about how their community should be governed or how important decisions should be made. But just as individual perseverance and insights are limited, so are the perseverance and insights of any immediate group of people. So we need to find ways of deepening and broadening the wisdom available to us. We need to look beyond what our own little circle possesses at this particular point in history.

GROWING IN CHRISTIAN PRACTICES: AN EDUCATIONAL APPROACH

People eager to talk about practices can also take steps to grow in understanding and living them. Those who are Christian are eager to know what guidance the Bible, theology, and the experience of people of faith can offer as we search for a way of life that is good. In addition, we experience the pressures contemporary society puts on basic human activities, and we want to be able to understand and respond appropriately to these pressures. Gathering in groups to explore practices together may provide the opportunity for which we long. There we can reflect and learn, thinking more deeply about the patterns of our lives and also beginning to change them.

This is what happened, rather spontaneously, for a group of busy professionals. One Monday, after all had whined at lunch about how much work they had taken home over the weekend, one remarked that they seemed to be awfully complacent about their violation of the commandment to observe the Sabbath. "I know that we sometimes break the other commandments as well," she observed, "but at least we don't sit around boasting about it." How was it, this group began to wonder, that they had become so heedless of something of supposed value within the Christian faith they all professed? What was that value, anyway? They knew they needed rest, but they had not thought about that need in relation to their faith. Research followed, and then an informed discussion about the nature of God's gift of Sabbath rest to the world. Afterwards, the subject lingered in the air among them, and a few patterns began to change—not enough to satisfy strict Sabbatarians, certainly, but that was not the point. Rather, in ways suited to their own circumstances, members of this group grew in their lived awareness of the holiness of time and creation, in regularity at worship, and in opposition to injustices in the distribution of work and wealth in our society.

A congregation in Washington, D.C., came to the study of a practice from a different direction. Homeless people on the sidewalk called the church's members to the practice of hospitality. Then the challenges of real-life hospitality led them to study it. What shape and meaning, they wanted to know, should this practice take, in light of God's care for creation and Christ's special love for the poor? How did what they were doing share in the activity of God's Spirit in the world? Part of the answer is now evident in what they do to provide housing for the poor, food for the hungry, and welcome for the refugee. Another part of the answer is articulated in their mission statement, which appears in the church bulletin: "Hospitality is the shape of ministry at Luther Place. . . . The congregation of Luther Place believes itself to be guests in God's Creation and servants in and through this House and Village. We welcome you to share the joyful responsibility of being faithful 'innkeepers' who are called to make room for others."

Growing in the Practices of Faith

Exploring the range and depth of a single practice could take a lifetime. That is partly because each is so rich and various. Every practice has taken an astonishing variety of specific forms, in history and around the world today. Moreover, every practice is a place of mystery: a gracious vessel where people participate in God's activity, but also a vessel that can be broken by loveless acts. Practices call for a lifetime of exploration because we are constantly learning more about what it means to do them well—and learning it right in the middle of our doing.

Education in Christian practices is always going on within the life of Christian communities. It happens as parents teach children the economics of a household or as friends surround a widow in her time of grief. Our most important education for practice happens in the course of life-in-community. It is education that takes place in the ongoing patterns of life together. This is like belonging to a congregation at song: you learn, even as a child, to take your pitch from others, to clap along or not to, to anticipate certain melodies at certain times of the year. You use your whole body, and you draw on the musical tastes and training you have developed outside the church as well as in it. You may discover that you have special talent; or you may not, in which case you keep on singing along anyway but let others do the solos. This kind of learning—communal but unplanned—takes place all the time.

But there is also a place for more deliberate efforts to help one another grow in understanding and doing the practices in light of our faith. This can be the focus of graduate study in theology or, with a different approach, of youth group retreats. It will flourish most fully when trust and mutual respect are present, for the agenda needs to include an honest look at the ways in which our practices—and therefore ourselves and our world—are broken. The deepest learning will happen when people practice as well as talk, and when they are willing to look closely at the concrete acts that give a practice its shape.

Education in Christian practices can occur in many different places and forms. Specific groups of people might find that a certain practice opens the door to learning in a particularly relevant way. Teenagers yearn intensely to know the human body as a place of honor, a place alive with the movements of creation, incarnation, and resurrection. The very old yearn for this also, in a different way. People in either age group could benefit from the help of pastors and teachers as they try to find their way through clouds of cultural confusion to practices that honor their bodies as images of God. Or college students, facing some of the most important choices of life, could covenant to explore the ancient practice that insists that a yes is always tied to a no, and vice versa. Parents trying to resist the pressures of consumerism could gather to consider the economics of their homes in the light of faith, as some of the groups described in this book did. They could even lead their children in an exploration of this practice in its biblical, theological, social, historical, and ethical dimensions.

A GUIDE TO EXPLORING CHRISTIAN PRACTICES

What, specifically, should people who want to explore practices consider? The chapters in this book provide clues and models, but the exploration will take different shapes in different communities. Still, in each case, it will be helpful to pay attention to certain dynamics, as we have in this book:

• Consider the practice in relation to basic human needs. Try to identify how and why it is important to the flourishing of human life. Pay close attention to how it affects the flourishing of specific groups of people in and beyond your own community.

• Inquire into its ethical dimensions. Has it sometimes been shaped in ways that hurt or oppress? Are there obstacles that keep us from engaging in the practice in ways that are good for ourselves and others?

• Consider the ways in which different communities—Christian and those of other traditions—have shaped this practice. What have Christian churches or other religious groups done, in history and today, to sustain it?

• Reflect on how a practice enables us to participate in the activity of God's Spirit in the world. This will require serious engagement with the biblical texts concerning this practice.

• Be concrete. Observe what people actually do when they are engaged well in a particular practice. Think of people or communities that conduct the practice with exceptional grace and skill: think of a grandmother's hospitality, or a teacher's power of discernment, or of the saints of Christian history. How do people draw one another into a practice, and how do they learn it from and teach it to one another? How do they pass on the lore and the craft of a practice?

- Worship together, and see whether you can find the practice crystallized in the liturgy.

- Practice together—not after you have studied and talked but at the same time. You will bring better questions to your study, and greater sensitivity to your action.

- Sharpen your vision to the ways in which the practice can go wrong. Sometimes people cannot enter a practice because the very structures of society oppose it: the poor cannot keep a Sunday Sabbath when a job becomes available; the homemaker cannot purchase the products of "right labor" if every material is woven in sweat shops; and people cannot shape communities aright when some are excluded. The structures of society can deform and block. Eyes attuned to the promises of Christian practices should become alert to seeing the evil that thwarts human good. And Christians-at-practice should consider how faithful practice can resist this evil—not so that our own practice will be somehow purified, but so that the world will become more just for all.

Entering more deeply into a Christian practice, we do not just learn the practice. When practices are faithful, they teach us surprising things about God, our neighbors, and the world. Honoring the body, we grow in our knowledge that every person, even if diseased or misshapen, is made in God's image, and we act with greater compassion. Keeping Sabbath, we learn more deeply the truths that God created the world, liberated the people, and triumphed over death, and we see the promise of these truths for the world we live in today. Singing our lives, we find ways to give voice to our deepest lament or praise, surrounded by a great cloud of witnesses, and we cannot be deaf to the sorrow and joy of humankind. Practices are filled with meaning, and the meaning goes far beyond our own spiritual life to touch all the suffering of humanity. Taking part in Christian practices can cultivate qualities we did not have before and open our eyes and hearts to the activity of God's Spirit in the wider world. This may satisfy some of the yearning with which we began, but it also introduces yearning of a deeper sort—a yearning for divine justice and peace for all.

CHRISTIAN PRACTICES AND THE RENEWAL OF CHURCH AND WORLD

Deliberate efforts to help one another grow in the Christian practices require commitment and constancy. Throughout history, people who share a common yearning for deeper Christian life have covenanted with one another to strengthen their understanding of and participation in certain practices. Beginning in ancient times, groups of women or men have founded religious orders defined by "rules" that order the practices of the members. More recently, the marginalized people of Latin America have gathered in base Christian communities for study, prayer, and action.

Not all committed groups are as radical as these—at least not in obvious ways. But regular and committed engagement with Christian practices has been a source of renewal, both for individuals and for communities of Christians. The Methodist movement began in this way in the 1700s, long before it was a separate church: people gathered regularly in small groups ("class meetings") for prayer, Bible study, and mutual support in practices such as visiting prisoners and discernment. Today, Covenant Discipleship Groups in many United Methodist churches have retrieved this form, and groups with different names but the same purposes also exist in other denominations. Many members report that this weekly or monthly experience has reshaped the way they live and pray. Sometimes groups like these also have surprising effects beyond themselves, becoming the yeast for renewal in a whole congregation.

Two essential Christian practices are always present in groups like these. In fact, it is impossible to imagine renewal and education in the Christian practices without them. These two are so essential to the others, and indeed to the Christian way of life as a whole, that the authors of this book chose not to separate them out in chapters of

Growing in the Practices of Faith

their own but rather to fold them into every chapter. They are prayer and Bible study. Without either one, the twelve practices we have discussed, and other practices as well, would collapse.

Every Christian practice requires prayer, as Christians doing things together attune themselves to take part, with trust, in the risky activities of God. In prayer, we open ourselves to respond to God's presence and notice the light of God as it shines on the world, exposing fault yet also promising hope. We pay attention in a special way, focusing our yearning to be partners in God's reconciling love. We ask for God's help in saying yes to that which is life-giving in the deepest sense and in saying the specific no that will loosen whatever chains bind us and others to destruction. We thank God for life and love, and we beg God for mercy and strength, for ourselves and all creation.

Every Christian practice also depends on a living encounter with the Bible. In each chapter of this book, we have searched the Bible for insight into the practices, but this is only a beginning. You, too, will find it valuable to do this, in small groups and alone, listening and probing, asking of the Bible the fresh questions that are sure to arise as you engage in practices in the world. You will discover there a well of wisdom and the stories of people-at-practice not unlike ourselves. And you will learn about what God's active presence and love for the life of the world really look like.

The best place to find these two central practices and all the others woven together is a Christian congregation. This may not be obvious to a newcomer, and even the most loyal members can become forgetful of the treasures available there: prayer, in sighs too deep for words; Word, breaking through the ordinary to disclose what God's activity consists of; worship, that dark and rich distillation of a way of life; Christian practices, doing things together that participate in God's creative and transformative activity, not only within the community of Christian faith but even more so as members live out their days in workplaces, homes, and the larger society.

Members of one small congregation devised a wonderful way of reminding one another to pray, study, worship, and practice. The method emphasized the great importance of the members' constancy and commitment to each other in these things, for the sake of their faithfulness in God's world. Its visible emblem was a simple black

PRACTICING OUR FAITH

loose-leaf notebook, which sat on the communion table next to the bread and wine and offering basket. The cover was inscribed "The Book of Disciplines of the Community of Christ," and inside were covenants and promises written and affirmed by members of the congregation. Every six months, these had to be renewed or changed. Some of the promises or covenants were shared by the community as a whole and were affirmed by each member with a signature; other promises, added beside the signatures, expressed individual vows. Sometimes the notebook was opened and read, sometimes not. But everyone knew it was public, and everyone also knew—from Discipline No. 1—that she or he was remembered in prayer by name by each of the others every day.

Commitments like these raise our hopes for renewal, for fullness of life. It is good and right that they do. But it is important also to acknowledge—as the members of this community surely would have—that even groups of people with commitments such as these will be far from perfect. They will experience pressures from without and from within, some of them very painful. They may also, we hope, grow in their capacity to engage in Christian practices, including the practice of forgiving one another.

A WAY OF LIFE

Woven together, Christian practices form a way of life. This way is not shaped primarily by a certain cultural style, class, nationality, or age; on the contrary, the way can embrace people in every circumstance, taking different shapes in different times and places. It becomes visible as ordinary people search together for specific ways of taking part in the practice of God, as they faithfully perceive it in the complicated places where they really live. It is like a tree whose branches reach out toward the future, even when the earth is shaking, because it is nourished by living water.

The authors of this book invite other searching people to join us in exploring Christian practices at this turning of the centuries. It is a time when the Earth seems to shake from the forces of change, and there is no way to foresee what specific forms an authentic Christian way of life will take in coming years. We do know, however, that the people who join in this search are not alone amid these changes. We are instructed by the wisdom of an ancient, global, and still developing tradition. We are surrounded by other human beings who share our hungers and joys. We are sustained by a creative and redemptive God. Knowing this, we enter the new century eager to live in ways that express our grateful response.

References

CHAPTER ONE: TIMES OF YEARNING, PRACTICES OF FAITH

The quotation by Martin Luther King Jr. is from a sermon on Christmas Eve, 1967, in James M. Washington, ed., *A Testament of Hope: The Essential Writings of Dr. Martin Luther King, Jr.* (San Francisco: Harper San Francisco, 1986), p. 254. The idea of "practices" has received much attention from philosophers and social scientists in recent years. Our use of the term is loosely based on the work of the moral philosopher Alasdair MacIntyre (see *After Virtue: A Study in Moral Theory,* 2d ed. [Notre Dame, Ind.: University of Notre Dame Press, 1984], pp. 187–188). Craig Dykstra led the way in exploring how this idea can address our yearning for a Christian way of life as the unnamed author of *Growing in the Life of Christian Faith* (Louisville, Ky.: Theology and Worship Ministry Unit, Presbyterian Church [U.S.A.], 1989).

Chapter Two: Honoring the Body

An important source for the historical material on Christianity and the body in this chapter is Peter Brown, *The Body and Society* (New York: Columbia University Press, 1988); the excerpt from Jerome's letters is from p. 317. The Jane Kenyon quotation is from her poem "Cages" in *From Room to Room* (Farmington, Maine: Alicejamesbooks, 1978), p. 35. The Simone Weil excerpt is from *Waiting for God*, trans. Emma Craufurd (New York: HarperCollins, 1951), p. 114. Tikva Frymer-Kensky's prayers are in *Motherprayer: The Pregnant Woman's Spiritual Companion* (New York: Riverhead Books, 1995). The excerpt from Margaret of Oingt's *Mirror* is translated and with an introduction by Renate Blumenfeld-Kosinski in *The Writings of Margaret of Oingt: Medieval Prioress and Mystic* (Newburyport, Mass.: Focus Information Group, 1990), p. 45. Other useful works about this practice are Caroline Walker Bynum, *Holy Feast and Holy Fast: The Religious Significance of Food to Medieval Women* (Berkeley: University of California Press, 1987), and *The Resurrection of the Body in Western Christianity, 200–1336* (New York: Columbia University Press, 1995); and James B. Nelson and Sandra P. Longfellow's *Sexuality and the Sacred: Sources for Theological Reflection* (Louisville, Ky.: Westminster/John Knox, 1994). My colleague Paul Wadell, C. P., gave valuable commentary.

Chapter Three: Hospitality

An important work on the dynamics of the "stranger" is Thomas Ogletree, *Hospitality to the Stranger: Dimensions of Moral Understanding* (Minneapolis: Augsburg Fortress, 1985); the excerpt is from pp. 2–3. The section on biblical perspectives relies on John Koenig, *New Testament Hospitality: Partnership with Strangers as Promise and Mission* (Minneapolis: Augsburg Fortress, 1985). I have also drawn from my longtime association with the Roman Catholic parish of St. Peter's in the Mission District of San Francisco and from personal and pastoral engagement with a variety of communities in California and Chicago. The stories of Christian hospitality represent a composite of the Latino experience in this country rather than particular events.

CHAPTER FOUR: HOUSEHOLD ECONOMICS

Useful sources for reflection on the new global commons and its implications for the formation of faith and practice are Laurent A. Parks Daloz, Cheryl H. Keen, James P. Keen, and Sharon Daloz Parks, *Common Fire: Lives of Commitment in a Complex World* (Boston: Beacon Press, 1996); and Richard J. Barnet, "The Global War Against the Poor" (Washington, D.C.: Church of the Savior—Servant Leadership Press, 1995). This chapter is also informed by Juliet Schor, *The Overworked American: The Unexpected Decline of Leisure* (New York: Basic Books, 1991); M. Douglas Meeks, *God the Economist: The Doctrine of God and Political Economy* (Minneapolis: Augsburg Fortress, 1989); Richard J. Foster, *Freedom of Simplicity* (San Francisco: Harper San Francisco, 1981); and Margaret R. Miles, *Practicing Christianity: Critical Perspectives for an Embodied Spirituality* (New York: Crossroad, 1990).

Useful sources regarding the practices of Quakers and Mennonites are *The Journal of John Woolman, and A Plea for the Poor* (Secaucus, N.J.: Citadel Press, 1961), quotations from pp. 129 and 211; Douglas V. Steere, ed., *Quaker Spirituality: Selected Writings* (New York: Paulist Press, 1984), the source of the quotations from Thomas Kelly, pp. 302–303; David Burns Windsor, *The Quaker Enterprise: Friends in Business* (London: Frederick Muller, 1980); *The Compassionate Community,* writings for the Mennonite Central Committee (pamphlet; n.d.); and Calvin Redekop, Stephen C. Ainlay, and Robert Siemens, *Mennonite Entrepreneurs* (Baltimore: Johns Hopkins University Press, 1995). The Quaker queries are from *Faith and Practice* (Philadelphia: Philadelphia Yearly Meeting of the Religious Society of Friends, 1955). On Dorothy Day and the Catholic Worker community, see Robert Ellsberg, ed., *By Little and by Little: The Selected Writings of Dorothy Day* (New York: Knopf, 1983). Kate Daloz, a student at Oberlin College, wrote the reflection on consumerism at Christmas. The factory fire story is from the Boston *Globe,* Dec. 15, 1995. On the Church of the Savior, see Elizabeth O'Conner, *Servant Leaders, Servant Structures* (Washington, D.C.: Servant Leadership School, 1991). The Wendell Berry excerpt is from his *Sex, Economy, Freedom and Community* (New York: Pantheon Books, 1992), p. 107. The excerpt by Duane Elgin is from his *Voluntary Simplicity: Toward a Way of Life That Is Outwardly Simple, Inwardly Rich,* rev. ed. (New York: Quill/Morrow, 1993), p. 27, and the excerpt by Sarah van Gelder is from *Yes! A Journal of Positive Futures,* Spring-Summer 1996, p. 13. Other excerpts are from a public television broadcast of *The Frugal Gourmet* in July 1994; *A Pastoral Letter on Catholic Social Teaching and the U.S. Economy: Economic Justice for All* (National Conference of Catholic Bishops, 1986), p. 91; and *Time,* Aug. 28, 1995, pp. 52–53.

CHAPTER FIVE: SAYING YES AND SAYING NO

Whenever I want to think critically and prayerfully about the spiritual life, I have found the works of Dorothee Soelle and Rosemary Haughton challenging. Important for this chapter are Haughton, *The Passionate God* (Mahwah, N.J.: Paulist Press, 1981) and *The Transformation of Man: A Study of Conversion and Community* (Springfield, Ill.: Templegate, 1980); and Soelle, *Choosing Life* (Minneapolis: Augsburg Fortress, 1981), quotation from p. 89. "Examination of conscience" is an old and enduring Christian practice. The collection *Hearts on Fire,* ed. Michael Harter, S.J. (St. Louis, Mo.: Institute of Jesuit Sources, 1993), is a good introduction. For very helpful works on prayer, see Anthony Bloom, *Beginning to Pray* (Mahwah, N.J.: Paulist Press, 1970); and James M. Washington, *Conversations with God: Two Centuries of Prayers by African Americans* (New York: HarperCollins, 1994). Anthony's admonition is from *The Sayings of the Desert Fathers,* trans. Benedicta Ward (New York: Macmillan, 1975), p. 2. Excerpts are from T. S. Eliot, "Choruses from 'The Rock,'" in *The Collected Poems and Plays, 1909–1950* (Orlando, Fla.: Harcourt Brace, 1971), p. 96; Francis Sullivan, "Vision with Its Outcome," in *Spy Wednesday's Kind* (New York: Smith, 1979), p. 75; *Be Friends of God: Spiritual Readings from Gregory the Great,* trans. John Leinenweber (Cambridge, Mass.: Cowley, 1990), p. 74; Marcus J. Borg, *Meeting Jesus Again for the First Time: The Historical Jesus and the Heart of Contemporary Faith* (New York: HarperCollins, 1994), p. 86; and Dorothee Soelle and Fulbert Steffensky, *Not Just Yes and Amen: Christians with a Cause* (Minneapolis: Augsburg Fortress, 1983), pp. 41 and 40.

CHAPTER SIX: KEEPING SABBATH

Abraham Joshua Heschel's short classic, *The Sabbath: Its Meaning for Modern Man* (New York: Farrar, Straus & Giroux, 1952), has strongly influenced recent Jewish and Christian reflection on the importance of the Sabbath; pp. 89, 17, and 28 are quoted here. Samuel H. Dresner, *The Sabbath* (New York: Burning Bush Press, 1970), provides another insightful Jewish account; the excerpt is from p. 21. Excellent recent works by Christians are Marva Dawn, *Keeping the Sabbath Wholly: Ceasing, Resting, Embracing, Feasting* (Grand Rapids, Mich.: Eerdmans, 1989); and Tilden Edwards, *Sabbath Time: Understanding and Practice for Contemporary Christians* (New York: Seabury Press, 1982). Dresner, Dawn, and Edwards include suggestions for individuals and families who seek to deepen their Sabbath observance. Eugene Peterson's report on how pastors can keep Sabbath is in "The Good-for-Nothing Sabbath," *Christianity Today,* Apr. 4, 1994, pp. 34–36. The poem by Wendell Berry is from *Sabbaths* (San Francisco: North Point Press, 1987), p. 19. Information on the economic crisis that frames this practice is from Juliet Schor, *The Overworked American: The Unexpected Decline of Leisure* (New York: Basic Books, 1991), quotation from p. xv. A very rich compendium of biblical, theological, and historical material is gathered in Tamara C. Eskenazi, Daniel J. Harrington, and William H. Shea, eds., *The Sabbath in Jewish and Christian Traditions* (New York: Crossroad, 1991); John H. Primus's essay in this volume includes the quotation by Martin Luther, p. 100. "Good Sabbaths Make Good Christians" is a chapter title in Winton U. Solberg, *Redeem the Time: The Puritan Sabbath in Early America* (Cambridge, Mass.: Harvard University Press, 1977). The prayer of invocation is adapted from the Presbyterian Church (U.S.A.), *Service for the Lord's Day* (Louisville, Ky.: Westminster/John Knox, 1984).

CHAPTER SEVEN: TESTIMONY

James Cone's words are from "Sanctification and Liberation in the Black Religious Tradition," in *Sanctification and Liberation,* ed. Theodore Runyon (Nashville, Tenn.: Abingdon Press, 1981), p. 175.

The quotations by Thomas G. Long are from *The Witness of Preaching* (Louisville, Ky.: Westminster/John Knox, 1989), pp. 45 and 44. The quotation from Joseph Sittler is from "The View from Mount Nebo," in *The Care of the Earth, and Other University Sermons* (Minneapolis: Augsburg Fortress, 1964), pp. 80–81. The quotation and excerpt by Paul Ricoeur are from "The Hermeneutics of Testimony," in *Essays on Biblical Interpretation,* ed. Lewis S. Mudge (Minneapolis: Augsburg Fortress, 1980), pp. 119–120 and 128–129. The excerpt by Richard K. Fenn is from *Liturgies and Trials* (Cleveland, Ohio: Pilgrim Press, 1982), p. 27. John Newton wrote "Amazing Grace" in 1779; John Fawcett wrote "Blessed Be the Tie That Binds" in 1782; see *The New Century Hymnal* (Cleveland, Ohio: Pilgrim Press, 1995), hymns 547 and 393. The conversion narrative by the former slave is not a direct quotation but a composite. Many such narratives were collected by Fisk University and are published in *God Struck Me Dead: Religious Conversion Experiences and Autobiographies of Ex-Slaves,* ed. Clifton H. Johnson (Cleveland, Ohio: Pilgrim Press, 1969).

CHAPTER EIGHT: DISCERNMENT

The primary source for Ignatian spiritual discernment is Ignatius of Loyola himself. See Louis Puhl, *The Spiritual Exercises of St. Ignatius* (Chicago: Loyola University Press, 1951); the excerpt is from Exercise 315, pp. 141–142. Other helpful sources are Thomas Green, *Weeds Among the Wheat* (Notre Dame, Ind.: Ave Maria Press, 1984); L. Patrick Carroll and Katherine M. Dyckman, "Prayerful Decision Making," in *Inviting the Mystic, Supporting the Prophet* (Mahwah, N.J.: Paulist Press, 1981); Philip Boroughs, "Using Ignatian Discernment," *Review for Religious,* 1992, *51*(3), 373–387; Jules Toner, "A Method for Communal Discernment of God's Will," in *Studies in the Spirituality of the Jesuits,* 1971, *3*(4); and Mary Benet McKinney, *Sharing Wisdom: A Process for Group Decision Making* (Allen, Tex.: Tabor Publishing, 1987). For biblical material, see Jacques Guillet's essay in Jacques Guillet and others, *Discernment of Spirits,* trans. Sister Innocentia Richards (Collegeville, Minn.: Liturgical Press, 1970). On Quaker discernment, see Michael Sheeran, *Beyond Majority Rule:*

Voteless Decisions in the Religious Society of Friends (Philadelphia: Philadelphia Yearly Meeting of the Religious Society of Friends, 1983); the excerpt by Isaac Pennington is from p. viii, and the one from the *Quaker Book of Discipline* is from p. 47. The story of consensus decision making is from Margaret Bacon, *The Quiet Rebels: The Story of the Quakers in America* (New York: Basic Books, 1969), pp. 174–175. Casiano Floristan and Christian Duquoc, eds., *Discernment of the Spirit and of Spirits* (New York: Seabury Press, 1979), is an important source on liberation theology and discernment; the excerpt by Jon Sobrino is from p. 14. The story about East Los Angeles is from Leonardo Vilchis, "Learning to Walk in the Middle of a Tempest," *Desde la Base,* 1991, *1*(4), 6–7. The excerpt by Sandra Schneiders is from "Spiritual Discernment in the Dialogue of Saint Catherine of Siena," *Horizons,* 1982, *9*(1), 48.

Chapter Nine: Shaping Communities

The most important source for the material on leadership and the story of Ruckelshaus and the EPA is Ronald A. Heifetz, *Leadership Without Easy Answers* (Cambridge, Mass.: Belknap Press, 1994); the excerpt is from p. 184. The treatment of Jewish and early Christian communities draws substantially from James Burtchaell, *From Synagogue to Church: Public Services and Offices in the Earliest Christian Communities* (Cambridge: Cambridge University Press, 1992); John Dominic Crossan, *Jesus: A Revolutionary Biography* (San Francisco: Harper San Francisco, 1994); N. T. Wright, *The New Testament and the People of God* (Minneapolis: Augsburg Fortress, 1992); and John Koenig, *Charismata: God's Gifts for God's People* (Louisville, Ky.: Westminster/John Knox, 1978). Discussion of the relationship of governance in these communities to society in our time is informed by John De Gruchy, *Christianity and Democracy: A Theology for a Just World Order* (Cambridge: Cambridge University Press, 1995); James P. Mackey, *Power and Christian Ethics* (Cambridge: Cambridge University Press, 1994); and Larry L. Rasmussen, *Moral Fragments and Moral Community: A Proposal for Church in Society* (Minneapolis: Augsburg Fortress, 1993). Other excerpts are from Martin Luther King Jr., *Where Do We Go from Here: Chaos or Community?* (New York: HarperCollins, 1967),

p. 167; and Beverly Wildung Harrison, *Making the Connections: Essays in Feminist Social Ethics* (Boston: Beacon Press, 1985), p. 20.

CHAPTER TEN: FORGIVENESS

A more extended account of the themes developed in this chapter is found in L. Gregory Jones, *Embodying Forgiveness: A Theological Analysis* (Grand Rapids, Mich.: Eerdmans, 1995). The quotation from Lincoln and the King excerpt are both found in Martin Luther King Jr., *Strength to Love* (Minneapolis: Augsburg Fortress, 1981), pp. 54–55. The quotation from Nicholas Lash is from *Believing Three Ways in One God* (Notre Dame, Ind.: University of Notre Dame Press, 1993), p. 119. The story from Jon Sobrino is from "Latin America: Place of Sin and Place of Forgiveness," *Concilium,* 1986, *184,* 50; the quotation by Christian Duquoc is from "The Forgiveness of God" in the same *Concilium,* p. 41. The quotation from C. S. Lewis is from *Letters to Malcolm* (Orlando, Fla.: Harcourt Brace, 1964), p. 106.

Other works I have found useful for thinking about the practice of Christian forgiveness are Rowan Williams, *Resurrection* (Wilton, Conn.: Morehouse-Barlow, 1994), excerpt from p. 52; Elsa Tamez, *The Amnesty of Grace,* trans. Sharon Ringe (Nashville, Tenn.: Abingdon Press, 1993), excerpt from p. 163; and Dietrich Bonhoeffer, *The Cost of Discipleship,* trans. R. H. Fuller (New York: Macmillan, 1963), including his famous critique of "cheap grace." Powerful depictions of Christian forgiveness can also be found in the films *Places in the Heart* (1984) and *Romero* (1989).

CHAPTER ELEVEN: HEALING

For overviews of healing ministries within the church, the two works I have found most useful are Morton Kelsey, *Healing and Christianity* (Minneapolis: Augsburg Fortress, 1995; first published 1973); and Una Kroll, *In Touch with Healing* (London: BBC Books, 1991), excerpt from p. 35. The first quotation is from Paul Tillich, *Systematic Theology* (Chicago: University of Chicago Press, 1967), vol. 3, p. 277. The quotation from Avery Brooke and some of the data that informed my discussion of St. Luke's School of Christian Healing came from a phone interview with her; see also her book *Healing in the Landscape of Prayer* (Cambridge, Mass.: Cowley, 1996). Information on Grace Lutheran Church is from "The Congregation as a Place of Healing," *Second Opinion: Health, Faith, and Ethics,* 1990, *13,* 75–137; quotations from Stephen Schmidt are from pp. 105 and 107; the latter provides the quotation by "one man" early in this chapter. The testimony by Douglas Anderson is from the same source, p. 117. The quotation by Sister Kathleen Popko is cited in Martin E. Marty, "The Tradition of the Church in Health and Healing," in the same issue of *Second Opinion,* p. 65. The account of Tilda Norberg's ministry and the liturgical words she used are from a personal interview; the credo comes from her brochure, "A Training Opportunity." The excerpt is from Tilda Norberg and Robert Webber, *Stretch Out Your Hand: Exploring Healing Prayer* (New York: United Church Press, 1990), p. 11. The excerpt by Richard Foster is from his *Prayer: Finding the Heart's True Home* (San Francisco: Harper San Francisco, 1992), pp. 206–207. The hymn by Thomas H. Troeger is hymn 264 in *The New Methodist Hymnal* (Nashville, Tenn.: United Methodist Publishing House, 1989).

CHAPTER TWELVE: DYING WELL

Nicholas Wolterstorff's book *Lament for a Son* (Grand Rapids, Mich.: Eerdmans, 1987) was important in my reflections on death and dying, for both its theological depth and its emotional intensity; quotation from pp. 38–41, 63. Other quotations are from William M. Shea, "Theologians and Their Catholic Authorities: Reminiscence and Reconnoiter," *Horizons,* Fall 1986, p. 345; John Donne, Sermon of March 8, 1621, in *Eighty Sermons* (London, 1640); Paul Ramsey, *The Patient as Person* (New Haven, Conn.: Yale University Press, 1970), p. 156; John Calvin, *Institutes of the Christian Religion,* ed. John T. McNeill (Louisville, Ky.: Westminster/John Knox, 1960), bk. 3, ch. 3, sec. 3; Eve Kavenaugh, "Prayer of the Flesh," *Other Side,* May–June 1993, p. 59 (excerpt from p. 58); and Vigen Guroian, "Death and Dying Well in the Orthodox Liturgical Tradition," *Second Opinion,* July 1993, p. 57. The quotation about death as a "friendly companion" is from Elizabeth Kübler-Ross, *Death: The Final Stage of Growth* (New York: Macmillan, 1969), p. 6. Other excerpts are from Luz Beatriz Arellano, "Women's Experience of God in Emerging Spirituality," in Virginia Fabella and Mercy Amba Oduyoye, eds., *With Passion and Compassion: Third World Women Doing Theology* (Maryknoll, N.Y.: Orbis Books, 1988), p. 146; and Thomas A. Dorsey, "Precious Lord, Take My Hand," in *The Presbyterian Hymnal: Hymns, Psalms, and Spiritual Songs* (Louisville, Ky.: Westminster/John Knox, 1990), hymn 404. Conversations with my colleague Burton Cooper, who has written and thought deeply on these issues, were formative for me. I recommend his book *Why, God?* (Louisville, Ky.: Westminster/John Knox, 1988). Other resources that were helpful to this chapter include the 1989 film *Shadowlands;* the compassionate but unflinching look at death and modern medical practice in Sherwin B. Nuland, *How We Die: Reflections on Life's Final Chapter* (New York: Knopf, 1994); Bonnie J. Miller-McLemore, *Death, Sin, and the Moral Life* (Atlanta: Scholars Press, 1988); David Power and Kabasele Lumbala, eds., *The Spectre of Mass Death* (London: SCM Press, 1993); and, for historical background on Christian practices surrounding death and dying, J. G. Davies, ed., *The New Westminster Dictionary of Liturgy and Worship* (Louisville, Ky.: Westminster/John Knox, 1986).

CHAPTER THIRTEEN: SINGING OUR LIVES

Several sources have helped to shape my chapter, including Ivor H. Jones, *Music: A Joy for Ever* (London: Epworth Press, 1989); Gabe Huck, *How Can I Keep from Singing?* (Chicago: Liturgy Training Publications, 1989); William B. McClain, *Come Sunday: The Liturgy of Zion* (Nashville, Tenn.: Abingdon Press, 1990); Gail Ramshaw, *Words That Sing* (Chicago: Liturgy Training Publications, 1992); and Erik Routley, *Church Music and the Christian Faith* (Carol Stream, Ill.: Agape, 1978). A recent video that explores words and music in contemporary Christian worship, featuring several of us who compose, is *When We Sing: Conversations with Alice Parker and Friends* (Chicago: Liturgy Training Publications, 1994). The quotation from Saint Augustine is from his letters *(Epistola* 55:18–19) quoted in *The*

Study of Liturgy, ed. Cheslyn Jones and others (New York: Oxford University Press, 1978), p. 441. The hymns "When in Our Music God Is Glorified," by Fred Pratt Green; "God of the Sparrow, God of the Whole" by Jaroslav J. Vajda; and "Lift Every Voice and Sing" by James Weldon Johnson and J. Rosamond Johnson are in *The United Methodist Hymnal* (Nashville, Tenn.: United Methodist Publishing House, 1989) and other recent hymnals. The story of the young martyr may be found in Mark Danner, "A Reporter at Large: The Truth of El Mozote," originally in the *New Yorker* (Dec. 6, 1993), cited by Kathleen Norris in *A Tremor of Bliss,* ed. Paul Elie (Orlando: Harcourt Brace, 1994), pp. 267–268. The excerpt from Huub Oosterhuis is from *Prayers, Poems and Songs* (New York: Herder & Herder, 1970), p. 104. The Dietrich Bonhoeffer excerpt is from his *Life Together* (New York: HarperCollins, 1954), p. 59, and the James Baldwin excerpt is from *Another Country* (New York: Dell, 1962), p. 106. The John Wesley quotation is from his preface to *A Collection of Hymns for the Use of the People Called Methodists* (London, 1780).

Chapter Fourteen:
Growing in the Practices of Faith

On Luther Place, see John Koenig, *New Testament Hospitality* (Minneapolis: Augsburg Fortress, 1985), p. 140. Information on the Community of Christ is from Larry Rasmussen, who was a member from 1972 to 1986.

The Contributors

DOROTHY C. BASS is director of the Project on the Education and Formation of People in Faith at Valparaiso University and a minister in the United Church of Christ.

M. SHAWN COPELAND, a Roman Catholic laywoman, is associate professor of theology at Marquette University.

CRAIG DYKSTRA is vice president for religion at Lilly Endowment Inc. and a minister in the Presbyterian Church (U.S.A.).

THOMAS HOYT JR., a New Testament scholar, is a bishop in the Christian Methodist Episcopal Church.

L. GREGORY JONES is a United Methodist minister and dean of the Divinity School at Duke University.

JOHN KOENIG is academic dean at the General Theological Seminary in New York and a priest in the Episcopal Church.

SHARON DALOZ PARKS, a member of the Society of Friends (Quakers), is a fellow at the Whidbey Institute, Clinton, Washington.

STEPHANIE PAULSELL is director of ministry studies at the University of Chicago Divinity School and a minister in the Christian Church (Disciples of Christ).

AMY PLANTINGA PAUW, a Presbyterian, is associate professor of theology at Louisville Presbyterian Theological Seminary.

ANA MARÍA PINEDA, a member of the Sisters of Mercy, is director of the Hispanic Ministries Program at the Catholic Theological Union, Chicago.

LARRY RASMUSSEN is Reinhold Niebuhr Professor of Social Ethics at Union Theological Seminary in New York City. He is a member of the Evangelical Lutheran Church in America.

FRANK ROGERS JR., a Roman Catholic layperson, is associate professor of religious education at the Claremont School of Theology.

DON E. SALIERS, a United Methodist minister, is professor of theology and liturgy, and director of the Master of Sacred Music program, at Emory University's Candler School of Theology.

Index

Beethoven, L. von, 189
Berry, W., 47, 77, 208, 209
Birmingham, Alabama, testimony in, 91
Birth, and honoring the body, 13–15, 20
Black Church, testimony in, 91–97,
    100–102
Bloom, A., 208
Body. *See* Honoring the body
Boff, L., 102
Bonhoeffer, D., 187, 212, 215
Borg, M. J., 67, 208–209
Boroughs, P., 210
Brooke, A., 154–155, 213
Brown, P., 206
Burtchaell, J., 211
Bynum, C. W., 206

C

Calvin, J., 12, 170, 213
Campaign for Peace, 117
Carroll, L. P., 210
Catholic Worker Movement, 49
Catholics. *See* Roman Catholics
Central America. *See* Latin America
Central American Resource Center
    (CARECEN), 35–36
Change, and community, 3–4
Chicago: and immigrants, 39; settlement
    houses in, 49; therapeutic touch in,
    23
Christianity, early: and asceticism, 60;
    and body, 17; and funerals, 169; and
    healing, 150, 152; and hospitality,
    33; and Sabbath, 82–83; and shap-
    ing communities, 125–127; and
    singing, 183
Christmas, 30, 38, 43, 50, 140, 193
Church, as alternative community,
    127–129; as source of hope, 164. *See
    also* Grace Lutheran Church, St.
    Luke's Episcopal Church, St.
    Peter's Parish, Trinity Christian
    Methodist Episcopal Church
Church of the Savior, and household
    economics, 57–58
Clean Air Act of 1970, 122
Communities: approach for, 119–132;
    challenge for, 129–130; and change,

3–4; churches as alternative,
    127–129; as a practice, 7, 10, 196,
    200; discernment in, 110–113, 115,
    116–117; faith-sharing, 71–72; of
    forgiveness, 143–145; governance
    and leadership for, 121–123, 127,
    131–132; for growth in practices, 7,
    12, 196, 198, 202–203; and honoring
    the body, 19, 24; and hospitality,
    2–3, 31, 35–37; and household eco-
    nomics, 56–58; legacy for, 123–126;
    shaping, 130–132; and testimony,
    92–94, 98–99; as way of life, 120–121
Community democracy, for community
    shaping, 125, 128, 130
Companions, in practices, 4–5
Cone, J., 95, 97, 210
Congregationalists, and community, 128
Conscience, examination of, and saying
    yes, 69–71
Constantine, 83
Cooper, B., 214
Copeland, M. S., 59
Council of Jerusalem, and discernment,
    111
Creative deviance, for community shap-
    ing, 125, 128, 130
Crossan, J. D., 211
Cumber, and household economics,
    45–47

D

Daloz, K., 207
Daloz, L., 207
Danner, M., 215
Darien, Connecticut, healing in,
    154–155, 157
Davies, J. G., 214
Dawn, M., 209
Day, D., 49, 63, 207
Death. *See* Dying well
DeGruchy, J., 211
Democracy, community, 125, 128, 130
Deviance, creative, 125, 128, 130
Discernment: applications of, 116–118;
    approach to, 105–118; in communi-
    ties, 110–113, 115, 116–117; concept
    of, 107; and deception, 113–116;

and household economics, 57; for individuals, 107–110, as a practice, 7, 10, 195, 196, 200

Discipleship, in community, 125–126

Donne, J., 164, 213

Dorsey, T. A., 175, 214

Dresner, S. H., 81, 209

Duquoc, C., 140, 211, 212

Dyckman, K., 210

Dying well: approach to, 163–177; attitudes toward, 164–166; circumstances for, 166–167; and judgment, 172–174; and lament, 167–168; meaning of, 176–177; and mercy, 174–176; and song, 191; and thanksgiving and hope, 169–172

Dykstra, C., 1, 195, 205–206

E

Easter, 10, 26, 82, 87, 169, 188–189

Economics. *See* Household economics

Edwards, T., 85, 209

Egypt, asceticism in, 62

El Salvador: forgiveness in, 146; song in, 191; testimony in, 103

Elgin, D., 51, 208

Eliot, T. S., 65, 208

Elizabeth of Hungary, 63

Ellsberg, R., 207

Embodiment, and honoring the body, 16, 17

England: asceticism in, 62; healing in, 153; household economics in, 52

Enoughness, in household economics, 58

Environmental Protection Agency (EPA), 45, 122–123, 132, 211

Epiphany, 16

Esau, 48

Eskenazi, T. C., 209

Eucharist, eucharistic, 9, 36, 117, 130–132, 146, 154, 156, 160, 162, 170, 177

Examination of conscience, and saying yes, 69–71

F

Faith-sharing groups, for saying yes, 71–72

Fawcett, J., 210

Fenn, R. K., 99, 210

Fisk University, 210

Floristan, C., 211

Forgiveness: acts of, 137; approach to, 133–147; communities of, 143–145; and dying well, 173; legacy of, 140–143; obstacles to, 135–138; as a practice, 8, 9, 11, 195; process of, 138–139; as way of life, 134–135; and worship, 146–147

Foster, R. J., 151, 207, 213

France, Revolution in, 77

Francis of Assisi, 63, 128

Franklin, A., 190

French Revolution, 77

Friends. *See* Quakers

Frymer-Kensky, T., 24–25, 206

G

Gandhi, M., 101

Germany: household economics in, 53; song in, 189

Governance, for communities, 121–123, 127, 131–132

Grace Lutheran Church, and healing, 155–157, 158–159, 213

Grant, A., 190

Green, F. P., 183–184, 187

Green, T., 210

Gregory the Great, 66, 208

Guests, as hosts, 32–35

Guidance, and discernment, 105–118

Guillet, J., 211

Guroian, V., 177, 214

Gutierrez, G., 143

H

Harrington, D. J., 209

Harrison, B. W., 126, 212

Harter, M., 208

Haughton, R., 208

Healing: approach to, 149–162; future of, 161–162; integrated practice of, 159–161; legacy for, 152–154; ministries of, 154–157, 160–161; as a practice, 7, 8, 10, 200; paradox of, 151–152; vocation for, 157–159

171; and hospitality, 35–36, 40–42; renewal in, 201; testimony in, 103

Latinos, and hospitality, 29–31, 35–36, 38–39, 41–42

Lazarus, 170

Leadership, for communities, 121–123, 127, 131–132

Lent, 10, 26, 164

Lewis, C. S., 146, 212

Lincoln, A., 139, 212

Long, T. G., 97, 101, 210

Longfellow, S. P., 206

Lord's Supper, 26, 83. *See also* Eucharist

Los Angeles, discernment in, 116–117

Lumbala, K., 214

Luther, M., 12, 83, 128, 209

Luther Place, and hospitality, 197

M

MacIntyre, A., 205

Mackey, J. P., 126, 211

Margaret of Oingt, 26, 206

Marginal living, testimony from, 94–95

Martha, 34, 169–170

Marty, M. E., 213

Mary (and Joseph), 29–30, 42, 183, 193

Mary (and Martha), 170

Maurin, P., 49

McClain, W. B., 214

McKinney, M. B., 210

Meeks, M. D., 46, 207

Mennonite Central Committee, 207

Mennonites: and community, 128; and household economics, 50, 53, 54–57. *See also* Amish community

Mercy, and dying well, 174–176

Methodists: and community, 128; Covenant Discipleship Groups of, 201; and healing, 153, 160; and song, 185, 193

Miles, M. R., 207

Miller-McLemore, B. J., 214

Miriam, 99–100

Missoula, dying well in, 175

Montgomery, Alabama, bus boycott in, 49

Moses, 20, 33, 78, 82, 99

Music. *See* song

Mutual aid, in household economy, 49–53, 55–56

N

National Conference of Catholic Bishops, 52

National Religious Partnership for the Environment, 57

Nelson, J. B., 206

Netherlands, household economics in, 53

New York City, hospitality in, 49, 63

Newton, J., 210

No. *See* Yes, saying

Norberg, T., 158, 160–161, 213

Norris, K., 215

Nuland, S. B., 214

O

O'Conner, E., 207–208

Ogletree, T., 35, 206

Oosterhuis, H., 180, 215

P

Parker, A., 215

Parks, S. D., 43, 207

Paul, 14, 21, 34, 50, 59, 60, 96, 97–98, 103, 114, 115, 119, 120, 124, 125, 127, 139, 144, 145, 168, 170, 171, 172, 177, 183, 184, 188

Paulsell, S., 13

Pauw, A. P., 163

Pennington, I., 107, 211

Pentecost, 96, 98

Peter, 9, 19, 96, 98, 145, 150

Peterson, E., 85, 209

Philoxenia, 33–34

Pineda, A. M., 29

Popko, K., 157, 213

Portuguese community, and hospitality, 37

Posada, and hospitality, 29–31, 36, 37, 38

Power, D., 214

Practices: approach to, 1–12; for community shaping, 119–132; concept of, 5–10; for discernment, 105–118; for dying well, 163–177; education for,

196–199; for forgiveness, 133–147;
growing in, 195–204; guide to
exploring, 199–201; for healing,
149–152; for honoring the body,
13–27; for hospitality, 29–42; for
household economics, 43–58; as
interrelated, 10–11; as life-giving,
2–3; need for, 1–2, 6–7; as rehears-
ing, 8–10; and renewal, 201–203;
for Sabbath keeping, 75–89; for
saying yes and no, 59–73; for song,
179–193; for testimony, 91–103; as
way of life, 203–204; as way of
thinking, 6–8

Prayer: and forgiveness, 146; and healing, 151–152, 154–156, 162; and
honoring the body, 24–25; and
renewal, 202; and saying yes, 68–69

Preaching, as testimony, 97–99

Presbyterian Church, and prayer, 86,
209; and household economics, 57

Primus, J. H., 209

Puhl, L., 210

Q

Quakers: and community, 128; and discernment, 111–112, 211; and household economics, 45, 50–54, 56; and
Sabbath keeping, 83; song of, 181

R

Ramsey, P., 165, 213

Ramshaw, G., 214

Rasmussen, L., 119, 212, 215

Redekop, C., 207

Religious Society of Friends. See
Quakers

Resurrection, 8–9, 26–27, 76, 82–85,
140–142, 150, 164, 169–171, 174,
176, 185–186, 193, 198

Richards, I., 211

Ricoeur, P., 93, 101, 210

Ringe, S., 212

River Forest, Illinois, healing in,
155–157

Rogers, F., Jr., 105

Roman Catholics: and dying well, 174;
and forgiveness, 143; and healing,

157; and household economics, 49,
52; and Sabbath keeping, 83

Romero, O., 103, 170

Routley, E., 214

Ruckelshaus, W., 122–123, 132, 211

S

Sabbath: approach for keeping, 75–89;
gift of, 76–77, 85–87; good from,
88–89; growth in keeping, 197, 200;
in Judaism, 79–81, 82, 84, 88; legacy
of, 77–83; obstacles to, 83–85; as a
practice, 9, 10, 11, 197, 200; time
for, 75–77, 85

St. Luke's Episcopal Church, School of
Christian Healing of, 154–155, 157,
213

St. Peter's parish, and hospitality, 29, 36,
206

Saliers, D. E., 179

San Francisco, hospitality in, 29–31,
35–36

San Jose, hospitality in, 37

Sarah, 33, 34

Saying yes. See Yes, saying

Schmidt, S., 156, 213

Schneiders, S., 114, 211

Schor, J., 75–76, 207, 209

Schroeder-Sheker, T., 175

Scriabin, A. N., 181

Self-control, and saying yes and no,
59–73

Seventh-Day Adventists, and Sabbath
keeping, 83, 84

Sexuality, and honoring the body, 15, 17,
18, 24–25

Shaw, R., 189

Shea, W. H., 209

Shea, W. M., 164, 213

Sheeran, M., 211

Shelter. See Posada

Siemens, R., 207

Simeon, 183

Simeon Stylites, 62

Simon, 19

Simplicity, in household economy, 49–53

Singing our lives. See Song

Sittler, J., 99, 210

Index of Scripture References

INDEX OF SCRIPTURE REFERENCES